A

PRIVILEGED

JOURNEY

From Enthusiast to Professional Railwayman

David Maidment

Above: Painting by railway artist David Charlesworth, commissioned by the author, of 30777 *Sir Lamiel* on the 5.9pm Waterloo–Basingstoke passing Surbiton, February 1960.

Cover: 4087 *Cardigan Castle* at Reading West on the down '*Mayflower*', the 5.30pm Paddington–Plymouth, April 1958. (*R. C. Riley*)

Contents: Ready for departure — 30777 *Sir Lamiel* at Waterloo on the 5.9pm to Basingstoke, May 1960.

Back cover: 5063 *Earl Baldwin* on the 2:10pm Paddington - Wolverhampton, passes Subway Junction, Paddington, 10.9.60.
(*R. C. Riley*)
46226 *Duchess of Norfolk* waits to take over a Glasgow - Euston express at Carlisle Central Station, 27.5.59. (*R. C. Riley*)
5038 *Morlais Castle* leaves Newton Abbot with the 8am Plymouth - Liverpool. (*R. C. Riley*)

All photographs in the book are by the author, except where otherwise credited.

First published in Great Britain in 2015 by
Pen & Sword Transport
An imprint of Pen & Sword Books Ltd
47 Church Street, Barnsley South Yorkshire S70 2AS

ISBN 9781783831081

Pen & Sword Books Ltd incorporates the imprints of Pen & Sword Archaeology,
Atlas, Aviation, Battleground, Discovery, Family History, History, Maritime,
Military, Naval, Politics, Railways, Select, Social History, Transport, True Crime, and
Claymore Press, Frontline Books, Leo Cooper, Praetorian Press, Remember When,
Seaforth Publishing and Wharncliffe.

For a complete list of Pen and Sword titles please contact Pen and Sword Books
Limited 47 Church Street, Barnsley, South Yorkshire, S70 2AS, England E-mail:
enquiries@pen-and-sword.co.uk Website: www.pen-and-sword.co.uk

Typeset by Milepost
Printed and bound in India by Replika Press Pvt. Ltd.

All royalties for this book will be donated to the Railway Children charity
(reg no. 1058991)
(www.railwaychildren.org.uk)

Acknowledgements

To those who stimulated and shared my interest in railways and especially the steam
engine - my father, Jack Maidment, Great Uncle George, Aunt Enid, Cedric Utley,
John Crowe, Alastair Wood...

Contents

Preface

David Charlesworth's representation of 4087 *Cardigan Castle* on Llanvihangel
Bank with a Plymouth–Manchester express c1963 — a painting commissioned
by the author and used on a Christmas card for the *Railway Children* charity.

This book has been written for fellow railway enthusiasts — particularly those
seduced by the magic of the steam locomotive. For some, hopefully these
chapters will elicit similar memories and permit them to revel in unashamed nostalgia.
For others — perhaps those who were not fortunate enough to experience Britain's
steam railways in their heyday — it may give a feel of what it was like to live and
work on the railway when Britain had more than 18,000 working steam locomotives.
From the age of two I was entranced by railways and their trains. By the time I was
eight I was a trainspotter, and by the age of eleven I was being allowed to travel
unaccompanied to London to pursue my hobby. Later I decided to turn my hobby
into a career.

In 1960 it was still acceptable to admit to being an enthusiast and become a
railway manager. For many senior managers at that time it meant that they knew you
were motivated, were aware of the basics of the job and had a more than average
awareness of the geography of Britain's vast railway system. Later, as the new traction
began to appear, interest in steam locomotives became a handicap that one had to
hide if one was ambitious. Steam locomotives were old-fashioned, and showing

an obvious interest in them meant you were backward-looking, not the thrusting, positive 'young turk' that the new generation of managers was seeking. I was nearly removed from the Western Region's management-training scheme in 1962 when my report on the three months' training at Old Oak Common had too much to say about the efficiencies or otherwise of the run down of steam, rather than dwelling on the opportunities for quicker 'dieselisation'. Perhaps they should not have sent me to train at a depot that in May 1962 still had 170 steam locomotives and only 20 diesel shunters. The Assistant General Manager, Lance Ibbotson, castigated me for not visiting the new Landore diesel depot within days of taking up my new training schedule in South Wales. The fact that at the time it was just a muddy building site held no excuse. So I became more circumspect about my enthusiasms and survived.

This book relies for some of the chapters on articles I've written over the years for the monthly magazine *Steam World* and a couple from *Steam Days*. Other chapters are entirely new, and all have been added to, amplified or updated. The photographs are from my vast collection taken with relatively cheap black-and-white-print cameras — a folding Kodak Brownie with fixed f8 aperture and 1/25sec standard shutter speed, followed in my teenage years by an Ensign Selfix that was still restricted by its slow shutter speed but had a superb lens. In the following pages I recall my experiences and railway training to the end of 1962; the intention is that a second volume will cover the final days of British steam until 1968, followed by a frantic rush round the railways of Europe before steam disappeared there too, and will also explain how my later railway career allowed me to continue to experience steam at home and abroad.

I owe thanks to a large number of people, but I'll select a few for special mention: firstly my parents, for encouraging and then tolerating my hobby, and my wife, Pat, for permitting it to be such an important part of my life; also my childhood friend Cedric Utley, who accompanied me on my earliest train-spotting trips, Martin Probyn, Conrad Natzio, Philip Balkwill, Jim Evans and other members of the intrepid Charterhouse Railway Society, Alistair Wood, who taught me the rudiments of train timing (although he was always sceptical of my accuracy and Western Region bias), Colin Boocock, who encouraged and helped me to write about my experiences, and those BR colleagues who encouraged me in those early days (or at least tolerated my interests) — Rodney Meadows, who, as Assistant Train Operating Officer (Bristol), supervised a 'short work course' which opened my eyes to a possible railway career, WR Assistant General Manager George Bowles, who recruited me, and Ray Sims, Shedmaster at Old Oak Common, who indulged my enthusiasm; then, much later, Frank Paterson, who encouraged me to reflect on my 'railway life' by getting me to give several long interviews on tape for the National Railway Museum's oral-history archives, recalling many of the experiences that gave rise to this book.

All royalties from this publication will be donated to the Railway Children charity, which I founded in 1995 with the help of colleagues in the railway industry. A description of how this came about and of the work it undertakes can be found in my self-published history of the charity — *The Other Railway Children* — and on the charity's website (www.railwaychildren.org.uk).

Chapter 1

In the beginning

I am four years old. I am sitting in a nursery school howling my head off. In front of me on the plastic table I have made a barricade of toy bricks and in it placed my book, opened at my favourite page, a picture of the big green steam engine called *Lord Nelson*. The teachers sent my mother away saying, 'leave him, he will soon get over it once you have gone away'. They are wrong. I have howled all morning, through lunch, and now it is early afternoon. The other children are doing their best to ignore me; the teachers are getting frustrated because of the din. They cannot phone home. We have no phone. They persuade me in the early afternoon to look at another book. For a few minutes I stare at a photo of the royal princesses — I remember a long hard look at the seven-year-old Princess Margaret Rose, ignoring her older sister — and then I return to my train book. They wait until my mother comes, and then they say 'it's no good, don't bring him tomorrow; bring him only when he's old enough to start primary school.' I am still sobbing, although I've run out of tears. The bricks are cleared away. My books are closed and put safely in my mother's cycle saddlebag.

A year later I go to school. It is the same place, but different. I am a year older. There is something active to do. I want to learn to read and write. My father is still away in the army. I do not know what he does or where he is, but sometimes he comes home on leave, and we see him off again at the station. He always takes me to see the engine. He told me once that he remembered *Queen Guinevere*. We get into the train before departure time to say farewell, and I panic because I think the train will take us with him, and we have to get out lest my mother should be embarrassed by my piercing screams. I don't understand train timetables yet. I receive small letters from my father. He always draws the picture of an engine in the top right-hand corner of the notepaper — stylised like my toy train I pull around on the carpet.

My earliest memory of all is of standing at the bottom of steps to the platform of Shrewsbury station (we had been evacuated to Shropshire for a while) waiting for my father to book his soldier's warrant ticket and being lifted to the top just in time to see the tail light of the London express disappearing along the platform. I can remember the frustration of not being allowed to look out of the window on the next train (two hours later) because it was dark and the blackout. I was three years old. I'm told that even earlier I insisted on my mother taking me for a walk in my pushchair the two miles from our home in East Molesey to Esher Common to see 'proper' trains (the electrics at Hampton Court apparently didn't count) — you couldn't do that easily now as the growth of trees and shrubs would obscure the view.

The author's favourite 'Castle', 4087 *Cardigan Castle*, surprises him at Paddington, arriving with the 9.30am Minehead, 9 August 1952.

My first proper 'engine' memory is travelling home from Bristol near the end of the war. I can visualise a double-headed train at Bristol with 'Castle' No 4087 and a 'Hall'. The date: 26 December 1944 (Boxing Day). I know because I still have the ticket — soldier's-leave child return, Shirehampton to Hampton Court. The place is Bristol Temple Meads, I am six years old. We are going home, and there are crowds on the platform. But my father takes me to see the engine; he always did, and I associate my father's army departures and arrivals with being taken to see the engine. And there they are, two engines, 4087 *Cardigan Castle* and an unremembered 'Hall'. And when we get to Paddington, there on the buffer-stops is just the one, *Cardigan Castle*. I can see it now and feel the small boy's puzzlement. How can it be? What happened to the other engine?

When, a couple of years later, my father bought me my first Ian Allan 'ABC' I underlined 4087 in that pristine book before I left the house on my first train-spotting trip. And there it's always stayed. In later years it was always special, I was at the end of Platform 8 at Paddington with dozens of other small boys in the summer of 1952 and fired my simple Kodak camera at a number of incoming expresses with mixed success, and suddenly one was revealed as 4087. It was the only shot I took that day that really satisfied me.

Years later I was stationed on BR's Western Region for my management training. During my time at Old Oak Common in the spring of 1962 (described in Chapter 15) I was on the footplate of 4704 on the night goods to Oxley when I spied 4087 on a night fast freight for the West of England, gleaming in the reflected lights of Paddington goods yard, and was tempted to change footplates ... And a few days later, after a superb ride from Swansea to Paddington on No 5056, I was returning to my Twyford digs on the rather mundane 7906 when, around Taplow, the 12.5pm Milford Haven–Paddington swept past with Laira's 4087, nearly ten minutes early — why, oh why, had I not waited at Swansea for the next up express? (And what was a Laira 'Castle' doing on a Landore 'Castle' turn?) Six months later I was practising Work Study techniques in Laira diesel depot in the snow, and there she was again — stored but lovingly cared for, ready to be restored to traffic the following month. Finally, in the spring of 1963, waiting at Pontypool Road for the 2pm Plymouth North & West express, I saw the familiar white painted smokebox-door hinges, the missing front numberplate, the Davies & Metcalfe lubricator high up beside the smokebox and I knew, 4087 again. Climbing Llanvihangel Bank in the setting sun, I'm hanging out the window, listening to the crisp exhaust as we make light of the gradient, the new foliage glistens, the Sugar Loaf broods over us. A magic memory!

Our first postwar holiday was at Brighton and we travelled there by the '*Brighton Belle*'. I must have been a typical bored boy on the journey and I can still hear my father saying — in some exasperation — 'Well, why don't you collect train numbers like other boys?' So I did. I still wonder how much he later regretted that chance remark. A favourite maiden aunt who lived in Brighton soon cottoned on to my interest, and every time we met she enhanced her reputation by producing a new 1/6d Ian Allan booklet in the series '*My Best Railway Photographs*'; my first was of the Great Western by Maurice Earley, the second a book of Southern photos by O. J. Morris.

Guildford's shed pilot (and the author's first footplate experience), Hawthorn Leslie 0-4-0ST 30458 *Ironside*, at Eastleigh 1954 after withdrawal. *(Manchester Locomotive Society collection)*

Uncle George's one-time engine, 'D15' 466, at Eastleigh in the 1930s.
(*J. M. Bentley collection*)

I have to admit that my loyalty was for the Great Western (the imprint of No 4087 and all those photos in Maurice Earley's book did their job only too well), but although my career developed on the Western Region, I lived until 1962 on the Southern, so its trains were the familiar ones.

I can't really explain my passion for trains, which began at such an early age. Perhaps I associated trains with meeting my father when he was so often absent during the war years. My only other railway connection was my Great Uncle George, husband of my paternal grandmother's sister. She, Aunt Kate, had been one of Queen Mary's maids in the Brunswick Tower at Windsor Castle with my grandmother, and after her marriage to George Newman, an engine driver, had moved to Guildford. Uncle George had worked Guildford top-link turns on the Waterloo–Portsmouth direct line during the 1920s with his 'own' engine, Drummond 'D15' 4-4-0 466, but had retired through ill health in 1929. (He eventually died aged 98 in the 1970s!) In the late 1940s, when I was nine or ten, I'd visited them for the day, and my uncle, as a treat, took me down to Guildford engine shed and put me on the footplate of the shed pilot, 0-4-0 saddle tank 30458 *Ironside*. My main memory is of being in the diminutive cab as we hauled a dead locomotive onto the turntable and burning my shins on the open fire, as I was wearing only short trousers.

In the autumn of 1949 I started at Surbiton County Grammar School and travelled daily from Hampton Court. The school stood beside the South West main line, just on the Waterloo side of Surbiton station, high above the embankment there. A few of us collected each morning in a small clearing above the line (you can't do it now — the undergrowth is too thick, and the school is gone) to see the action before

'King Arthur' 30455 *Sir Launcelot* on a semi-fast train from Basingstoke passes just below the point at which Surbiton County Grammar schoolboys trainspotted before the morning bell sounded, 6 February 1957.

30749 *Iseult* passes Surbiton with a semi-fast to Basingstoke — a replica of the scene the author had witnessed in 1950. *(Robin Russell)*

the school whistle blew at 9 o'clock. We watched the 8.30am Waterloo–Bournemouth with its Nine Elms 'Merchant Navy' or 'West Country' sidle beneath the high road bridge, braking for the Surbiton stop. And simultaneously and almost noiselessly apart from the distant whistle as it approached the main up platform at speed would come a malachite-green 'Lord Nelson'. We soon lost interest in this because within weeks we'd copped the whole class!

The evening, whilst waiting for the 4.25 home on Surbiton station, was even more interesting. School finished at 4pm sharp and although I couldn't get the 4.5, I was at the station at least by 4.10 in time to see the up *'Atlantic Coast Express'* roar through with its Exmouth Junction 'Merchant Navy' (usually 35022, 35023 or the newly painted blue 35024) and almost simultaneously see the 3.54pm Waterloo–Basingstoke come bucketing down the track working hard with one of its collection of Nine Elms veterans — Class T14 'Paddleboxes' 444, 445, 447, 460, 462 and the already renumbered 30446 and 30461, which would leave a fog of pungent brown smoke hanging under the wide platform overbridge. These would be increasingly interspersed with one of the Urie 'H15s' or Class N15X 'Remembrances' or one of the Urie or 'Scotch' 'King Arthurs' — I can still recall in my mind's eye 30741 *Joyous Gard*, 30753 *Melisande*, 30776 *Sir Galagars* and 30791 *Sir Uwaine*. Most of the 'Arthurs' were in malachite-green livery with 'BRITISH RAILWAYS' painted on the tender in the old Southern style.

Two of the Drummond T14 4-6-0s, that regularly hauled the 3.54pm Waterloo – Basingstoke in 1949-50, 444 and an unknown sister at Nine Elms in 1950, alongside 34023 *Blackmore Vale*. *(Lewis Coles/MLS Collection)*

13

'Merchant Navy' 35024 *East Asiatic Company* (in blue) passes Surbiton on the 3 o'clock Waterloo–West of England c1952. *(Robin Russell)*

30806 *Sir Galleron* between Brookwood and Woking with the Eastleigh van train — still the same as seen daily in 1950, but recorded in 1960.

After a couple of down-line electrics, taking some of my friends to Oxshott and Esher respectively, the 'ACE' would be followed by the Eastleigh van train — mixed ECS and parcels, with the possibility of almost anything at the front end. Although booked for an Eastleigh-based 'Arthur' or 'H15' it was obviously used for running-in ex-works locos. I remember seeing at least one 'L12' (30424), and just once the unfamiliar outline of a large-diameter-chimney 'Schools', 30917 *Ardingly*, surprised us all and caused extraordinary scenes of merriment among the crowd of small-boy witnesses — after all, few of us at that stage could afford a trip to Charing Cross from our meagre pocket money.

Finally, just before my own electric slunk around the corner from under the high bridge below the school, the Clapham Junction milk empties, a train on which No 34031 *Torrington* performed for months, would charge through the station amid the clatter of its six-wheelers, followed by the pungent smell of Kentish coal. And all the time a 'K10' or 'L11' 4-4-0 would be slithering up and down the adjacent coal yard (now a car park) — more often than not 30406, or one of its sisters 405 and 413. On one memorable occasion it was, of all things, the malachite-green royal 'T9', 30119. If for any reason I got out of school early I would see an up Basingstoke local with an 'N15X' (Nos 32328 *Hackworth* in lined BR black and 32330 *Cudworth* in malachite green stick in my memory) and a pick-up freight with one of Feltham's magnificent 'H16' Pacific tanks (30516-20). For some obscure reason I used to circle the numbers of the engines I'd 'copped' in green biro in my Southern 'ABC' instead of underlining as most other boys did.

Looking back now, I realise that in those two years I never failed to see those four steam services between 4.5 and 4.25pm, and the sheer consistency of the Southern Region's punctuality could be taken for granted. One of my schoolmasters at Charterhouse, which I attended after 1951, lived near Worplesdon, his garden backing onto the Woking–Guildford main line, and he told me that his party trick was to take visitors to see the hourly fast Pompey electrics crossing each other at the bottom of his garden — and it never failed!

It would have been around this time that I discovered the monthly Ian Allan magazine *Trains Illustrated*. My first purchase was No 10, although since then I've managed to pick up a couple of the earliest editions. I used to long for the time each month when the new magazine would arrive and would pore over it until the next one appeared. I can remember those early editions and the photos much better than those in more recent magazines. It was the regular article by Cecil J. Allen on locomotive practice and performance that inspired me in particular and led later to my own interest in recording locomotive performance, although I compiled no serious logs until about 1956.

Then, a couple of years later, around April 1951 (we'd still maintained our interest), I was at the top of the cutting, waiting for the school bell to go, but on this particular morning, for some unknown reason, I was alone. There was something odd about the approaching westbound train — the whistle in the distance was a blood-curdling chime, and the approaching locomotive was not an air-smoothed Bulleid, nor was it an 'Arthur' or 'Nelson'. And suddenly it emerged from beneath the high bridge,

15

70009 *Alfred the Great*, a brilliant green apparition, and the scales tumbled from my eyes — because just a few weeks earlier I'd seen the dramatic photo of 70000 on the cover of the March 1951 *Trains Illustrated*. I couldn't wait to tell my friends. And they didn't believe me! It was such a let down. So I waited the next day — the others were losing interest and couldn't be bothered — and it was 70009 again. The next day I waited with trepidation, as my sceptical friends had turned out to call my bluff, and it was a 'West Country'. The others gave up until the following Monday, and then, to the surprise of all of us, it was not a Bulleid, nor 70009, but the other 'Britannia' that was loaned to the Southern while a couple of Bulleid Pacifics were tried out on the Great Eastern, 70014 *Iron Duke*. The relief when 70014 did not let me down before my friends!

Photograph of brand-new BR Standard Pacific 70000 *Britannia* on the cover of *Trains Illustrated* March 1951.

TRAINS
ILLUSTRATED

MARCH, 1951

70000

AN *Ian Allan* PUBLICATION

1/6

Tableau 1

Surbiton station, March 1950

It's a damp late afternoon in early March, and Cedric, Robert and I are scampering over the Ewell Road Bridge, our satchels bouncing on our backs, full of the homework set by our form master, Mr Bolt. The clouds have hung around all day, and although it's only just after 4 o'clock it already seems like dusk. We're hurrying because we want to be at the station before the 'Atlantic Coast Express' charges through. Then, as we leave the main road and turn off past the leafless bushes that screen us from the sight of the four tracks down below, Cedric and Robert begin to scuffle with two of the other boys in our class who are going in the opposite direction to us, to Berrylands and New Malden. I'm impatient. If we don't hurry the express will tear past, and we shall just see the smoke billowing through the trees and hear the howl of the mournful hooter. I make to go on ahead, ears straining for the distant sound. 'It's coming,' I yell. 'Come on, we'll miss it!'

My friends break off from their tomfoolery, and we clear the thicket and come onto the open pathway above the concrete embankment walls just in time, for there's a prolonged wail from the approaching express which bursts from under the station overbridge and tears past us in a blur of green, smoke swirling around the coaches labelled Padstow and Bude and Ilfracombe, the staccato thunder of the wheels drowning the soft exhaust of the 'Merchant Navy' already disappearing under the high bridge by our school.

'Holland-Afrika Line again,' moans Cedric. 'No need to have hurried — it's always the same.' It isn't, but I don't argue. You never know, it might be different one day. We hurry down onto the platform, for there'll be a train on the down line in a minute. We're at the bottom of the steps, and I can already see the billowing white smoke in the gloom, under the bridge. This train is working hard — I can hear the pounding of the engine, the deep roar from the chimney, the rhythmic 'pshht pshht' of steam from the cylinders — and as the malachite-green engine rocks past me, its exhaust richocheting off the overbridge and engulfing us boys on the platform, I read '30744' — Maid of Astolat. It's gone in an instant, its short train clattering past and hurrying westwards, the tail lamp just visible in the dusk, shining through the smokescreen now trailing in its wake.

Scarcely has the sound of its exhaust dwindled in the distance than Robert's electric train comes tentatively under the bridge, the station loudspeaker booming its familiar message, 'Esher, Hersham, Walton, Weybrdge, West Weybridge, West Byfleet, Woking, the front four cars for Brookwood, Ash Vale, Aldershot ...' The voice fades under the hum of the approaching train, brakes squealing as it stops, and Robert jumps in, shouting out some last comment on our Geography homework. At the same time there is a sudden thunderous slip behind us and a clanging of buffers as the coal-yard shunter, 'L11' 30406, jerks into action, drawing out a raft of wagons towards the throat of the sidings. Cedric and I both look round, turning our backs on the departing electric and stare at the sparks still descending. The glare from the open firebox door illuminates the driver tugging at the regulator, while the fireman is hanging nonchalantly out of the other side of the draughty cab. The engine slithers to a halt amid a further clanging of buffers, and we are so absorbed in this spectacle that we nearly miss the Eastleigh van train, which has been sidling up on us. We are alerted as we suddenly hear its engine open up as its driver spots the signal at the far end of the up platform change from double-yellow to green, and 'Scotch Arthur' 30770 *Sir Prianius* accelerates slowly past us with a long string of parcel vans. We count them; I make it nineteen, Cedric swears there are twenty, and we try to count again, but the 'N15' has got hold of its train now, and the empty vehicles are accelerating past us at an ever-increasing tempo.

It's nearly time for our train now. Will it come before the milk empties? We're at the front of our platform, ready to join the first car of our four-coach EMU, right opposite where 30406 is straining to haul another half-dozen wagons from the back of the coal yard. I'm not that bothered. Both the 'Arthurs' tonight were 'cops', and I'm satisfied. The milk train will only be *Torrington* again — it has been for over a fortnight now. And indeed I spy the 4.25 to Hampton Court coming under the bridge just as a wisp of steam appears above it, and I watch the 'West Country' gain on our slowing electric. And I'm wrong. It's a different Exmouth Junction 'West Country', *Yes Tor*. Three cops tonight. Cedric and I look at each other in glee. We dance a jig, and in our surprise and excitement we almost forget to join our train, which has now stopped silently behind us. We scamper in and slam the door, pull out the strap and let the window down with a clatter so we can breathe in the pungent smell of the brown haze left behind by the shuffling pacific and its clackety-clack six-wheelers. We set off in pursuit of it, but it's got too great a head start, and all we catch is the remnant haze of brown smoke drifting in the drizzle that is now swirling into our compartment. We close the window. The show is over for another day.

Overleaf: Pages from the author's 1949 Ian Allan 'ABC' trainspotter's book of BR Southern Region locomotives.

4-4-0   Class S11

Rbt. from engines Introduced 1903
Weights: Loco.   53 tons 15 cwt.
     Tender types : 17, 28
Pressure : 175 lb.   Cyls. 19" × 26"
Driving Wheels: 6' 0".   T.E.: 19 390 lb.

30395	30398	30401	30403
30396	30399	30402	30404
30397	30400		

Total 10

4-4-0   Class L11

(Class continued from No. 30175)

30405	30408	30411	30413
30406	30409	30412	30414
30407	30410		

(Class continued No. 30435)

4-4-0   Class L12

Rbt. from engines introduced 1904
Weights : Loco.   55 tons 5 cwt
     Tender types : 18, 28
Pressure : 175 lb. Cyls. 19" × 26"
Driving Wheels: 6' 7".   T.E.: 17,670 lb.

30415	30420	30425	30430
30416	30421	30426	30431
30417	30422	30427	30432
30418	30423	30428	30433
30419	30424	30429	30434

Total 20

4-4-0   Class L11

(Class continued from No. 30414)

30435	30437	30439	30441
30436	30438	30440	30442

Total 40 32

4-6-0   Class T14

Rebuilt from Drummond engines introduced 1911.
Weights : Loco.   76 tons 10 cwt.
     Tender type : 40
Pressure : 175 lb.   Cyls. (4) 15" × 26"
Driving Wheels: 6' 7".   T.E.: 22,030 lb.

30443	30445	30446	30447
30444			

(Class continued No. 30459)

4-6-0   Class N15

(Dimensions applicable only to this series)

Built 1925, assimilated to Class N15 introduced 1918

Weights : Loco. { 80 tons 19 cwt. (Nos. 30448-52) / 79 tons 18 cwt. (Nos. 30452-7) }

Tender type : 29
Pressure : 200 lb.   Cyls. 20½" × 28"
Driving Wheels: 6' 7".   T.E.: 25,320 lb.

30448	Sir Tristram
30449	Sir Torre
30450	Sir Kay
30451	Sir Lamorak
30452	Sir Meliagrance
30453	King Arthur
30454	Queen Guinevere
30455	Sir Launcelot
30456	Sir Galahad
30457	Sir Bedivere

(Class continued No. 30736)

0-4-0ST   Class 0458

Introduced 1890
Weight : 21 tons 2 cwt.
Pressure : 120 lb. Cyls. 12" × 20"
Driving Wheels : 3' 2". T.E.: 7,730 lb.

30458	Ironside

Total 1

4-6-0   Class T14

(Class continued from No. 30447)

30459	30460	30461	30462

Total 8 7 2

4-4-0   Class D15

Rebt. from engines introduced 1912
Weights : Loco.   61 tons 11 cwt.
     Tender type : 17
Pressure : 180 lb.   Cyls. 20" × 26"
Driving Wheels: 6' 7".   T.E.: 20,140 lb.

30463	30466	30469	30471
30464	30467	30470	30472
30465	30468		

Total 10

4-6-0   Class H15

(Class continued from No. 30335. Dimensions below applicable only to this series and Nos. 30491, 30521-4)

Introduced 1914
Weights : Loco.   79 tons 19 cwt.
         Tender type : 36
Pressure : 180 lb.   Cyls. 21″ × 28″
Driving Wheels: 6′ 0″.   T.E.: 26,240 lb.

30473	30475	30477	30478
30474	30476		

(Class continued No. 30482)

0-4-4T   Class M7

(Class continued from No. 30379)

30479 | 30480† | 30481†

(Class continued No. 30667)

4-6-0   Class H15

(Class continued from No. 30478. Dimensions below applicable only to this series, except No. 30491)

Introduced 1914
Weights : Loco.   81 tons 5 cwt.
         Tender type : 39
Pressure : 180 lb.   Cyls. 21″ × 28″
Driving Wheels : 6′ 0″. T.E. 26,240 lb.

30482	30485	30488	30490
30483	30486	30489	30491*
30484	30487		

(Class continued No. 30521)

* Dimensions as 30473-30478 series.

4-8-0T   Class G16

Introduced 1921
Weight : 95 tons 2 cwt.
Pressure : 180 lb.   Cyls. 22″ × 28″
Driving Wheels: 5′ 1″. T.E.: 33,990 lb.

30492 | 30493 | 30494 | 30495

Total 4

4-6-0   Class S15

(Dimensions below applicable to this series only)

Introduced 1920
Weights : Loco.   79 tons 16 cwt.
         Tender types : 28, 37
Pressure : 180 lb.   Cyls. 21″ × 28″
Driving Wheels: 5′ 7″.   T.E.: 28,200 lb.

30496	30501	30506	30511
30497	30502	30507	30512
30498	30503	30508	30513
30499	30504	30509	30514
30500	30505	30510	30515

(Class continued No. 30823)

4-6-2T   Class H16

Introduced 1921
Weight : 96 tons 8 cwt.
Pressure : 180 lb.   Cyls. 21″ × 28″
Driving Wheels : 5′7″. T.E. 28,200 lb.

30516	30518	30519	30520
30517			

Total 5

4-6-0   Class H15

(Class continued from No. 30491. For dimensions see 30473-30478 series)

30521 | 30522 | 30523 | 30524

Total 26

0-6-0   Class Q

Introduced 1938
Weights : Loco.   49 tons 10 cwt.
         Tender type : 19
Pressure : 200 lb.   Cyls. 19″ × 26″
Driving Wheels: 5′ 1″. T.E.: 26,160 lb.

(All except Nos. 30545/9 fitted with multiple-jet blast pipe and large diameter chimney)

30530	30535	30540	30545
30531	30536	30541	30546
30532	30537	30542	30547
30533	30538	30543	30548
30534	30539	30544	30549

Total 20

Chapter 2

What we were allowed to do in 1950

'M7' 30130 at Waterloo, 29 May 1950. *(Cedric Utley)*

Boys of twelve were allowed to put sandwiches, an apricot 'Harvest' pie and a bottle of Tizer in a duffle bag, buy a cheap day return to London and spend the day on their own going around the Circle Line, stopping off at Paddington, Euston Square, King's Cross & St Pancras and Liverpool Street before returning to Embankment and walking across Hungerford Bridge back to Waterloo in the hope of seeing a St Leonards or Bricklayers Arms 'Schools' poking its head out of Charing Cross station. Permission was granted even more easily if one went with a friend, although I suspect two heads on these occasions were marginally more enterprising and therefore more dangerous than one.

The first evidence I have of such a visit is a page of four rather amateurish photos taken by my friend Cedric thirteen days after my twelfth birthday. A splendid but not-quite-horizontal photo of *Arethusa* at St Pancras, complete with Fowler tender still showing 'L M S' very plainly, a far-from-horizontal photo of Hawksworth tank 1504 in the distance at Paddington (why that instead of Caledonian-blue 'Kings' and Brunswick-green 'Castles'?), a distant shot from Platform 8 of the locos around the turntable in King's Cross yard — an 'N2', *Dante*, *Raby Castle* (I think) and what looks like an 'L1' — and a fine photo of 'M7' No 30130 at Waterloo, awaiting its next ECS duty. Cedric became my bosom pal. He'd just moved to East Molesey from Yorkshire, and we joined the 8.25 from Hampton Court to Surbiton together to go to our grammar school.

But the Southern's Western Section engines amid all the electrics seemed too humdrum, and so we made our plans to look for more exotic sights in London, and our mothers acquiesced. It was 29 May 1950, that first trip that I remember. A Saturday, of course; it was compulsory Church and Sunday School on Sundays. The old pre-Grouping three-car unit, augmented to four cars by the addition of a Bulleid trailer, all-stations to Waterloo in exactly the same time as the scarlet Class 455 units do it now, would be in Waterloo before 9am. We would look out for an old second-class compartment, long since downgraded to third, because it gave more legroom for standing around the window trying to catch a glimpse of mysterious goings-on in Stewarts Lane before looking for engines backing out of Nine Elms, awaiting their turn to parade at Waterloo.

It was the Northern Line to old Euston, in time for our first quarry, the '*Royal Scot*'. A quick look to see what had arrived at platforms 1, 2 and 3, usually night sleepers still slumbering at the stop-blocks, or perhaps something already backing its train up Camden Bank towards Willesden carriage sidings, then all haste to platform

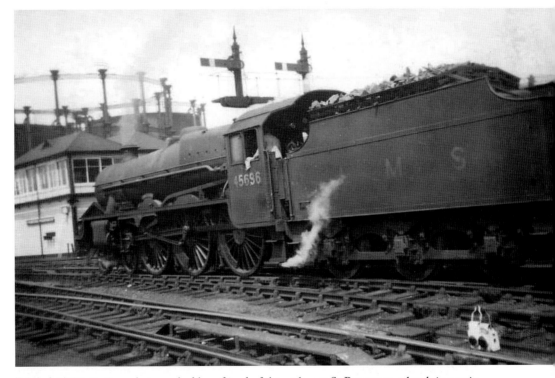

'Jubilee' 45696 *Arethusa* photographed by a friend of the author at St Pancras on a lunchtime train for Derby, 29 May 1950. *(Cedric Utley)*

13, in time to wait with trepidation for the tender of the 'Duchess' to appear in the distance, descending the bank — rumour had it that the train was diagrammed for a Polmadie 'Duchess', no less, to our innocent eyes a rare exotic beast. It was blue, of course, 46227 *Duchess of Devonshire* — not just my first Polmadie locomotive, but my first 'Duchess' too. The business end of platform 13 was timbered and very narrow, so the spotters were crammed into a small space, all pushing for a glimpse into the holy cab and the roaring fire, as the engine deafened us by suddenly expulsing a tirade of steam. After its departure (and, I suppose, the 10.40 to Perth, which I cannot remember) the station seemed strangely quiet. The arrival side was now empty, the sleeper trains now safely stowed at Willesden. I just remember an apple-green 'Royal Scot', 46169 *The Boy Scout* in its experimental livery, and an unrebuilt and unnamed 'Patriot', 45509, simmering halfway down the platform lit by shafts of sunlight pouring through the smoky roof.

Disappointed at the lack of further action, we walked to Euston Square and made for Paddington, emerging on the Hammersmith platform amid 'sixty-oners' ('Large Prairie' tank engines of the '61xx' class) on non-corridor locals for Slough and Reading, and looked across at the phalanx of 'Kings' and 'Castles' ranged at the head of platforms 1-5 in glorious symmetry. We would run across the passenger bridge halfway down the platforms lest a train steal a march on us and leave before we had gained its precious number.

At first we used to join a few boys at the far end of platform 1, beside the metal advertisements on the brick walls for 'Tangye Oil Pumps', in order to be subsumed into the thunderous exhaust of departing trains as the smoke and steam crashed back

'Star' 4007 *Swallowfield Park* arriving at Paddington c1950 with a train from Worcester. *(Anon)*

24

An array of locomotives waiting to depart Paddington on 14 February 1958. From left to right are 5935 *Norton Hall*, 70021 *Morning Star* on the 1.55pm to West Wales, 5029 *Nunney Castle* on the 1.50 relief and 6020 *King Henry IV* on the 2.10 to Wolverhampton.

from the bridge under Bishop's Bridge Road. That first day I remember the filthy tender of the erstwhile royal engine 4082 *Windsor Castle* backing around from the parcels deck (platform 1A), its front end swathed in steam, onto a Worcester train — before, that is, it swapped identities with *Bristol Castle* for the King's funeral and became 7013 for evermore, outliving the 25-years-younger 4082 by several months. I remember 5093 *Upton Castle* racing in past the majority of small boys on platform 8 with the 'Red Dragon' and (now of greater interest) underlinings in my notebook of a couple of 'Princesses' — Nos 4051 and 4052 and an early survivor, 4007 *Swallowfield Park* — and not realising their rarity or that of the lone 'Saint' I saw in London, 2949 *Stanford Court*, that lunchtime. Seen from platform 1, incoming trains surprised the unguarded spotter by arriving suddenly from behind a motley collection of small hutments and entered the platforms with unusual rapidity.

On we went to King's Cross, using the Hammersmith Line so that we could see action up to the moment the tube train appeared from Subway Junction. A quick nip into St Pancras produced the one 'namer' — the aforementioned 45696 *Arethusa* — but a solitary 'Black Five' was the only other offering, apart from a couple of Stanier 2-6-2 tanks, so we sought bigger scalps next door. A couple of 'A1s' graced the arrival platforms, one being *King's Courier*, but we joined the throng at the end of platform 8 with its vista to the yard, agog to see what would emerge from the Gasworks Tunnel, which seemed always on the brink of producing its magic from the smoke curling from the tunnel portal, several minutes after the last action. While we waited we remembered our soggy sandwiches and took a swig of Tizer, for we had been so absorbed and excited that we had not noticed any hunger pangs. Then a shadow formed in the swirling smoke, a corridor tender emerged, and the cry went up long before we saw the streamlined shape, a 'Streak'. *Walter K. Whigham*, 60028. 'N2s' chugged out from the 'drain' with their archaic sets of quad-arts but went virtually unnoticed — a scrawled number to underline later, but no picture etched on the inner eye. A 'V2' clanked in from the north over on the far side, but the eyes of small boys were drawn inexorably to the glamorous pacific. Who was Walter Whigham? Did it matter? The driver played his chime whistle for us, a short peep at first; then, as he left with the Newcastle express, he exhibited its full glory, a spine-tingling chord in crescendo, and repeated the plangent and prolonged orchestration as the 'A4' plunged into the tunnel, the coaches disappearing smoothly, one by one into the murk, and silence descended on the awestruck assembly.

This first time we felt obliged to return home in time for tea. We dragged ourselves away from our steamy temple, learned a bit more of the Underground system and the long walk between the Piccadilly and Northern lines at Leicester Square and had time for just one photo of the 'M7' at the end of platform 11, by the empty barrows and milk churns. The solitary pacific waiting to depart was given little attention — we'd seen *Blue Funnel* so many times before — but we took more interest as it drew alongside between Queen's Park and Clapham Junction, and for a few seconds we watched the flailing rods and saw the glow from the fire illuminate the sweating

'N2' 69523 (since preserved as GNR 1744) climbs out of the 'Drain' at King's Cross alongside 'A3' 60112 *St Simon*, 13 September 1958.

fireman. Then we were slowing to stop, and 35013 uttered its low melancholy hoot as it shut off steam to negotiate the curve and glided out of sight.

Only now was I really aware of one of the consequences of this day, as I found I was scratching my eye, blinking the smarting tears as the smuts irritated the iris. The sensation got worse, and when I finally reached home I was shepherded to the next street, where my cousin, a district nurse, rolled up my eyelid with the help of a matchstick and removed the offending cinders. I blinked once more, felt the relief and ran home, filthy, tired and already anxious to see when I could afford another trip from my savings — pocket money 1/3 a week — and dare another request from my indulgent parents. The evening was spent carefully underlining my 'cops' in virgin Ian Allan 'ABCs'.

Just once we went out to Clapham Junction to see the LBSC engines off the line to/from Victoria. I remember seeing a few of the efficient 'I3' tanks (32028, 32081, 32089) on the Oxted services just before the LM Fairburn tanks took over, but the star that night was the 6.10pm from Victoria, which swept majestically through the station behind my first sight of an 'Atlantic', malachite-green 32422 *North Foreland*. The roll as she took the curve through the station was graceful, and there was only a slight haze from the chimney as the train glided past. Then, as the last coach passed us, there was a billowing of white steam as the engine was opened up on its climb out to Balham. The vision was so fast, over in a few seconds, yet I can still conjure up the slight lurch of 32422 in my mind's eye as it hit the curve through the platform. My friend and I stood mesmerised as the last traces of smoke drifted into the trees on the embankment at the southern end of the station.

That summer we had another London day in late July; memories fade, as, for some reason, we had no camera with us. 46224 *Princess Alexandra* was our second Polmadie 'Duchess', and I recall a sparkling 4059 *Princess Patricia* of Gloucester shed on the mid-morning Paddington–Cheltenham at platform 1, so we must have made a quick getaway from Euston immediately after departure of the '*Royal Scot*'. However, a few days later I was Cedric's guest for three weeks in his native Yorkshire, staying with his aunt, a schoolteacher, in Hatfield, near Doncaster, on the line to Scunthorpe and Cleethorpes. I think the idea was for him to visit relatives and me to keep him company as a friend, but we spent most of the time, when not playing 'fivestones' in front of the aunt's hearth, on the old cattle dock at Doncaster station, noting the numbers of innumerable 'B1s'.

We were accompanied by his dad to King's Cross and put aboard the train while he was despatched to the front end to collect the number of our train's locomotive (grown-ups didn't really understand that number-taking by proxy doesn't count). He scrawled '60033' in the condensation on our window and then '60067' for the '*Flying Scotsman*' at the adjacent platform; if we peered out of the window toplight we could just make out its silhouette in the distance. Of course, at Doncaster we did it properly and spent a good few minutes staring at the blue *Seagull* that had hauled us from King's Cross on the 10.10 to Leeds.

Most days we were packed off by bus into town and joined the throng of twenty to thirty youngsters watching the antics of 'J52s' shunting portions on and off Hull

'A1' 60141 *Abbotsford* on the up *'Yorkshire Pullman'* at Grantham, 1953.
(J. M. Bentley collection)

Locally allocated 'B1' 61036 *Ralph Assheton* in the up parcels bay at Doncaster station, 1953. *(J. M. Bentley collection)*

and Leeds trains to London, the stored hulk of one of the last Ivatt Atlantics (62877) over towards 'The Plant', the thrill of pacifics at frequent intervals and the sight of 60082 *Neil Gow* in full cry on the up '*Flying Scotsman*'. 'Directors' came in on trains from Lincoln or Sheffield — 62661 *Gerard Powys Dewhurst* and 62668 *Jutland* spring to mind — along with yet more 'B1s'. Unfortunately we couldn't afford train fares to visit other locations but took buses to Leeds and Sheffield; the latter's Midland station produced two original Midland Compounds (41015 and 41019) and a couple of 'Jubilees', but Victoria was a great disappointment. When we tried to enter the barrier the ticket collector told us that train-spotters were banned, then relented when he found we came from London. All that for what? One paltry 'B1'! We paid a visit to relatives in Scunthorpe, which prompted the only train journey of the holiday apart from the outward and return trips from London. We picked up the Cleethorpes-bound train from Thorne behind the highest-numbered 'B1', 61409, and returned behind one of Doncaster's common 'namers', 61249 *Fitzherbert Wright*. Was any train stopping at Doncaster not hauled by a 'B1'?

We visited Cedric's grandmother in Cudworth and, I'm told, upset the elderly lady by making our excuses as fast as we could and visiting the line by Cudworth engine shed; I cannot find such a shed in my records now; I suspect it was Royston (20C), which was populated mainly by '4Fs' and '8Fs'. Somewhere from the top of a bus I spied my only Great Central Atlantic, 2909 (in large florid numerals); another time, also from atop a bus, while waiting at a level crossing en route to York, we saw *Cock o' the North* on a northbound train of fish empties. York itself was a revelation — besides a few old North Eastern 'D20' 4-4-0s there were lots of 'D49s', especially the 'Hunts'; I remember seeing my first, 62751 *The Albrighton*, running light-engine above us on some brick embankment wall, but others were pottering off to Harrogate and Scarborough from the north end of the station. We visited the old York Museum and saw *City of Truro* in its cramped shed. When it was finally time to return home we were ushered into a crowded Thompson SK (not even a window seat — grown-ups just did not understand) that had just been hauled into the station by yet another 'B1', 61167, and our disappointment was overwhelming until we found we were being hauled out backwards to be attached to the train that had just run in from Leeds at the opposite platform behind blue 'A1' 60141 *Abbotsford*. What a relief!

Chapter 3

My first camera

Brand-new 'Battle of Britain' 34110 *66 Squadron* at Bournemouth Central on a semi-fast morning train to Waterloo, watched by thirteen-year-old trainspotter David, 16 May 1951. *(Jack Maidment)*

I spent most Saturdays at my paternal grandparents', only a five-minute walk from my home, but in the winter of 1950/1 my grandmother died quite suddenly, and various routines changed. She left me £10 in her will 'to buy something to remember her by', and with this bequest I bought my first camera, a simple folding Kodak with a basic 1/25sec shutter speed and fixed f8 aperture. Of course, there was only one objective I had with this camera. I've scanned my first photo album for photos of people, and apart from a couple of shots of my 'O'-gauge model railway laid out temporarily in our allotment with my dad and sister in the background and a shot of me on my thirteenth birthday gazing admiringly at brand-new 34110 *66 Squadron* at Bournemouth Central (taken by my father) I can find none.

I regret now that I have only a couple of photos of my youngest sister (who was just two at the time), one posed photo of my family around then, with our cat, and a couple of beach photos of that May holiday in Bournemouth, but I must have put them in a separate album. I have just one photo, rather distant, of my grandfather and never took a photo of my maternal grandmother, who lived until 1957, and only two doors away.

So, a week after the purchase of this precious object, on 3 April 1951, I spent another day in London with my friend Cedric, of whom, interestingly, I have no photos either. Euston and the '*Royal Scot*' was again our initial target, and I have that first photo of 46231 *Duchess of Atholl* swathed in steam, backlit, the sun gleaming off the boiler side. A more fortunate choice of subject was a side-on shot of 46148 *The Manchester Regiment* running to the turntable tucked away on the west side of the station, for it was still unrebuilt, and I don't recall ever again seeing an unrebuilt 'Royal Scot' engine.

Left: The author's first photograph with his new camera: Polmadie's 46231 *Duchess of Atholl* on the '*Royal Scot*' at Euston, 3 April 1951.

Below: Unrebuilt 'Royal Scot' 46148 *The Manchester Regiment* runs down to the turntable at Euston, 3 April 1951.

Trainspotters on Paddington's platform 8 admire blue 'King' 6008 *King James II* after arrival with a train from Wolverhampton, 3 April 1951.

After that it was Paddington for late morning and lunchtime and a rather nondescript shot of a Landore 'Hall' (5902 *Howick Hall*) — taken, I suspect, because of its rarity value for us young London spotters — and a better one of a blue 'King', 6008 *King James II*, and a group of admiring spotters at the place that was to become my favourite vantage-point, the business end of platform 8, beyond the Bishop's Bridge Road overbridge. By lunchtime it had obviously clouded over, and a photo I took of Canton's spotless 5020 *Trematon Castle* on the 1.55pm Paddington–Swansea and West Wales express shows the white steam gushing from the safety valve merging with a pure white sky. However humdrum the photo, it made a great impression on me; the engine is posed perfectly to show off its handsome lines, it is burnished and gleaming (as Canton's top-link engines always were), and it was fitted with one of the Hawksworth flush-sided tenders, which, I have always thought, made the 'Castles' look more svelte.

I think we gave King's Cross a miss because of our Doncaster holiday (recounted in the last chapter) and went to explore Liverpool Street instead. Film was of course expensive then, and the Ilford film I bought had just eight exposures. I'd left some for Liverpool Street, but the dull midday had turned into a late afternoon of steady rain, and the old terminus never rejoiced in the best light for taking railway photos.

With such a new toy, I took no pictures there, partly from fear of getting my new camera wet and partly from the well-founded belief that little would come out anyway. I therefore have to rely on my memory. I'm sure Liverpool Street must have abounded in those derided (by me) 'B1s', and we can't have seen any of the brand-new 'Britannias', because I would have remembered them. I can remember looking down on 'Sandringham' 61619 *Welbeck Abbey* — we were standing on the raised road for arriving taxis, between the two sides of the station — and 61671 *Royal Sovereign*, the 'B17' rebuilt by Thompson as a two cylinder 'B2' and based at Cambridge for royal train duties to and from Sandringham. My overriding memory of Liverpool Street is of those endless yo-yos of 'N7'-hauled articulated sets rushing in and out on services to Chingford and Enfield and the constant pounding of Westinghouse brake pumps, as though the station had innumerable live heartbeats. On subsequent visits I attempted more photos, some reasonably successfully, but it always seemed murky down there.

In May the family took a short break in Bournemouth, and I must have spent several mornings before the boarding-house breakfast on the road bridge above the London end of the Central station. I have a nice shot of 34106 *Lydford* departing on the '*Royal Wessex*'.

'Canton's immaculate 5020 *Trematon Castle* ready to depart Paddington with the 1.55pm to West Wales, 3 April 1951.

I went to Southampton on my own, spotting, coincidentally travelling down behind 34010 and back with 34009. For some reason I did decide to take photos of one or two veterans as well as the Bulleids, and a photo of 'S11' 30404, in the bay at Southampton Central is very clear. A couple of days later, on 19 May, I recorded sister 'S11' 30403 on a parcels train at Bournemouth, but the weather intervened again, to its detriment.

In contrast the obligatory summer holiday day in London on 28 July was swelteringly hot and full of the atmosphere of summer Saturdays when the whole country decamped by train to the seaside. We were greeted at Euston by the sight of blue 'Princess Royal' 46203 *Princess Margaret Rose* just arrived on the '*Ulster Express*'; 46230 *Duchess of Buccleugh* was the Polmadie Pacific on the '*Royal Scot*', and I have several other 2½x3½in prints taken in the bright light — 46253 *City of St Albans* picking up a vanfit to add to a holiday express (passengers' luggage in advance or some scout group's camping gear?), 45686 *St Vincent* with its crew chewing the fat before departure for Birmingham, 45525 *Colwyn Bay* (before the addition of smoke-deflectors) basking at platform 14. Three weeks later I'd saved enough pocket money for another outing (without Cedric this time) and, again in glorious sunshine, took a photo which to me captures the atmosphere of those summer spotter trips — 46120 and 46162 crammed at the end of the wooden platform 13, spotters squeezed between them, both engines blowing off steam furiously prior to departure for North Wales on the '*Welshman*' and its relief.

'West Country' 34106 *Lydford* leaving Bournemouth Central with the up '*Royal Wessex*', 17 May 1951.

Drummond 'S11' mixed-traffic 4-4-0 30404 at Southampton Central, 17 May 1951.

Summer Saturday at Euston, with spotters standing between 46120 *Royal Inniskilling Fusilier* on the '*Welshman*' for Holyhead and its relief headed by 46162 *Queen's Westminster Rifleman*, 18 August 1951.

Back at Paddington I shot 'Castles' and 'Halls' (5042, 5063 and 4974) on ECS duties, the record-breaking 5006 *Tregenna Castle* on the 3.55pm to Cardiff and West Wales, showing off its Canton shine in the bright sunlight, and the 4.10 to Wolverhampton and the 4.15 to Plymouth via Bristol, with 7026 *Tenby Castle* and the doyen 6000 *King George V* respectively, side by side. A mogul — Collett-built 9310, with side-window cab — made an appearance, and I first became aware of the Paddington arrival-indicator board's habit of showing all arriving trains to be 99 minutes late, as it had no space to show three digits under each train heading! Then it was home to my district nurse cousin for the removal of a bumper crop of smuts garnered during this torrid day.

In between my London train-spotting trips I accompanied my Aunt Doris and Uncle Vic (the district nurse's parents) to visit a friend of theirs in Axminster. To my disappointment we went in Uncle's Ford V8 — I think they thought it was a treat for me, as no-one else in the family owned a car. We had a day excursion to the sea at Exmouth, and to my relief we were all too many to get in Uncle's car, so I volunteered (!) to go by train. A Salisbury 'S15', 30826, hauled our three-coach stopping train to Sidmouth Junction, and 'M7' 30030 deposited us at Exmouth in time to meet up with the rest of the family. I was saddled with the host family's daughter (a bit older than I was) for the return journey, and we were dropped at the station just in time to see the branch train for Budleigh Salterton and Sidmouth Junction disappearing. I remember everyone being astounded at my nonchalance (and encyclopaedic railway knowledge) as I stated that we'd go via Exeter instead. 'M7' 30023 was waiting with an Exeter train, and I had a high old time train-spotting at Exeter Central before a stopper

Canton's 5006 *Tregenna Castle* waiting to depart Paddington with the 3.55pm to West Wales, 18 August 1951.

An evening scene at Liverpool Street in 1958, featuring 'B1' 61378, '*Britannia*' 70002 *Geoffrey Chaucer* at the head of a Norwich express and an 'L1' tank on empty-stock duties.

for Yeovil Junction turned up behind 'H15' 30330. I'm not sure what I did with my charge during my enforced stay in Exeter — I don't think she was amused.

In early September, before starting at a new school, I was despatched to spend a week with a cousin in Chelmsford. She was a teacher of primary-age children and had me decorating her 'maths cards' with small drawings of trains to provoke more interest from the young boys she taught. I escaped to Chelmsford station a couple of times to pursue my hobby — by this time the new 'Britannias' were much in evidence. In fact my journey from London to Chelmsford had been behind 70002 *Geoffrey Chaucer*, and most of the early series (70000-13, apart from 70004 on '*Golden Arrow*' duties) were well in evidence. The chime whistle was much used, and I recollect a wedding party joining a London-bound train, the best man giving a half crown to the driver, with a plea to sound celebratory whistles as he departed over the viaduct towards the city. Unfortunately the loco on this train was a mere 'B1', 61234, so the ensuing shrill whistles were not the symphony that an enthusiastic 'Britannia' driver could have performed. A couple of days later a group of boys tried to persuade a 'Britannia' driver to use his chime whistle to such effect, but he declined on the basis that he did not wish to cause all the mothers of sleeping babies to complain to head office.

I spent a day at Shenfield in order to observe the Southend trains as well as those for Ipswich and Norwich, travelling there behind an 'L1', 67737, and back behind 'B1' 61201, and achieved reasonable shots of a 'B12' (61546), a 'B2' (61644), a new 'Britannia' (70006) and a filthy 'K2' (61777), of a class which I do not really associate with the East Anglian main line. I was taken one evening to see the comedy 'Charlie's Aunt' in London, and our return was on the 10.30pm Liverpool Street–Norwich mail train, with Ipswich 'B12' 61535, an engine that has featured in Dick Hardy's tales about his time at Ipswich when 'B12s' were allocated to regular crews and included this important train in their diagrammed work. At the time I was disappointed, as I was hoping for a named locomotive — a 'Sandringham' or 'Britannia'. However, it went well, and in later years I appreciated having experience of this class in its heyday.

At the end of the week I was taken to Chelmsford station to catch the next train back to London, but I determined to stay until I got a 'namer' on my train. I therefore watched a string of 'B1' departures and was about to give up when a train from the Clacton line drew in behind 'B2' 61639 *Norwich City*, and I took that with gratitude.

Early the following year (1953) I was again a guest at my aunt's in Chelmsford. My cousin Eileen (the primary-school teacher) accompanied me from Liverpool Street, so I had no choice of train and instead of a 'Britannia' got 'B12/3' 61566 on a semi-fast — I now value her choice! I chose to spend one bleak January day train-spotting on Shenfield station. This added a few more 'B12s' to the diet of 'B1s' and 'B17s' (and brand-new 'Britannias') on the GE main line (the 'B12s' seeming to monopolise the Southend workings). Around midday it started to snow, and reason advised me to join a down express, which pulled in behind 'B1' 61201. However, I'd already had a couple of runs with this loco and decided to wait for the next train. The snow got harder, and nothing came in either direction. A light-engine ('N7' 69654) appeared eventually off the Southend line and stood on the far platform. The driver, peering out into the blizzard, took pity on the frozen waif on the other platform and beckoned me across. So my second footplate run was a few yards down to the water column whilst I roasted myself before the glowing fire. It started to get dark; still no other train arrived, and eventually a member of station staff appeared and told me that there would be no service for at least another two hours. On looking at my ticket, he retired into his office, and an 'L1' (67734) miraculously appeared with a couple of coaches from the carriage sidings to form a special to Chelmsford, just for my benefit! But I got my 'Britannia' (70005 *John Milton*) on my return to London the following day.

Back to January 1952. Before returning to my boarding school I spent a further day in London and found out the hard way the limitations of my simple camera. A reasonable shot of a 'B1' (!) on the turntable at Liverpool Street and a passable shot of 6013 *King Henry VIII* leaving Paddington on the 'Cornish Riviera' were acceptable, as was a panned photo of 5979 *Cruckton Hall* leaving Paddington with a semi-fast for Oxford, giving the impression that it was attempting the speed blue riband to Subway Junction. However, 5087 departing Paddington in swathes of steam and a blurred 5034 arriving demonstrated to me that my shutter speed was not up to such movement in the poor light of winter. A subsequent attempt at a shot of 34007 passing through Surbiton in drizzling rain as I returned to school proved the point beyond all doubt.

I seem to have allowed myself one trip to London each school holiday. My Easter-holiday excursion furnished more 'Castles' and blue 'Kings' at Paddington,

The winter 'Cornish Riviera' departing Paddington behind 6013 King Henry VIII, 5 January 1952.

which was most memorable for my first sight of gas-turbine locomotive 18000, nicknamed 'Kerosene Castle'. The 1952 summer visit produced a crop of photos from Paddington, distinguished by a shot of my favourite 'Castle', 4087, arriving from Minehead (no camera blur this time) and another of 4705 after arrival with a summer-holiday express. I made a brief visit to see the Tilbury three-cylinder Stanier tanks at Fenchurch Street and took another photo on Liverpool Street's turntable, this time in the sunshine showing off 'B12' 61549, with which I won my school Railway Society's photo competition in 1953.

On subsequent London trips I began to take local trains out to places like Southall, Willesden, Hendon and Finsbury Park to see freight services and take photos of trains on the move, although my limited shutter speed always made that a gamble. I was rewarded by the sights of wheezing 'G2' and 'G2a' 0-8-0s at Willesden, the occasional '28xx' en route to Acton and Swindon 'Dukedog' 9023, which seemed quite out of place in the metropolis. Motive power on my short journeys was usually restricted to '61xx' out of Paddington and Fairburn and Fowler 2-6-4 tanks out of

'B12/3' 61549 on the turntable at Liverpool Street, 4 April 1953.

Euston and St Pancras, although I do remember a couple of 'Black Fives' and one Kentish Town 'Jubilee', 45557 *New Brunswick*, on a non-corridor all-stations train to Bedford, which I took as far as Cricklewood. The best was getting back to King's Cross from Finsbury Park, especially in summer, when a succession of expresses would stop there in the queue to reach the terminus. I could jump a train and savour snippets behind such Pacifics as 'A2' 60533 *Happy Knight* and 'A4' 60029 *Woodcock*, although on one occasion I came unstuck when I joined a train behind a rare named 'B1', 61027 *Madoqua*, and finished up at Broad Street.

For Christmas 1953 I received a 'do-it-yourself' photo-printing kit, and my photos for the following year display an inconsistency of quality that arose from my early efforts. Some are 'muddy' in the extreme, but as I began to learn the techniques of shading the foreground (to bring out the smoke and sky effects) and got more practice, some worthwhile scenes were preserved for posterity. By this time, though, I was fifteen years of age, nearing sixteen, and the lone trips I undertook are no longer worthy of comment. Looking back at those early years, however, it is remarkable how much we were allowed to do without supervision. I do not recall ever getting into any situations that would be considered dangerous, apart from those assaults on my eyes by the smuts that were a constant hazard of train journeys in steam days — especially for young boys who insisted on sticking their heads out of carriage windows.

Tableau 2
Euston–Willesden, 1953

I'm home from boarding school, and we've a fortnight before we go to Devon for our annual summer holiday. I've loaded the Ilford film into my folding Kodak camera, eight negatives awaiting my activation, and at the very first opportunity, a Saturday, I'm away to London. It's already warm, and I've just emerged from the Northern Line at Euston station. My sandwiches, notebook and all four Ian Allan 'ABCs' are in my old satchel slung across my shoulder, and my camera case hangs in front of me, ready to be opened as soon as I spy anything that takes my fancy. I make my way first to the arrival side, to platforms 1, 2 and 3, and see at once that all three are still occupied, two by night sleepers whose coaches have not yet been removed to Willesden. I glance swiftly at a 'Scot' and a Camden 'Duchess', 46235 *City of Birmingham*, that's no cop, but my eye fastens on the sleek shape of a 'Princess Royal' pacific at the buffer-stops at platform 2, still sporting the '*Ulster Express*' headboard. As I push my way through the holiday crowds already mustering I see it's 46203 *Princess Margaret Rose*, and there's something strange about it. My eyes adjust to the glare reflected from the roof, and I notice that it's dark blue.

I undo the catch on my camera case. This is a 'must', although — despite the sun — the object of my desire lies in the shadow. I could take it in the classic pose alongside the 'Scot' peeping behind it at Platform 1, but for some reason I move back towards the tender and peer through the viewfinder at the large numerals on the cabside and the elongated boiler of the pacific, the top reflecting the shafts of sunlight piercing the opaque glass panels of the roof blackened by decades of steam locomotives that have stood in this very spot. One exposure gone. Will it come out properly? Or was the shadow too great? Will the negative be underexposed? I linger a short while, savouring the moment of spotting my first engine of this class, much more handsome, I think, than the other LM locomotives, more like my favourite 'Kings' and 'Castles'. Then I drag myself away and buy a platform ticket to enter the main-line departure platforms and join the gaggle of spotters already crammed into the narrow end of platform 13.

I'm tempted to take more photos — another 'Scot' has backed into the centre platforms to pick up a van, and a gleaming ex-works 'Compound', 41144, has just slipped in over the far side of the station, but I wasn't quick enough, and it was probably too far away to get a decent photo. Anyway, I'm meant to be saving my shots for later, for I've decided to go out to Willesden Junction to see, hopefully, some freights. It's getting hot now — I'm wearing a shirt and tie (!) and school blazer; train-spotters are still nattily and inappropriately dressed. I purchase a day-return ticket to Willesden Junction and, having made my way to the front of the train of eight non-corridor coaches standing at platform 7, find a filthy 2-6-4 tank, 42118 of Willesden, at its head. Luckily the train is nearly empty, so I bag a compartment and I dash to windows on either side to catch everything I can. We bark up Camden Bank, and I'm hanging out the window as we pass Camden shed — too quickly for my liking, as I can scarcely write down the numbers of the assembled 4-6-0s and pacifics crammed together in the cramped depot — 46228, 46240 and 45703, I scribble; there was another 'Jubilee' which I missed and a 'Black Five' over the back, but it's too late: we're plunging into Primrose Hill Tunnel, and I'm struggling with the strap to close the window, choking as the smoke pours into the compartment, bouncing off the tunnel walls.

I'm still wafting the smoke out of the compartment through the now fully opened window when the brakes screech on; we're through another tunnel, luckily steam now shut off, and it's Willesden Junction, where I scramble out, making sure I don't leave any of my precious cargo behind. I explore my new surroundings. We have drawn up in the middle platform between the fast and slow lines, and even as 42118 pulls away, the wheezing of a dirty old LNWR 'G2a', 49061, takes my attention; I hastily unfasten my camera case, but the old engine has slipped behind some wagons and is tortuously easing itself and a few wagons away in the direction of Wembley. Suddenly there is a prolonged hoot in the distance. I look up to see a train advancing fast on the up line. Before I can even contemplate taking a photo the double-headed train sweeps past, its '2P' 4-4-0 pilot lurching wildly as it takes the curve through the platform. I just get its number, 40674, but the 'Jubilee' behind is gone in a blur. Was it 45634 or 45643? I look them up in my 'shedbook' later and find they're both Crewe (5A) engines, so I'm no wiser. Perhaps coming to Willesden was a mistake. Then an '8F' trundles towards me from the Kensington line, and I take a photo of 48623 as it clanks past with a row of vanfits. I've hardly put my camera away when I hear the steady pounding of an engine working hard, and a shape I don't recognise bursts from Kensal Green Tunnel. I hurriedly get my camera out and am just in time to get a quick snap of my first sight of a BR 'Standard 5', 73042, on a relief train for North Wales. It's going well, and as soon as I've clicked the shutter I realise that I'll be lucky if it isn't just a blur, as 1/25 of a second is not enough to stop that sort of movement.

I retreat to the up slow platform to give myself more of a chance to get the numbers of trains which are still speeding past in the up direction and take photos of slower-moving trains on the slow lines, and am rewarded with a shot of unrebuilt 'Patriot' 45511 *Isle of Man* coming steadily down the line with a long train of northbound perishables. I watch a couple more expresses hurl themselves through the station, nearing their destination, steam already shut off — 46144 *Honourable Artillery Company* on a train from Liverpool, then a rebuilt 'Patriot', 45525 *Colwyn Bay*, blowing off steam furiously as it freewheels past with a train from Manchester and Stoke. But there are no more freights. Most engine crews are required for the holiday passenger traffic, and freight work is minimal on summer Saturdays. Suddenly a 'Black Five', 45375 of Rugby, bustles into my platform with a semi-fast from Northampton, and I have to make up my mind. Do I go back to Euston and then to Paddington in time for lunchtime trains or wait to see if there is anything more here? The 'Black Five' takes the decision for me. It'll be the first LM tender engine I've travelled behind, so my mind is made up. I take it.

Locally allocated unrebuilt 'Patriot' 45511 *Isle of Man* passes Willesden Junction with a northbound fitted freight, 8 April 1954.

Chapter 4

Devon holidays

6863 *Dolhwyel Grange* at Paignton on the early-morning stopping train to Exeter,
19 August 1952.

After several years of 'boring' seaside holidays on the South Coast my family decided to become more ambitious and booked into a boarding house in Paignton for August 1952. We caught a Summer Saturday train from Surbiton; Nine Elms 'Scotch Arthur' 30787 *Sir Menadeuke* took us to Salisbury, and Salisbury's blue 35007 *Aberdeen Commonwealth* covered the next leg to Exeter Central.

Exeter westwards was a mystery to me, and I was amazed when three (!) locomotives backed on to take us down the bank to St Davids. An Exmouth Junction 'cop', 34025 *Whimple*, had 'T9' 30702 and one of the 'E1/R' bankers, 32135, returning to its base to await the next service requiring a push up the hill to Central. I remember standing transfixed as the three locomotives stood blowing off steam furiously under the bridge at the end of the platform — I could only just see the details of the 0-6-2T at the front. The descent to St Davids is only three quarters of a mile, but for me on that occasion it was a magical journey. And from St Davids I enjoyed my first run behind a Great Western engine since 4087 — a packed Cardiff–Kingswear train behind clean lined-black 4968 *Shotton Hall*. We were squashed in the corridor, but it didn't matter. I was in for two weeks' heaven!

Every morning before breakfast I'd be on the overbridge at the London end of Paignton station, train-spotting by the level crossing. I recall a frequent visitor was 6863, with what was to me an unpronounceable name *Dolhywel Grange* (I think 'Dollywell' was my best guess). Another was 6817 *Gwenddwr Grange*, with equally mysterious spelling, and a third common engine was 6845 *Paviland Grange*, on which I was to have a footplate run during my management training at Old Oak Common ten years later. One day my sister had returned from the beach early, as she'd been feeling unwell, and claimed to have seen 5021 *Whittington Castle* as she passed the station going westwards — 5021 was an Exeter engine and rare in London, but despite hanging around the railway the next day the only 'Castle' I saw was 7019 of Bristol on the early-morning stopper. Most days we walked to the beach at Goodrington, which backed onto the line as it began the climb to Churston and on to Kingswear. Paddling and sandcastle-building could be accompanied by train-spotting — one of the few occasions on which I have successfully multi-tasked. I can remember on several evenings seeing a polished 5050 *Earl of St Germans* barking up the gradient as we were beginning to pack up and head back to our lodgings for the evening meal; I now realise it was the Shrewsbury engine on the alternate-day double-home working between Shrewsbury and Newton Abbot — it would go through to Kingswear and return to Newton Abbot on a local before picking up the 8am Plymouth–Liverpool the next day. Of course, Teignmouth was even better than Goodrington, and I persuaded our family to make a day trip there so we could sunbathe — with parents and sister looking out to sea and me facing the sea wall! Our stopper from Newton Abbot was hauled by a grubby blue 'King', 6022 *King Edward III*.

Blue 'Merchant Navy' 35007 *Aberdeen Commonwealth* observes a signal check at Surbiton. *(Robin Russell)*

'Star' 4056 *Princess Margaret* rushes into Kingswear station with the 8.5am Cardiff, 23 August 1952.

A few days later I was playing cricket with my dad on a small grassy park between the railway line and Goodrington beach. I'd been pestering to play cricket, but my sister wouldn't oblige, so my dad had become a reluctant bowler. Suddenly I heard something coming and halted my father in mid-stride as I ran to the boundary hedge and peered through at the oncoming light-engine. Oh joy! It was the legendary 111, the former *Great Bear*. My father was annoyed. 'Do you want to play cricket or not?' he shouted in exasperation. I didn't mind then either way. I could just see the advancing 'Castle' frontage and that magic smokebox-door numberplate, 111.

When I first went train-spotting at Paddington 'Saints' and 'Stars' were not uncommon — my first visit there, as noted earlier, 'copped' Nos 2949, 4007, 4051 and 4052. Later I saw 2945, 4049, 4053, 4054, 4059 and 4061, as well as 4021 *British Monarch*, which I saw several times on semi-fasts from Didcot or Oxford. For some reason I had always had a soft spot for 4056. (I think as a five-year-old I developed a crush for a photo of the seven-year-old princess in one of my picture books.) I first saw it that year at Kingswear — we had spent our middle Saturday (23 August) on the Dart river steamer and were returning to Paignton behind 4091 *Dudley Castle*. I was just photographing the 'Castle' when 4056 rushed into the station on a train from Cardiff, taking me by surprise, and the hurried shot only just got the front end in focus!

A couple of days later we took a day excursion from Paignton to Plymouth. We were hauled to Newton Abbot by tender-first 'Modified Hall' 6994, which ran round at the latter station and was then piloted by 7813 *Freshford Manor* over the South Devon banks. To my disappointment our evening train home was a stopping service headed by, of all things, 'West Country' 34017 *Ilfracombe*, which I'd seen so many times at Surbiton; I learned later that this was to maintain Southern Region crews' knowledge of the GW coast line from Exeter in case of diversions, while the WR crew and a '63xx' had a daily turn over the North Devon line.

My father was a keen walker, and one swelteringly hot day our family (four of us, including my eleven-year-old sister and me, newly a teenager) embarked on a full-day hike to find Fingle Bridge, somewhere on South Dartmoor, by the Bovey or Teign river. I don't even know if this is its correct name (it might be Fingal's Bridge, with a passing allusion to the Hebridean coast), but I've looked in vain at Ordnance Survey maps in my possession. We took the train from Newton Abbot to Lustleigh behind 5557, a loco which had already graced locals between Paignton and adjacent stations more than once on this holiday. Then we set off along deserted lanes, all scenery hidden by the towering hedgerows. We walked and walked, and I grumbled and grumbled. My father kept consulting the map — another two miles, then another … I'm sure this so-called beauty spot was a figment of either my father's imagination or the cartographer's.

Eventually we sat by the roadside and ate our picnic, intended for a grassy slope beside the mythical bridge, and began to undermine my father's confidence that he had read the map correctly. Another couple of miles' trudge in the full August afternoon heat, and still no relevant signpost appeared, so my complaints and that of my put-upon younger sister paid off. My father reluctantly abandoned the goal, and we swung westwards (?) towards Moretonhampstead, which we, the map and roadsigns all recognised. It was pure chance what time we would arrive and whether we'd find a train waiting, but we were in luck. Under the simple dead-end canopy of a typical GW branch terminus stood the local back to Newton Abbot, and there, simmering at its head, was 4547, still emblazoned with 'G W R' across its tank sides. It was a great relief and joy — the sheer pleasure at arriving somewhere known and finding a waiting train, particularly one headed by one of the earlier Churchward tanks I'd previously only seen shunting the pick-up goods in Goodrington sidings. The rest of the family was weary and fed up with not having achieved our goal; I, however, now perked up and was to be found an hour later dashing up and down the long Newton Abbot platforms whilst waiting for the next Kingswear-branch train, all tiredness mysteriously gone.

We started our journey home on a holiday relief for the West Midlands headed by a Didcot 'Hall', 4994, transferring at St Davids to a train from Ilfracombe headed by Light Pacific 34058 *Sir Frederick Pile*, banked up the 1 in 37 to Central by 'E1/R' 32124. To my disappointment 34058 ran through to Basingstoke, where we picked up a semi-fast to Surbiton headed by Urie 'H15' 30334.

The following year — again to my disappointment, as I was keen for a run behind one of the exotically named Urie 'Arthurs' — we watched 'N15' 30744 *Maid of Astolat* depart from Surbiton, as we had to wait for the following service, on which we had reservations. My family was accompanying a party of girls to a Girls' Life Brigade camp at Newton Abbot, run by my aunt, and blue 35015 *Rotterdam Lloyd* worked throughout to Exeter Central. I can't remember what took us down the bank — I think it was a single 'West Country' — but the Western train we picked up was headed by 'Castle' 5069 *Isambard Kingdom Brunel* of Bristol Bath Road. The train was again packed, and my one effort to look out of the window around Starcross was met by a stinging smut in the eye, from which I suffered for the rest of the day. I am ashamed to admit that the fifteen-year-old boy was more interested in train-spotting at Exeter and Newton Abbot than taking the opportunity provided by the proximity of twenty girls aged between twelve and fifteen! The second week the girls went home, and my family moved on for a further week at the Paignton guesthouse.

During the first week all the girls went on an outing to Teignmouth, and, despite my reservations at accompanying a load of females, another spell on the sea wall was too good to miss. The outward trip produced only a '45xx' 2-6-2T, but I took several photos in that well-known location and awaited the return evening train with anticipation. This was the through Liverpool express (the balancing turn of the 8am Plymouth, as I've now realised), and it came under the bridge from the sea wall and along the curved platform. Hiding behind the numerals '247' was a spotless 'Castle'; as it approached I could see the 84G shedplate, and my mind whirled to the few Shrewsbury 'Castles', because these were rare beasts for a London boy. 5097 *Sarum Castle* duly came to a stand, and I was ecstatic.

A couple of days later I escaped the female entourage and went train-spotting at Newton Abbot and took a trip to Dawlish for more photography. At Newton Abbot I caught ROD 3038 on a freight and 4077 *Chepstow Castle*, obviously just ex works, going off shed as the Newton Abbot engine for the Shrewsbury double-home job. At Dawlish I took a photo of 70021 and eventually found that the Liverpool had 5097 again, so I waited for the following Exeter–Kingswear local, with 5997 *Sparkford Hall*.

The girls finished their camp at the end of the week — I was even seduced into taking part in a midnight feast on the last night — and I helped my father pack their gear and get it to the station and see them off. Then I was allowed to spend the rest of the day watching the Western Summer Saturday procession while my parents and sister moved down to our Paignton guesthouse. I eventually took a Cardiff–Kingswear train, on which I'd travelled the previous year with 4968, and got another Canton 'Hall', 4963 *Rignall Hall*.

We had spent most days on Goodrington Sands the previous week and a couple of times had travelled back to Newton Abbot on a local with the engine off the down '*Torbay Express*', its headboard reversed, 5028 of Newton Abbot and 5047 of Worcester. (Apparently it was a triangular diagram involving Old Oak, Newton Abbot and Worcester 'Castles'.) The second week — tired and beladen with beach paraphenalia though we were — we had to walk the mile or so back to our 'bed &

5097 *Sarum Castle* brings the Shrewsbury double-home diagram on the 9.10am Liverpool into Newton Abbot, 17 August 1953.

breakfast' lodging house. One evening, as we walked along the little overgrown path beside the railway, I saw something unusual in the Goodrington carriage sidings. An excursion train was stabled there, and at the head was the last 'Saint', 2920 *Saint David*. Regretably I did not have my camera with me that day, and by the time I'd rushed back from the guesthouse it had gone. It was clean and shining in its coat of black paint and LNWR lining, although it was only another couple of months before its withdrawal. But what I picture most of all are the brass and scarlet name- and numberplates.

On the last day of our stay we had to return to Exeter by a specified service, as all returning holidaymakers were 'regulated'. Our train was one of many hauled by a succession of 'Halls' — 5990 *Dorford Hall* was ours. From Exeter it was a Bulleid Light Pacific, 34032 *Camelford*, which once more to my disapointment did not change at Salisbury. We alighted at Basingstoke to pick up a semi-fast stopping at Surbiton behind another Urie 'H15', 30332.

In 1954 we stayed at the Methodist Guild House in Sidmouth, and I spent a few glorious summer days scuttling behind the Sidmouth-branch 'M7', 30025, to the Junction and Tipton St John's, connecting to the Exmouth branch, where I encountered more 'M7s', ex-LMR Class 2 2-6-2 tanks 41313 and 41314 and a few BR

2920 *Saint David*, in the condition in which the author saw it in August 1953.
(Neville Stead)

'Standard 3' 2-6-2 tanks, 82011/3/7-9, which were beginning to replace the 'M7s'. I managed one excursion to the Lyme Regis branch still in the hands of the venerable Adams 4-4-2 tanks — we had 30583 — and another to spend the mid-Saturday again at Exeter St Davids, where I captured 4703 on a Paignton–Nottingham train, among others. We had travelled down from Surbiton to Sidmouth Junction behind Salisbury's 34052 *Lord Dowding* and returned with 30025 for the last time to the junction and then to Salisbury behind 34026 *Yes Tor*, which was replaced there by 73112 one of the brand-new (and as yet unnamed) 'Standard 5s' allocated to the Southern Region's Western Section.

In 1956 we found accommodation in Ilfracombe. The 7.38am Waterloo–Ilfracombe was hauled by 34009 *Lyme Regis*, which should have worked through to Exeter but failed at Salisbury with injector trouble. After a short pause the watercart tender of one of Salisbury's 'Eastleigh Arthurs' backed around the corner, and 30449 *Sir Torre* duly coupled up with the 11-coach, 385-ton-gross train. By this time an 'Arthur' on an express over the Salisbury–Exeter switchback was a rarity. Clearly *Sir Torre* had been commandeered at short notice, and the start out to Wilton was painfully slow, with clouds of sulphurous smoke as the fireman got the fire into some sort of shape. Once we got going, however, 30449 performed admirably, and this must have been the first journey I had logged (see Appendix, Table 1). From the slow start, clearing Semley at 53mph was a nice surprise, and 80 at Sherborne and a minimum of 26 on Honiton Bank, recovering to 28 in the tunnel, was good for an

'Arthur' with this crowded train. *Sir Torre* was replaced at Exeter Central by 34003 *Plymouth* for the run through to our destination at Ilfracombe, which ended with a descent of the steep (1-in-36) gradient from Mortehoe to the terminus poised over the town below.

I had a couple of forays taking photographs of a succession of Bulleid Light Pacifics making a fuss of climbing out of the station, then on the middle Saturday boarded a train for the Midlands hauled to Exeter by WR Mogul 7311, which I took just as far as Mortehoe, the first stop. I spent the day walking from Mortehoe to Braunton, some seven miles, keeping close to the railway line, which for the last four and a half miles climbed to Mortehoe Summit at a steady 1 in 40. I met a series of trains climbing the bank from Waterloo and photographed 34062, 34034, 34003, 34051 and 34059, as well as a solitary 'N', 31837, and an 'M7', 30671, on a short freight. I ended my day somewhat weary — it had been a hot day — behind another WR Mogul, Exeter's 6322, banked to Mortehoe Summit by 'M7' 30254. We also spent a day in Barnstaple, where I was able to take a few photos of trains crossing the bridge over the river between the Junction and Town stations, before our annual holiday was over, and it was back to Surbiton, via London this time, with No 34028 *Eddystone* as far as Salisbury and then, to my dismay, a filthy Maunsell 'H15', 30523, which coasted most of the way at 50mph, emitting a haze of brown smoke, arriving very late.

Adams 4-4-2T 30583 being hand-coaled at Axminster before working the Lyme Regis branch train, photographed during a family holiday to Sidmouth, 3 September 1954.

'Battle of Britain' 34062 *17 Squadron* approaches Mortehoe Summit with a Waterloo–Ilfracombe express, 8 August 1956.

34059 *Sir Archibald* Sinclair leaves Braunton with a very late-running express from Waterloo to Ilfracombe, 8 August 1956.

Tableau 3

Goodrington Sands, August 1952

It's a hot day and we — my father, mother, eleven-year-old sister Jill and I — have traipsed the mile from our Paignton lodgings to the beach at Goodrington Sands. We are struggling with all the things necessary for a day by the seaside — windbreak, buckets and spades, towels, costumes, picnic lunch. We'll pay a shilling each for deck-chairs on the beach; three will be set up facing the surging water, tide now coming back in, while mine resolutely faces the other way. No, I've not quarrelled with the rest of the family yet, though carrying all that baggage in the heat was not really my idea of a holiday. It's just because the railway line from Newton Abbot to Kingswear runs right at the back of the sands, on the embankment behind the bathing huts.

In order to get here we've walked along the footpath by the railway track — nothing passed us — and the three carriage sidings on the upside between Goodrington and Paignton stations. They were empty of locomotives, although a couple of coach sets slumber there, roused only at the weekend. As we emerge onto the beach and choose our spot I'm alert for signs of activity on the railway behind me. Trains from the east announce themselves, whether they're just starting from Goodrington Sands Halt or are getting a run at the bank from their Paignton stop. But trains coming down the bank from Churston off the single line are silent, free-wheeling, unless they whistle for the footpath crossing that we traversed half a mile away, or there is a screech of brakes if the train is stopping at the halt.

My sister is stripping off her shoes and socks and is already dashing over the sand to paddle, then rushes back squealing, for the sea is cold, she says. It always is; I suppose I'll have to go in sometime, but not now. Not until I've seen a couple of trains and perhaps got at least one 'cop' under my belt. It must be half past ten already. My father has been impatient for some time to get us out here; he dislikes the tardy preparations. We did not have breakfast until 9 o'clock — the time the landlady stipulates — so I've been at Paignton station since 8 o'clock this morning and already copped *Chirk Castle* on a local from Newton Abbot and watched No 6836 *Estevarney Grange* sizzling in the station with the 8.30 stopper to Exeter. But that's a common one; I've seen it at least twice before already this holiday, and we're still in the first week.

Mum is already reading, and Dad is hammering the windbreak in — not that there is much breeze today, but it's a ritual. Then my ears prick up, for I can hear a shrill whistle in the distance and the steady bark of a Great Western engine as it's leaving Paignton. For a moment the sound recedes, overcome by the surging

4704, a locomotive the author drove in 1962 during his management training at Old Oak Common, tackles the 1-in-71 climb away from Goodrington with the 1.20pm Paddington–Kingswear on 15 July 1961. *(P. K. Bowles / R. Woodley collection)*

tide, then I hear it as its driver opens the regulator further to attack the two and a half miles of 1 in 71/60 to Churston. 7929 *Wyke Hall* bursts out from behind the pine trees shrouding Goodrington Sands Halt and charges past, accelerating its six motley Collett and Hawksworth carmine-and-cream coaches up the gradient, which is clarly visible from my vantage-point. I can still hear its strident, labouring exhaust as it hits the steepest part of the bank; five minutes later I can still hear 7929 chirrupping in the distance. All is silent once again as it nears Churston station, and the waves, the seagulls and the ice-cream vendor take over once more. Then, ten minutes later, I almost miss 2-6-2T No 5544, which, having passed *Wyke Hall* at Churston station, comes rushing, bunker-first, its four Mk 1 coaches forming a Kingswear–Paddington train that will be amalgamated with the Plymouth portion at Newton Abbot.

There is a lull during which I pester for an ice cream — I'm dissuaded, as it's too early. 'After lunch', I'm told, so I watch my sister constructing a crumbling castle in the dry sand. There's a long gap between trains, and I'm getting bored. I get into my swimming trunks, with much flapping of towels to protect my adolescent modesty, and wander down to the water's edge and discover for myself what my sister said. It's cold — too cold to think of immersing anything higher than my calves. While I'm in the sea there's a flurry of steam above the trees and a sharp 'peep' on a whistle, and a 'Small Prairie', 4582, puffs up the bank with a stopper from Newton Abbot to Kingswear. I've seen it every day all week; it's one of the local clutch of these engines — 4532, 4547, 4587, 5525, 5557 have all been underlined in my Western Region 'ABC' already, as well as the two I've seen this morning.

We're just getting ready for our picnic lunch when there's a shrill whistle, and into sight bursts a gleaming 'Castle', 4098 *Kidwelly Castle*, with the '*Torbay Express*' headboard and a long rake of the new BR standard carriages. And I've hardly noted that with satisfaction and bitten into a sausage roll when there's a pounding from the opposite direction, and 5019 *Treago Castle* whistles briefly and rushes the bank, its fireman hanging out of the cab, waving at small children who have paused from their sandcastle-building next to us and are waving frantically at the train. I get my promised ice cream and then persuade my father and reluctant sister and mother to join a game of beach cricket. We go down to the firmer sand, and I keep one eye on the ball and another on the track, which means I miss a catch but spot 6845 *Paviland Grange* also going westwards with a stopper from Taunton and Exeter. Dad shouts at me, and I chase the ball into the waves; then it's my turn to bat, and I hit the ball deliberately into the sea, where my sister has to wade to collect it. I hear another train whistle and stop my father in mid-stride to watch a train from Kingswear descending the bank, but it's only *Wyke Hall* coming back. The women take the opportunity of the pause to indicate that they think that the cricket match is finished, and we return to our deck-chairs to sunbathe — my parents to read, my sister to resume the digging of a moat around her elaborate sand construction to receive the water when the tide reaches this far (which I doubt it will).

I watch a string of trains passing throughout the afternoon, hauled by 6934 *Beachamwell Hall*, 6817 *Gwenddwr Grange*, 4954 *Plaish Hall*, Mogul 6322 of Exeter, '4575' tank No 5525 and finally another 'Hall', 6954. Soon it'll be time to rub the salt from our skin and dress again to go back to our lodgings for the evening meal, to be set inflexibly before us at 6 o'clock exactly. But just before we do there's one more train that barks firmly up the bank — a resplendent 'Castle', 5050 *Earl of St Germans* (a Shrewsbury engine, no less), hauling a string of coaches bearing Liverpool–Kingswear roofboards. This makes my day, and I watch it with awe as it thunders up the track, drowning the noise of the waves now lapping near our spot, and drawing admiring eyes from the crowds now packing up and making ready to return to their hotels and lodging houses, just like us. I sigh with satisfaction. I'm ready to go now.

5021 *Whittington Castle* climbs past the beach huts at Goodrington Sands with an Exeter–Kingswear stopping train, 8 June 1954. *(F. A. Blencowe)*

Chapter 5
The Charterhouse Railway Society

Maunsell 'U' 2-6-0 31800 with the only weekday steam working, the daily pick-up goods, passing Godalming, 21 June 1955.

I had won a Surrey County Council 'assisted place' at Charterhouse in 1951. I was deeply apprehensive about this new venture, although it provided some relief from bullying at the grammar school, as I'd been a bit of a 'teacher's pet', being acclaimed only too frequently as the first son of an 'old boy' to go there.

There was not much to see of interest on the local railway at Godalming. My new school had an odd rule: to cross a railway line was 'out of bounds'. That stopped unauthorised trips into the local towns of Godalming or Guildford but allowed plenty of latitude on the West and North side of the school.

I had an old bike (Raleigh, 1936 vintage) given me by my grandfather and between 1951 and 1956 frequently cycled the five or six miles to Wanborough (which meant a stiff climb over the Hog's Back), as two trains on the Reading–Redhill 'Rattler', as it was known, would pass near Wanborough station half an hour or so after our lunch finished. The westbound train would come first, huffing and puffing its three

56

'birdcage' carriages, the engine being normally a Guildford or Redhill Wainwright Class D 4-4-0 but occasionally a Class C 0-6-0 goods. Usually it was 31577 or 31586 (31075 and 31488 being the others I remember). On one occasion the eastbound train, which soon followed, was not the usual Maunsell mogul but bunker-first Standard 2-6-4 tank 80019, rushing in at a fair turn of speed for this line. The element of surprise at seeing my first '80xxx' Standard was my excitement at the time, but memory now reveres the ancient 'D' struggling to lift its period formation out of the station amid a cloud of black smoke and leaking steam.

Wainwright 'D' 31075 at Guildford with Reading - Redhill train, 12 June 1956.

Wainwright 'C' 0-6-0 31683 crosses the 'out of bounds' limit bridge at Wanborough with the 2.23pm Guilford–Reading, 16 June 1955.

More usual power for the 2.23pm Guildford–Reading: Class D 4-4-0 31586 near Ash Junction, 25 June 1955.

As a fourteen-year-old I had inherited the Chair of the school Railway Society, after a period of disinterest from older pupils — as my barber explained to me at home, if I wanted 'street cred' (I've forgotten what we called it in those days), I should give up trains and interest myself in fast cars or aircraft. I had the help of a few thirteen-year-olds — Martin Probyn as Secretary, Jim Evans (later, like myself, a BR senior officer) as Treasurer and the new boys, Philip Balkwill (who later became a master at the school and died of cancer tragically young a few years ago) and his friend, Conrad Natzio.

We were highly energetic, boosting the membership to over 300 (!) by putting on regular film shows using the marvellous BT films you can now see at the National Railway Museum (remember 'Train Time' and that corpulant WR Operating Manager on a desk festooned with the largest number of telephones you have ever seen?). We charged 3d a show or gave free admission to the four shows a year if you joined the Railway Club (annual subscription 6d), and, as entertainment in those pre-TV days was at a premium, we had a lot of takers. I vaguely remember that 'London to Brighton in Four Minutes' had a regular showing by popular demand, and a brief sighting of a train on an adjoining track and the possibility of a race (which failed miserably to materialise) was enough to get hordes of schoolboys jumping up and down in their seats, yelling the driver on! We also achieved a great coup in our early years by getting our little exhibition on 'Societies Day' opened by Sir Brian Robertson, Chairman of the British Transport Commission. He happened to be a friend of Jim Evans' uncle as well as being an Old Carthusian.

An austerity 0-6-0 tank, WD 118 *Brussels*, at Longmoor with a University College London Railway Society Special in 1958.

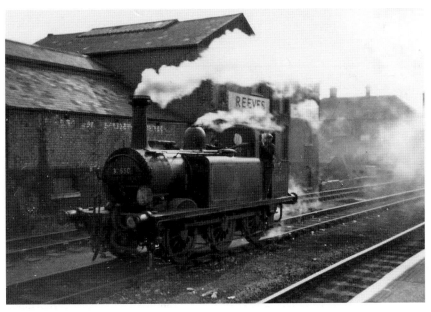

'Terrier' 32650 at Fratton, ready to take the next branch train to Hayling Island, 26 May 1956.

We had regular outings on half days — to London depots like Old Oak Common and Camden, to the Longmoor Military Railway and to the Hayling Island branch, with its 'Terrier' tanks, like 32640, 32650, 32661 and 32677, still working hard.

Every May the school would have a 'Societies Day', when a whole day was made available for club visits. In 1953 we caught the 9.30 Waterloo from Woking to Eastleigh behind 'Lord Nelson' 30858 *Lord Duncan* and visited the works, returning via Portsmouth — I was very surprised to find our train from Eastleigh to Portsmouth hauled by 6960 *Raveningham Hall* of Reading. In 1954 we planned a round-trip over Kent and Sussex branch lines, travelling from Redhill to Tonbridge behind 'H' tank 31261, going around Tonbridge shed, riding behind new 80014 to Tunbridge Wells and East Grinstead and then taking an electric ('2-PUL' units) to Pulborough, where we managed to leave our master ('Kipper' Leask), who was meant to be in charge, in the train's toilet when we disembarked. Now on our own, we caught 30051 on the Midhurst branch and eventually got back to Redhill, where our train back to Guildford produced a brand-new 'Standard 4' 2-6-0, 76054. Redhill got Nos 76053-62, which replaced many of the old Wainwright engines on the 'Rattler', and our local diet now became these and the various Maunsell moguls.

In April 1953, during the school holiday, I was entrusted with chaperoning a nine-year-old girl, Heather Swann (the daughter of a friend of my Aunt Doris, with whom she'd been staying), back to her home in Salisbury. We caught the 9.30am Waterloo–Bournemouth, which stopped at Surbiton, with Nine Elms 'Lord Nelson' 30858 *Lord Duncan* (again) as far as Basingstoke, where we changed to a local stopping train to Salisbury behind 30781 *Sir Aglovale* — a 'cop' and, as such, a much more acceptable steed. Later in the day, after the succesful handover of my charge to her father and in receipt of a copy of *Railway Magazine* — the reward for my trouble — I got, just to rub it in, *Sir Aglovale* all the way back to Surbiton. A year later, confidence in my escort service established, I was entrusted with Heather again, this time to get her to Tonbridge — out from Waterloo East with 34078 *222 Squadron* and back on a train from Hastings that ran in, to my delight, behind 30900 *Eton*. That Easter the family went to Chelmsford for my cousin's wedding, the highlight for me being the journey from Liverpool Street behind 70039 *Sir Christopher Wren*. But then the run home was with 70039 again. I can't remember anything about Eileen's wedding.

By 1955 I'd become a bit more ambitious with my primitive Kodak camera and started cycling to various locations nearby on the Redhill–Reading line, Shalford and Ash Junction in particular. And I'd begun to look further afield. In the Easter holidays I'd noticed a football excursion advertised for Arsenal fans for their away match at Cardiff, priced at a just-affordable 14/6d. Standing at the platform end at Paddington, I watched a glistening 5036 *Lyonshall Castle* and a somewhat dirtier 5004 *Llanstephan Castle* back down onto other trains. Then my heart sank as nothing better than a filthy Pontypool Road 'Hall', 4990 *Clifton Hall*, coupled up. Performance was not scintillating, but we got there in good time for the match, allowing me to visit Canton depot, take a trip to Barry Town and back behind a pair of 'Large Prairie' tanks (5195 and 4164) and watch 373, a former Taff Vale tank, bustle off to Bute Road (which, frankly, I now wish I'd chosen instead of the Barry trip). I was tempted

A wet Sunday at Shalford, with Maunsell 'U' Mogul 31631 on a Redhill–Reading train, 19 June 1955.

to join Canton's 5046 *Earl Cawdor* and the 5.30pm London express as we massed on the platform for our returning excursion, but that train was taboo without full-fare tickets, so I had to await 'Modified Hall' 6999 *Capel Dewi Hall*, destined to achieve fame later, when it replaced 4079 on the 1964 'Castle' swansong at Westbury. I still have no idea whether Arsenal won or not.

That summer term, after exams, we had half-day outings to Reading shed and branch-line trips — Guildford to Christ's Hospital with 'M7' 30048, on to Horsham with 'E4' 32511, back to Cranleigh behind another 'M7', 30108, and finally, to our great joy, the last 'D3' 0-4-4T survivor, 32390, from Cranleigh back to Guildford. My August holiday was spent at the Methodist Guild Hotel in Whitby, where cliff walks were interspersed with communal train trips to Robin Hood's Bay (out with 'A5' 69831, back with 69842), Staithes (out with 'A8' 69879, back with Standard 2-6-0 76023), up the Esk Valley (with 'A8' 69854 and back with 'G5' 67289) and a day on my own in York, where I was pleased to get 'A8' 69890 on the Whitby portion of the *'Scarborough Flyer'* to Malton, there joining with 'B16/3' 61472, and returning after a day's 'spotting' with named 'B1' 61237 *Geoffrey H. Kitson* and 69890 again. We all went to Scarborough for the day over the moors at Ravenscar, with the only 'Standard 3' 2-6-0 I ever travelled behind, 77014 (only to find, ten years later, it was the one transferred to Guildford!). The Saturday *'Scarborough Flyer'* home was a disappointment from York, as King's Cross 'V2' 60832 worked throughout, in contrast to our down run a fortnight before, which had produced a Top Shed 'A4', 60015 *Quicksilver*, as far as Grantham, where York 'V2' 60892 took over.

Maunsell 'U' 31616 with a Redhill–Reading train near Ash Junction in 1955.

An interloper — Nine Elms 'T9' 4-4-0 30724 near Ash en route from Guildford to Reading in 1958.

In 1955 we had fixed a visit to Rugby Locomotive Testing Plant for our 'Societies Day' outing. Having caught the 'Royal Scot' behind 'Duchess' 46250 *City of Lichfield*, we were abandoned by our master-in-charge at Rugby, where he announced he was off to see his aunt. We duly went around the shed, finding several '4P' Compounds in store, and were then met by the angry boss of the Testing Plant, who'd been watching us wandering unsupervised all over the shed and wanted to know who was in charge. When I admitted to this we got a safety lecture. (Our absentee master must also have got a rocket later, as he was replaced thereafter by the musical William Llewellyn, a true enthusiast, who really took an interest and inspired us.) After all this, disappointingly, nothing was moving, for although we found 'Royal Scot' 46165 on the rollers it had failed with a collapsed brick arch earlier that morning. I was looking forward to a fast run back to Euston on a mile-a-minute schedule behind a Bushbury 'Jubilee' and was astounded and dismayed to get one of the earliest diesel-electrics, 10203, which conversely delighted other members of the Society.

Another fond memory of Railway Society activities relates to the model-railway layout of a retired surgeon named Romanis, an 'Old Carthusian' who lived just half a mile from the school, in Hurtmore. In the summer term half a dozen of us would be invited every Sunday afternoon to operate his magnificent Gauge 1 layout — a system with twenty-five locos modelled on the late pre-Grouping period, with three signalling block posts and a 60- or 90-minute timetable we had to operate with precise punctuality. At the end of the session, if we had operated the layout to his satisfaction, we would round off the visit with a glass of cider in his beautiful mansion.

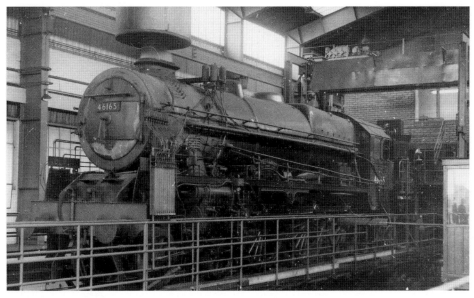

Rebuilt 'Royal Scot' 46165 *The Ranger (12th London Regiment)* on the Rugby Test Plant rollers during the Charterhouse Railway Society visit in May 1955.

My Housemaster, Jock Reith, was confident that I was capable of getting a scholarship place at Oxford University (wrong!), and so began a series of trips from Guildford to Oxford, sitting abortive exams and whiling away the cold evenings on Oxford station rather than in cold lodgings or stuffy pubs. In November 1955 I had my first attempt at Oriel College, travelling to Reading behind the venerable 'D', 31075, and thence 4083 *Abbotsbury Castle*. I can't remember much about the exam papers or the interviews, but I did travel to Radley one evening behind 4942 *Maindy Hall* and went to Abingdon and back with the push-pull train and 1420. Afterwards it was back to Reading with Oxford's 5026 *Criccieth Castle* and another 'D', No 31488, to Guildford. Further efforts in January and February produced memorable freezing evenings train-watching and a return one night to London in a pea-soup fog, with 6854 *Roundhill Grange* audible but invisible somewhere up front.

My efforts to gain entry through the illustrious portals of various Oxford colleges continued in 1956, equally unsuccessfully, although, since my railway training in later years included six weeks at Oxford station, I was able to drop 'my Oxford days' into the conversation when it mattered. A couple of November attempts, including a 'near miss' at Pembroke College, resulted in 'Castle' haulage to and from Paddington (5083, 5099 and 7005) and a final up run which was certainly different. I arrived at Oxford station in the early evening in another pea-soup fog and was genuinely surprised when 7004 *Eastnor Castle* pulled in early but stopped halfway down the platform. It cut off and disappeared into the murk, and to my astonishment a royal saloon backed down with another 'bulled-up' 'Castle', although by now the front of the platform had been cordoned off, and I was unable to ascertain its identity. Princess Margaret suddenly appeared, escorted by the top-hatted Stationmaster, and we set off punctually and with great gusto. The fog lifted momentarily as we rounded the Didcot curve to gain the main line, and from my position near the back of the train I could see the orange glow from the footplate and saw sparks fly high into the air as the regulator was opened wide to accelerate. The dense fog enveloped us once more in the Thames Valley, but despite this we made a cracking pace, and after Reading we were haring through the total darkness at an estimated 80mph when suddenly the train shuddered as a very heavy brake application was made. We screeched to a halt, and, peering out of the window, I could see little until I just made out the parapet of the bridge at Maidenhead over the Thames. We stood for about five minutes, then resumed our progress at a rather more sedate pace, but even so we were only six minutes late arriving at Paddington. We were all held back from alighting until the royal party had disembarked, and then, at last, I was able to identify our royal steed as Old Oak's 5040 *Stokesay Castle*, an engine frequently (with 5035) used by the depot on its VIP turns. I glanced at the arrival indicator on the 'lawn' and noted that, apart from our train, every other estimated lateness was the maximum 99 minutes! I later heard that the driver and inspector had been disciplined, as we had overrun a 'red' signal (a 'SPAD'), both men being over-confident that the road would have been cleared for a 'semi-royal', despite the weather.

Turning out years of accumulated papers, I've just come across a sheaf of faded handwritten foolscap, which meticulously describes an exercise that boys from Charterhouse carried out on a summer Saturday in 1956. At least, I think it must have been that year, although memory told me it was earlier; however, I have just laboriously gone back through calendars, allowing for leap years, and calculated that during my time there as a boarder this was the only year in which 28 July fell a Saturday.

Philip and Conrad were enthusiastic train-timers, and during my last summer at the school we decided that on the last Saturday of term we would attempt to log trains over the Weybridge–Basingstoke section of line. We got about ten of us with five stopwatches (borrowed from the athletics coach), synchronised them before we started at 12 noon, BBC time, and calibrated them at the end at 9pm, again checking them against the BBC News, adjusting passing times accordingly. We agreed to stand at the nearest quarter-milepost and log the passing time as the locomotive drew level.

We left school after lunch and cycled to our allotted posts — Weybridge station, Woking station, the summit at Milepost 30¼ and Fleet and Basingstoke stations. As boss I granted myself Woking and had borrowed a very ancient 8mm camera, the possession of the music master, Bill Llewellyn, who had responsibility for our Society, with which to record events. At one stage I left a colleague at Woking in charge and caught the 2.54pm Waterloo–Salisbury with 30454 to Farnborough, returning with 30449 on an up local, for filming purposes. I regret the film has long since disappeared. At Woking, the afternoon scene was one of constant activity, if not chaos, as the trains recorded were augmented by numerous electrics from the Portsmouth and Alton directions, with conflictions with the main line at the flat junction west of the station. This caused signal checks to nearly all services — trains hurtling through the station under clear signals were the exception (35027 on the very late 1.30pm Waterloo at 75mph, and two successive trains timed at 80mph+ on the up — 30751, on a boat train, followed by 34007, both engine whistles howling at the crowds still crammed on the platforms). This hive of activity contrasted with the sylvan scene near Milepost 30¼, where a small overbridge crossed the line just before the summit of the steady climb from Woking and where the peace was shattered by hard-working down trains and speeding up expresses just before sighting double-yellows announcing the Woking congestion.

The aim of our project was to time the passing of each train that afternoon at our respective posts, to estimate speeds and comment on the working as we observed it and to create logs of the trains of the thirty miles or so we were covering. Today these provide a fascinating insight into one of the busiest Saturdays of the year (known then throughout the railways as 'Black Saturday') at a time when rail-borne holiday traffic was at its postwar peak. I also received some information from the records of Ben Brooksbank, who travelled from Waterloo to Basingstoke on the same day, and some notes from the *Railway Observer* which have been made available to me with comments on earlier running on that Saturday morning and which offer some explanation for the late running noted by our Charterhouse team. The Charterhouse group concentrated mainly on up trains, which were the most numerous, being the afternoon returning holiday traffic. I have no timetable for the period to check, and at the time we used the booked arrival and departure times at/ from Waterloo to identify the trains.

A bit of background first from the RO notes referring to July 1956, for the magazine comments that the weekend scene on the Southern's Western Section showed a number of changes from previous summers. The influx of Standard Class 4 and 5 4-6-0s had caused former dependence on 'S15' and 'H15' classes to be much reduced, although 30476 was in action on a top-link job due to disruption earlier in the day, and 30497 was on the 1.24pm Waterloo–Salisbury semi-fast, appearing to be in some difficulty. Incidentally, the provision of Urie or Maunsell 'S15s' for the Basingstoke and Salisbury semi-fasts was common practice on summer Saturdays until the end of the 1950s. The absence of Urie 'H15s' is surprising (apart from the Maunsell rebuild, No 30491), but Maunsell 30476 on the fast 3.20pm Waterloo–Bournemouth was a sign of desperation, and it fared badly, being reported as 'winded' as it drifted over the summit near MP31 in the low 40s and a haze of brown smoke. The other main change was the use of 'U' moguls on the Lymington Pier trains after years of the Drummond 'D15' 4-4-0s, although this would be short-lived, as the 'Schools' transferred to Nine Elms from St Leonards had taken over these turns by the summer of 1958.

Punctuality was surprisingly poor. One always associates the Waterloo main line with exemplary timekeeping in the 1950s, but on this date things went badly awry, timings being already adrift by the time the survey commenced. The 1.24pm Waterloo–Salisbury hauled by the Feltham Urie 'S15' was 49 minutes late at Woking and clearly in trouble, with the following 1.30pm Waterloo–Bournemouth probably as far back as Hampton Court Junction, but most other down services that afternoon were between ten and twenty-five minutes late. The main note from the *Railway Observer* concerned a pointer to the root cause of the observed unpunctuality during the afternoon period. Two Urie 'N15s' seem to have fouled up the day by mid-morning. 30751 *Etarre* of Basingstoke shed was the engine for the 10.42 Waterloo boat-train special for Southampton Docks and apparently took 97 minutes to travel the 48 miles to Basingstoke, delaying the following West of England expresses so badly that several (34064, 35021 and 34027 on 'ACE' portions and 34009 on a Swanage-bound train) had to stop at Basingstoke to take water, although it was observed mid-afternoon tearing through Woking at over 80mph, whistle screaming, on a lightweight up '*Ocean Liner Express*'. The other culprit was 30739 *King Leodegrance*, labouring up the bank from Winchester to Roundwood Summit with a 13-coach Bournemouth–Birkenhead cross-country train which was fifty minutes late at Basingstoke. Both of these delinquents managed to stagger into Basingstoke at around the same time (12.15pm), with queues of trains behind them. One consequence was the late arrival in London of Bournemouth engines required for return diagrams and therefore either late departures or substitutions, like 30476 (off an up '*Ocean Liner Express*') on the 3.20pm Waterloo–Bournemouth, which should have had a 'Merchant Navy'.

On this summer Saturday the Southern Region managed to run at least thirteen 'Ocean Liner Expresses' — five down and eight up — in both directions running in the peak traffic flows. Unusually only one was hauled by a 'Lord Nelson'. Nine were

A Summer Saturday at Woking, as 'King Arthur' No 30779 *Sir Colgrevance* speeds past with a relief train for Bournemouth in July 1959.

hauled by 'King Arthurs', including four by Urie engines and three of the Basingstoke 'N15s' (30751, 30753 and 30771) worked boat trains in both directions. Two others were headed by Light Pacifics — one a Ramsgate 'Battle of Britain', possibly after repair at Eastleigh, although the survey notes only refer to it being in 'reasonable' condition. The remaining boat train was hauled by Eastleigh's Maunsell 'H15' 30476, which later graced the 3.20pm Waterloo–Bournemouth express.

In fact 'King Arthurs' of all descriptions were well represented during the day, Urie 30739/47/9-51/53, 'Eastleigh Arthurs' Nos 30448/49/54/56/57 and 'Scotch' Nos 30763/65/71/73/74/79-82/88-91 all being noted by either the Charterhouse team or Ben Brooksbank. Aside from the morning problems with 30739 and 30751 — and a comment by the Fleet observer that 30774 on the 3.30pm to Bournemouth seemed to be riding like a 'bucking bronco' — the general impression was that they were performing very competently. 30750 on an 11-coach Ilfracombe–Waterloo train was stopped outside Woking station awaiting a path, blowing off steam furiously, and two of the meagre number of trains actually seen on-time were both 'Arthur'-hauled — 30763 on the 5.30pm Waterloo–Bournemouth and No 30457 on the 7.9pm arrival from Bournemouth. One oddity was Urie 'Arthur' 30747 on an up Lymington Pier train; 4-6-0s were too long for the Lymington turntable, so where did 30747 take over? It was an Eastleigh engine, but as it was only eleven minutes late at Woking the engine change must have been enacted very smartly. Perhaps it had been sent down from Eastleigh to Lymington light-engine, already turned, following a failure of one of the rostered 'U' moguls.

The fastest runs were almost all by 'Merchant Navy' Pacifics — the six speediest all being still unrebuilt (Nos 35004/08/09/24/25/27). Four rebuilt pacifics were seen — 35018 on the 9 o'clock Waterloo–Plymouth, 35022 ex works up from Bournemouth, 35014 on the up '*Bournemouth Belle*' and 35020 running-in on the Clapham–West of England milk empties. In fact nineteen of the thirty large Bulleids were out on Western Section metals that day. Two Light Pacifics (34037 and 34110) were flyers, although many of the others were only mediocre. Only six of the 'Nelsons' put in an appearance (three during the Charterhouse Railway Club observations), compared with the twenty-four 'N15s'. The last serviceable 'N15X', 32331 *Beattie*, was in action at Basingstoke, taking over from a Western engine on a relief Birmingham–Bournemouth train. The influx of BR Standards was beginning to have a marked effect, and six of Nine Elms' series of 'Standard 5s' (73110-9) were seen, including 73118 on the Ilfracombe and Torrington portions of the down '*ACE*'. They were performing competently enough but excited little comment apart from No 73113, which was noted slipping at speed passing Weybridge after accelerating from signal checks. Three of Basingstoke's 'Standard 4s' (75075/78/79) were seen all on the Basingstoke–Reading route, and one from Bath S&D (!) — 75071 — which appeared on an unidentified up express with '258' headcode displayed on the smokebox.

Our observers at Basingstoke took notes (although not times) of the WR-SR cross-country services, and these have been augmented by notes made by Ben Brooksbank during a journey from Waterloo to Paddington via Basingstoke and Reading. Most of these trains changed locos at Basingstoke, although a few (30739, 30765 and 30864) ran through to Oxford, and 'Modified Halls' Nos 7911 and 7919 ran south towards Eastleigh and Portsmouth. The Western offered one of the earliest '43xx' still surviving (4375) and one of the three remaining 'Stars' (4061 of Stafford Road), as well as a 'Grange', three 'Halls' of the Collett series and no fewer than five Hawksworth 'Modified Halls', which were popular locos on WR Summer Saturday traffic.

Most of the services in the up direction were delayed approaching the junction with the Guildford and Portsmouth line at the west end of Woking, some severely. Electric services from that line and Alton were so frequent that they went unrecorded by the Woking observers. One of the earliest severely delayed up services noted was the 1.42pm Waterloo arrival from Bournemouth with a dirty Bournemouth 'Arthur' (30782), which managed to take 38 minutes from Fleet to Woking but was observed to be held outside Woking station for some time. 30782 was, however, going well enough past Fleet with its heavy train, and it should be noted that nearly all Bournemouth engines were noted as dirty or even 'filthy'. Someone told me at the time that all that depot's cleaners left to take seasonal jobs selling ice creams on the beach, but I cannot vouch for the veracity of this excuse for the state of its locomotives; all were affected, even the pacifics (except for the ex-works rebuilt No 35022). This was in contrast to most Nine Elms, Salisbury and Exmouth Junction engines, which were clean, even when high-mileage.

In fact only one up train was on time during most of the afternoon (No 35025 on the Bournemouth train, due at Waterloo at 4.14pm, closely following the late first portion of the *ACE*), although by early evening there were two other punctual services noted (30457 on the 7.9pm arrival from Bournemouth and 34023 on the 7.38pm arrival from Exeter). There were no punctual trains in the down direction until the 4.20pm and 4.35pm Waterloo–Bournemouth-line trains (both with Light Pacifics), the 5.30pm with 30763 and 6.30pm with 34108. The 5.0pm to Exeter with 35004 was early into Woking, but a very rowdy wedding party delayed its departure by more than ten minutes.

The survey was the brainchild of the late Philip Balkwill and his friend Conrad Natzio, and as far as I'm aware nothing similar — timing trains over a stretch of thirty miles and recording locomotive performance — has been attempted before or since.

Churchward mogul 5347 at Cardiff General on the 3.25pm stopping train to Swansea, photographed on the author's 'Arsenal – Cardiff City football excursion', 11 April 1955

Tableau 4

Oxford station, November 1956

It's cold and damp and foggy, and my room in College has a radiator that doesn't work and a single-bar electric fire. I had a reasonable meal at lunchtime between the examinations, so a sandwich and a bar of chocolate at the station will suffice. I've discovered that there are twenty-eight of us competing for one scholarship place, so I've decided that I might as well make the most of my brief sojourn here by spending my evenings watching trains rather than revising. Examinations on my knowledge of French and German language and literature were to be expected, but to write an essay on 'Black Magic' without any other option, as I was instructed to do earlier today, was not predictable. I know absolutely nothing about the subject except the box of chocolates of that name, so I wrote about that. It's therefore a lost cause, so I may as well indulge my hobby.

I've got all evening to while away. The last exam finished at 4 o'clock, and I'm here in the murky darkness less than an hour later, so I decide that sometime this evening I'll take a trip out to Radley and the Abingdon branch. I buy a cheap day-return ticket to Abingdon and wander onto the long up platform to see what's about. The mist is swirling around, and I wind my long school scarf tighter around my neck and stare at the '61xx' Prairie tank oozing steam at the platform with four non-corridor coaches for Thame. There are a lot of travellers huddled together on the far platform, and I can just decipher the muffled tones of the station announcer informing us of the late running of the Bournemouth–Sheffield express, now overdue by twenty minutes.

I wander down to the north end of the station and in the bay find the bulbous face of a 'B12' (61549) looming at me out of the mist, having arrived from Bletchley and Cambridge. There's nothing to be seen in the bay on the down side, but the sounds of something can be heard in the distance, and a ghostly 'King Arthur', 30783 *Sir Gillemere*, draws in slowly with the late-running cross-country train. I watch as the fireman drops down and goes to uncouple the Southern engine and observe it disappear into the fog, the orange glow from the fire visible as the shape of the 'King Arthur' merges with the mist. For a long time nothing happens, other than the sharp exhaust beats of 6122 departing for Thame. Then I see the faint shape of a Hawksworth tender backing out of the fog and can just make out the outline of a 'Modified Hall', though I can't identify it in the darkness at the far end of the station. I nip over the bridge and hurry forward, though there's no need to rush, as the driver of 6970 *Whaddon Hall* is still performing the brake test. I wait there to watch its departure until all I can see is the red glow of the tail lamp fading into the opaque blackness. But I stop to listen to the exhaust of the 'Hall', echoing for a long time in the still night, getting fainter, then becoming more distinct for a few seconds then fading again until the only sounds are the squealing of signal wires and the clatter as the starter semaphore beside me is restored to danger.

I wander back to the up platform and buy a cheese sandwich at the cafeteria, emerging just in time to see an Old Oak engine, 5035 *Coity Castle*, appear out of the darkness and come to rest with a short train of former GW carriages. It's displaying the express headcode, and to my surprise I hear the station announcer repeating that it's for London only, emphasising the words carefully so we are left in no doubt. I move up to the engine and feel the warmth emanating from between the cab and tender and watch the fireman shovelling coal into the fire, carefully lifting the firedoor plate with his left hand each time he throws another shovelful of coal into the seething furnace. The driver looks at me shivering on the platform. 'Want to come up and warm yourself for a few minutes? We're not due away yet.'

I accept with alacrity and stand directly in front of the fire, for the fireman has ceased his labour and is now hosing the footplate and coal at the front of the tender to lay the dust. The driver doesn't seem curious about my presence; he doesn't ask me if I'm travelling to London on his train. The fireman motions me to one side and places a few more carefully directed shovels of coal into the back corners of the fire, looking at the gauge which shows the steam pressure on the red line at 225psi, as it should be. 'Nearly time to go,' says the driver as I hear whistles being blown, and I climb down onto the cold platform. 'A fast one, this, just the hour to Paddington, but I doubt if we'll make it tonight. Nothing wrong with the engine, but it's foggy out there and worse nearer London.' Then a short, high-pitched whistle, and *Coity Castle* gives a series of satisfying thumps of exhaust, and the last coach slips past into the night as the train rapidly accelerates down the gradient out of the station and past the invisible cemetery.

Even as I stand there listening to the steady 'Castle' exhaust increasing in a crescendo echoing in the stillness I hear a second, slower beat and just make out the pale headlamps of a heavy freight which is plodding up the slope into the centre road, an LM '8F' with a long string of empty bogie bolsters destined, I presume, for somewhere in the West Midlands. The train is slowing, as the signals are against it, and the wagons buffer up as it screeches to a halt. A few minutes later there's another approaching train from the south, and the dark outline of another 'Castle' slips behind the freight into the far platform, followed by a string of coaches, dimly lit. I rush back along the platform and over the footbridge because I assume this is a Worcester train that will not stay here long. In fact I needn't have hurried, as the engine, 5083 *Bath Abbey*, is taking water from the column at the end of the platform. I stand in the freezing fog, trying to gain some heat from nearness of the locomotive; then whistles blow, and the driver hurriedly winds the handle to shut off the water supply while the fireman, standing atop the tender, slings the hose out, and water cascades onto the glistening platform. A green light sways in the mist back along the platform, and 5083 slips once, sets

71

off slowly, then, a couple of coach lengths past me, bursts into a harsh exhaust as the driver opens her up. I count the coaches — ten on, but most of the passengers have alighted at Oxford, for the train is less than half full as it disappears towards Moreton-in-Marsh and Evesham.

I return to the up platform and look at my watch, wondering how soon I ought to make my way to Radley. It's well after six o'clock now, and a train is drawing slowly into the platform — a 'Hall' showing the headcode for a stopping train. It draws alongside me, and I note a clean black engine with LNWR lining, 4942 *Maindy Hall*, bearing an 84C (Banbury) shedplate. I check it really is all stations to Didcot and get into an empty compartment, the steam-heat oozing under the seat and drifting up outside the window. We wait for ten minutes, then there's a short toot on the whistle, and we're off into the darkness, leaving the lights of Oxford behind us as we accelerate past Hinksey sidings, where the outline of a Churchward 2-8-0 is dimly seen but unidentified. It's less than ten minutes before we're slowing down for Radley, where I am the sole person to alight on the deserted platform.

I cross the bridge to the far platform, where the Abingdon auto-train is standing awaiting passengers. 0-4-2T 1420 is simmering quietly under a single feeble light, and I get in to the warm coach, its windows running with condensation. I suddenly realise that we are awaiting a connection from London or Reading and just make out the form of a 'Modified Hall' as it slinks past at the opposite platform. Doors slam and echo in the fog, and half a dozen passengers join the branch train, rubbing their hands to keep warm as they settle on the comfortable upholstery. They've scarcely got in, and the Oxford-bound train departed, before we jerk into motion and trot serenely through total blackness for about ten minutes; then I can just make out the lights of a station, and we're at our destination. The others get out, but I stay put. The guard looks at me quizzically and checks my ticket.

'Just out for the ride then? Not a good night for sightseeing, is it?' He must think I'm crazy. No-one else comes to join us, and after a fifteen-minute wait we're on our way back to Radley, once more in pitch darkness. I've not seen anything of Abingdon. When we arrive Radley station is deserted, and I've no idea how long I'll have to wait before there's a train back to Oxford. I consult the timetable display board and see I have a train in half an hour's time. The waiting room is locked, and 1420 and its single coach disappear off into the night. There's no light apart from the dim station lights, no wind, no sound, just the mist, one moment thick and impenetrable, the next thinning to give a brief glimpse of a wan moon before blanketing the station once more. I stamp my feet and twist my scarf a second time round my neck, then I hear an approaching train, pounding towards me. The glow from the engine pierces the gloom, and a Hereford/Worcester–London express hurls itself through the phantom station, sparks flying. I think I caught the sight of '7005' from the front numberplate as for a split-second the smokebox door was illuminated by the platform lamps, then it's gone. For several minutes the mist is swept into the slipstream of the speeding train, then stillness once more reigns, and the cold seeps into my bones. Perhaps I should have stayed in my lodgings after all, or found a café or pub, or at least stayed on Oxford station. I keep looking at my watch — the train was due five minutes ago, then ten minutes. There is no-one to tell me where this train is or when it might appear. Suddenly a door opens, and a lone porter appears; almost simultaneously I hear a train approaching and see the faint outline of express headlamps through the fog. My train back is a semi-fast from London to Worcester, and it's another of Worcester's rebuilt 'Stars', 5090 *Neath Abbey*, that delivers me back safely and in a fuggy warmth to Oxford station.

I could stay longer — it is still only half past eight — but the fog is getting thicker, trains are getting later, and Oxford station is deserted now. Enough! I'll go and get some hot soup somewhere and turn in for an early night. Tomorrow there's just one more examination, an interview, then after lunch it's back to school via Reading and Guildford until the next set of scholarship exams for which I've been entered, at Pembroke College, in a month's time.

Oxford station on 4 March 1957, with Collett 0-6-0 2236 on a stopping train to Thame and 6862 *Derwent Grange* passing with a northbound freight.

Chapter 6
Living in Woking, 1957-62

'Schools' 30907 *Dulwich*, newly transferred to Nine Elms following the Hastings-line dieselisation, ready to depart Waterloo with the 12.54pm to Salisbury, 19 March 1959.

I left Charterhouse at the end of 1956 and got a temporary job at Old Oak Common from then until I went to University in September 1957. I'll cover my time at Old Oak later, but a more mundane aspect of that period was commuting from Hampton Court to Waterloo and Willesden. By changing at Surbiton in the morning I could pick up the first Basingstoke–Waterloo service, one of the few steam trains that stopped at Surbiton other than on a summer Saturday. During 1957 it was almost invariably hauled by one of the massive Urie 'H15s' (30482-90) or the Maunsell rebuild (30491), although on two occasions one of the last Urie 'N15s' appeared (30748 *Vivien* and 30738 *King Pellinore*). (Some years later, in 1966, I picked up this same service from Woking and was astonished to find at its head, newly and uniquely transferred to Guildford, 77014 — a loco by which I'd been hauled in 1955 between Whitby and Scarborough!)

In November 1957 my family moved to Woking, and the County Council supplied me with a season ticket to Warren Street instead of paying for college hostel or lodging accommodation (University College London's male students only had access to 171 hostel places at that time). So began regular steam journeys to London. My first day was an eye-opener. The 8.47 Woking, which became my regular commuting train, left Salisbury at 6.45am and was booked for Salisbury's third 'Merchant Navy'. (It returned on the 1.0pm Waterloo–Exeter.) As Salisbury had only three 'Merchant Navies' (Nos 35004/06/07) we more often than not got one of its 'Battle of Britains' (34049-55/59), but on that first morning we got 35004 and a run to remember. This run was never surpassed in all my commuting days, and I've included its log in the Appendix, Table 7. I've also shown alongside it a 1959 run with 35007 (which by then was rebuilt) and a number of other runs from my morning commuting to London, for comparison.

At 5.30 that evening I saw 30457 *Sir Bedivere* tender-first on the buffer-stops at Waterloo with the stock for the 5.39 to Salisbury (a 'Standard 5' turn) and realised it was for the 6.9 to Basingstoke, first stop Woking. My first railway books (presents from a favourite aunt) were from that classic Ian Allan series '*My Best Photographs*' by Maurice Earley, Eric Treacy and O. J. Morris. The Southern volume included a shot of 457 emerging from Honiton Tunnel and a caption I always remembered — 'the best of them all'. I think this remark was a reference to 448-57 in general, but I have always associated it with 457 in particular. I eventually had thirty-six runs behind *Sir Bedivere* over the following three years of commuting, but none matched the feeling of satisfaction of that first evening and the realisation of the promise that my season ticket held.

College lectures were normally from 10am until 4pm — except on Thursdays, when we had an early lecture, necessitating my use of a 'Lord Nelson'-hauled train. In the evening I had a choice (ignoring the Pompey electrics, of course!). There was the 5 o'clock to Exeter, normally with an Exmouth Junction 'Merchant Navy' but occasionally a Light Pacific, or the 5.9pm to Basingstoke, which in my first year was almost invariably hauled by one of 70D's double-chimney 'Standard 4s', 75076-9. I almost always chose the Exeter train, whose locos had a wide variety of outlines and liveries in 1957/8 — rebuilt and unrebuilt, different cabs, tenders. My favourites were 35008 *Orient Line* and 35013 *Blue Funnel*, two of the most common, and an exciting run behind one of Salisbury's top-link drivers was usually on the cards. A number of logs of evening commuter services are shown in the Appendix, Tables 2, 8 and 9.

In my second and third years the 5.9 became much more interesting, as 'Arthurs' and 'Schools' from the Southern's Eastern Section were transferred to Nine Elms and Basingstoke. Initially on the 5.9 we got 'Schools' 30904, 30905 (with the high-sided tender that for years had been coupled to 30932), 30908, 30918 and 30923 and 'Arthurs' 30765, 30773, 30794 and 30795. A little later we got 30777 *Sir Lamiel*, best of the lot, which became almost a permanent fixture on the 5.9 in the latter part of 1959 and the first half of 1960. I searched in vain for any reference to 'Sir Lamiel' in Geoffrey of Monmouth, Chrétien de Troyes or the German mediaeval poets — until recently. Over lunch in a Carlisle pub, whilst No 5043 *Earl of Mount Edgcumbe* was being coaled and watered en route from its tour of Scotland, a colleague consulted an Arthurian expert on my behalf and elicited the response that 'Sir Lamiel' is referenced once in Mallory as 'Sir Lamiel of Cardiff'; nothing else is known about him. Perhaps No 30777 should bear the shedplate 86C.

30914 *Eastbourne* at Victoria on 12 June 1959, the penultimate day of Kent Coast steam, ready to depart with the 12.35pm to Ramsgate.

A unique event which I have described elsewhere but which bears repeating was a personal engine trial carried out one memorable week in 1959 by Driver Carlisle — a former GW driver by now based at Basingstoke. He decided to see which of the 70D 'King Arthurs', 'Schools' and 'Standard 4s' could get to Woking in the shortest time. I travelled on the train three times that week with 30794 *Sir Ector de Maris*, 30923 *Bradfield* and 75078. All got to Woking in less than 26½ minutes (schedule 31 minutes for the 24.4 miles) — not bad for a heavily loaded ten-coach train in the evening rush hour (see Table 9). The 'Schools' achieved the highest speed (83mph at West Weybridge, passing Brooklands), but 30794 won hands down overall by dint of an electrifying start from London, passing through Surbiton in 14½ minutes at 75mph. We held that speed thereafter and stopped at Woking in 25 minutes 45 seconds, this being the only time we beat the 26min barrier (indeed the only time in three years that I managed that with any steam train in either direction). 30794 was not Basingstoke's best 'N15' either, and it is interesting to contemplate what time might have been achieved with 30765, 30777 or 30795.

The 1959 Summer Timetable promised the introduction of electric traction on the Kent Coast via Chatham, so I took a day off studies to experience the last rites. I occasionally sallied forth between lectures (and as a change to the Waterloo–Woking trips, but of course this cost real money) from Victoria to Bromley South and back to travel behind the six-wheel-tender 'Arthurs'; 30800, 30805 and 30806 all obliged, as did a couple of 'U1' three-cylinder 2-6-0s on Ramsgate trains, and I managed to get one 'D1' 4-4-0 (31505) on the return. However, on the penultimate day of

30905 *Tonbridge* with the unique Schools high-sided tender passes Woking with a summer relief train for Bournemouth, July 1959

'U1' three-cylinder mogul 31891 at Victoria on the 1.35pm to Ramsgate in 1958.

steam, a Saturday in mid-June, I forked out for a day return to Chatham and found the first Victoria–Ramsgate express after my arrival at the terminus was headed by 30914 *Eastbourne*, which I was happy to take immediately, leaving me all day to select a choice return working. (I was hoping for a Wainwright/Maunsell 4-4-0 rebuild.) I took a number of photos at Chatham while I waited — 30911 *Dover* on the next service from Victoria and then 30803 *Sir Harry le Fise Lake* as it rushed through non-stop. The up services were disappointing — Bulleid pacifics and 'Standard 5s', not even an 'Arthur' or 'Schools'. I was just about to give up and determined to take the next service when it turned up behind a 4-4-0 — not a 'D1' or 'E1' rebuild but one of the Maunsell 'L1s', a rather down-at-heel 31788, which performed soundly enough. It could not have been too run-down, as it was transferred with sisters 31753 and 31786 to Nine Elms, where I had a series of runs later behind each of these on my commuter trains to and from Woking.

Of course, I did not always dash away from college straight after lectures finished but sometimes tarried with my friends over coffee or practiced my table-tennis with Gordon, a fellow member of the college third-league team. Waterloo's offerings after the 5.9 were the 5.39 (a Nine Elms 'Standard 5'), the 6.9 (one of Nine Elms' three 'Eastleigh Arthurs', 30455-7, for the first year and thereafter usually a 'Standard 5', once 73080-9 had been transferred from Stewarts Lane) or the 6.54 to Salisbury. This last was interesting, as during 1957 and the early part of 1958 it was rostered for one of Salisbury's 'S15s' in the 30823-32 series, then one of its regular 'King Arthurs' (30448-54) until 1959, when Nos 30796, 30798 and 30799 were reallocated from the Eastern Section to Salisbury and took their share of this turn. The most common was 30453 *King Arthur* itself; I had fifty-five very efficient runs with this loco — a performance matched only by No 30777 (fifty-three runs in total, mostly on the 5.9 Waterloo).

30453 *King Arthur* awaiting departure from Waterloo with the 2.54pm to Salisbury in May 1960.

An evening excursion to Hackney Downs in the summer of 1958 yielded this view of 'N7/1' 69603 approaching with a local for Chingford.

I regularly attended the weekly college MethSoc discussion group (more like full-blooded arguments most weeks) at Hinde Street Chapel, near Bond Street tube station. The meeting was not until 7.30pm, so after a day's study I would often retire in the meantime to Liverpool Street for immersion in the station's sulphurous, murky atmosphere. The constant raspings of Westinghouse brake pumps as 'N7s' scuttled to and fro, together with Sandringhams or 'B12s' tender-first at the buffer-stops, awaiting their next assignments, were an enticing draw. In the early evening there was always a 'Sandringham' on empty stock at platform 8 or 9, and I would look eagerly at it to judge whether I wanted to buy a ticket to Broxbourne or Bishops Stortford, or even just to Tottenham Hale, to accompany its next northbound foray. My memories are of dark, damp wintry fogs, glistening wet platforms, hordes of scurrying commuters, the panting brake pumps and down-at-heel 'B17s' such as No 61601 *Holkham* or 61618 *Wynyard Park* or a 'B2' such as 61616 *Falloden*, behind which I would make that modest journey past Hackney Marshes, with a drunken syncopated apology of an exhaust drifting past the cracked-open window of my compartment. I would take it as far as Tottenham Hale, or Broxbourne if I was not too impecunious, returning as often as not behind a Stratford 'N7' or 'L1'. Occasionally, if the best 'Sandringham' looked set for the GE main line, I would go to Shenfield and be treated with another 'Footballer' or 'Sandringham' on the return. Real fireworks were unusual, but one evening the driver of 61613 *Woodbastwick Hall* decided to keep steam on going down Brentwood Bank, and we nearly made an '80' — but I couldn't quite get beyond 79mph on the watch. The poor loco paid for it that night — on arrival at Liverpool Street the bottom half of the smokebox door was glowing an angry red!

Thompson 'B2' rebuild 61616 *Falloden* on the 4.36pm Liverpool Street–Kings Lynn 'Fenman', 1958.

Over three years I was at college I amassed a fair mileage behind the 'N15s', which were always my SR favourites. In all I had 585 runs behind this group of fifty-four engines (I'm ignoring the Urie 'N15s', behind which I only had two runs — 30748 and 30755) at an average of 10.8 runs per individual locomotive. In those years I had no engine failure with any of them (come to think of it, nor with any of the other classes, except for the previously mentioned 34009, one 'Standard 5' and a couple of horrendous efforts by 'Lord Nelsons' — always the most vulnerable of locos, of which more anon). Nor do I remember a single trip on which we lost any time due to locomotive reasons with the 'Arthurs'. The 'N15s' were very effective engines for six-coach semi-fast trains to Basingstoke or Salisbury, surefooted and with good acceleration, although rarely touching 80mph. (I had a couple of 80s — one with 30777 and one with 30765 — and the 1956 run with 30449, but I think that was it.) The evening commuter services (the 10-coach 5.9 and 11-coach 6.9) taxed them more but not unduly so.

On Saturday afternoons I would often slip down to the Farnborough Railway Enthusiasts' Club beside the main line and catch up on the latest news from Swindon from 'Griff' Evans whilst watching the succession of summer reliefs powered by 'Arthurs' and the occasional 'Schools'. On one occasion I was spotted on the platform at Woking awaiting the Saturday 1.24pm Waterloo and beckoned onto the footplate of No 30777 for the ten-mile run to Farnborough.

You may be wondering how I managed to amass so many runs behind these locos in just four years of commuting. Well, I sort of cheated! During my second and third college years I had many free periods in which I was meant to study German mediaeval- and modern-literature texts, and I presume I was expected to work in the college library. Often there would be a whole day free for study. If I stayed in college the temptations for endless coffees and other pursuits with friends were too great. If I stayed at home the temptation to lie in bed for half the day was equally strong. So, often, I would join the 8.47am or, more likely, the 9.8 (a 70D 'Arthur', 'Schools' or 'Standard 4') or the 9.48 (a stopper from Bournemouth with a 70A 'Arthur' or 'Standard 5') and spend the rest of the day see-sawing backwards and forwards from Woking to Waterloo, reading German poetry and drama texts as I went! I could get in four return trips (eight locos) in normal hours and five if I was still game and there was something interesting about. I've put a number of logs from these trips in Appendix Tables 3, 10 and 11, although I rarely timed these trains, as I did have work to do. One of the problems was that if the train ran at a certain speed the rail-joint rhythms would coincide with a poem's metre (especially Middle High German mediaeval texts), and I could arrive at Woking or Waterloo with a dozen pages read and not a word comprehended, as I had read it too fast!

30448 *Sir Tristram* saunters into Farnborough with the 2.54pm Waterloo–Salisbury, July 1959.

81

Normal motive power for the 9.48am Woking–Waterloo as Nine Elms Standard Class 5 73118 *King Leodegrance* draws into Woking in 1959.

Once or twice a week I would stay in college for the evening for extramural activities — the regular table-tennis league matches or various college society meetings — and this meant dashing for the last steam train back to Woking, the 11.15pm Waterloo–Basingstoke. This was an interesting train — normally four coaches diagrammed for a 70A 'N15' (usually 30763, 30774, 30778 or 30779) — but as it was a light job (the loco returned on a freight) Nine Elms would turn out any spare engine, often a 'foreign' 'Arthur' or a high-mileage pacific that was on 'restricted' working. At that time of night few people were about (and certainly no loco inspectors), so I found myself one night invited onto the footplate of Eastleigh's 30784 *Sir Nerovens* and offered the regulator before reaching Clapham Junction. Unfortunately I made a mess of it, as the regulator was very stiff; I failed to get it open early enough to recover from the Clapham speed restriction through the station, and our climb to Earlsfield was painfully slow. However, with only four coaches we soon recovered time afterwards.

The most memorable run on this train (for all the wrong reasons) was with 35005 *Canadian Pacific*, still in unrebuilt form. It was, as the driver remarked, 'running out' and was overdue a visit to Eastleigh Works, where it would undergo rebuilding. From the start things happened. We slithered and slipped with our four-coach train the length of platform 8, making all sorts of weird syncopated noises — the valve settings were all to pot — and took five minutes to get past Vauxhall, then something clicked and we accelerated at tremendous speed, rocketing around the (40mph) Clapham curve at 61mph without touching the brake. By Wimbledon we were doing 75; we were hurtling towards Hampton Court Junction when the brakes were slammed on, and we screeched to a halt, straddling the crossover to the slow line beyond the 'box, having just passed the signal at danger. (For some reason this night the signalman was to put us to the slow at Hampton Court Junction, instead of Esher as usual.) An angry altercation broke the silence of the very misty night, after which we set off down the slow, only to run into a fog so thick down by the River Mole between Esher and Hersham that we reduced speed to walking pace to search for signals. The fireman had actually to climb the signal post just before Hersham station to 'feel' its aspect! Finally, after our arrival in Woking twenty-five minutes late, there was a sudden 'whoosh' as 35005 went up in flames, and the fire brigade rushed to the scene. I wonder how many HMRI inquiries would have been instituted into that run in today's world!

In between travelling to and from London, when I had little opportunity for photography, already carting around so much paraphernalia, my briefcase full of textbooks and removable parts of my bicycle, I made an occasional foray on a Saturday to the wooded cuttings just to the west of Woking station or a little further west to an overbridge near the summit of the rise from Woking to Milepost 31. It was about this time that I swapped my faithful old camera for a second-hand Ensign Selfix — still a slow fixed shutter speed, but with a beautiful lens that gave high definition as long as the trains were not moving too fast. This was fine for the environs of Woking, as long as I photographed trains stopping there or took them at a reasonably head-on angle. I later found another favourite location near one of the many nearby golf courses, halfway between Woking and Brookwood.

30453 *King Arthur* passing Woking Golf Course with the 2.54pm Waterloo–Salisbury, September 1959.

'Merchant Navy' 35030 *Elder Dempster Lines* nears the summit at Milepost 31 with the 3pm Waterloo–West of England, 11 July 1956.

30804 *Sir Cador of Cornwall* with a down ballast train near Woking Golf Course, September 1959.

From August 1960, the proud possessor of a second-class honours degree and a letter from the Ministry of Defence informing me of the abolition of National Service, I obtained employment as a clerk in the London Divisional Passenger Office of the Western Region Operating Department, continuing my regular commuting to Waterloo until I started as a Western Region Management Trainee in the autumn of 1961. As I had to be at Paddington by 9am the 'Nelson'-hauled 7.51 Woking, due Waterloo at 8.22, was ideal. During this period I became pretty familiar with the performance of the regular locomotives and crews. I had a lot of experience of the 'Lord Nelsons', behind which I'd previously travelled every Thursday on this train (which set off from Southampton Terminus at 6.4am) in order to be present for the one weekly college lecture that started at 9am, and often, during my daytime meanderings, on the 10.54am Waterloo–Basingstoke as far as Woking. Altogether I clocked up 383 runs behind the Maunsell 'Nelsons' between 1957 and 1962 — and not one of them was memorable in the positive sense of the word. They were known to all local enthusiasts as 'Nellies', and the word that comes to mind when describing them on the move is 'waffle', which perhaps sums up my impression of them overall. Of course, their soft exhaust from the wide Bulleid chimney and the eight beats per revolution (save in the case of 30865) reinforced the impression that they shuffled along in a very 'understated' way.

'Lord Nelson' 30865 *Sir John Hawkins* leaving Woking with the 11.53am Woking–Waterloo, a semi-fast from Basingstoke, 29 December 1958.

I cycled to Woking from my home and left my bike in the bushes outside the station (I couldn't afford 1/3d a week to leave it in the station lock-up) and would run across the forecourt as the haze of brown smoke drifted lazily from the loco's chimney as it slunk into the station — always a couple of minutes late. (I relied on this, as 7.51am is an early hour for students!) I could give no other morning train this latitude. I would set up my beach stool in the corridor (I hardly ever got a compartment seat) and watch the countryside roll gently past as the 'Nellie' took usually 5 minutes to clear West Byfleet ('King Arthurs' would do it in 4 minutes and Bulleids anything from 3½ to over 5, depending on how much they slipped). Cruising speed around Hersham/Esher was usually around 60-65mph; a good run would make 68mph, and 14-15 minutes to clear Surbiton was the norm. My 'par' on other trains was 70-75mph around Esher and 13½ minutes to Surbiton. (For typical runs on this train see Appendix, Table 4.)

I talked to many drivers during this time, and the general view of the 'Nelsons' was that they was hard to fire compared to the Bulleids, Standards and 'King Arthurs' — they had a long firebox requiring careful firing, and few Eastleigh firemen in the late 1950s were really masters of them. As a result they were rarely steaming well by the time they reached Woking, and in winter we used to joke that we could have steam heating or get to Waterloo on time but never both! In reality that was false, because we rarely reached Waterloo at 8.22 anyway (it was usually between 8.25 and 8.28), but I can remember some classic occasions when the insides of the carriage windows froze over, and bowler-hatted city gents were rolling up the *Financial Times* and shoving it up their trouser legs! (And I'm not joking!)

On the 10.54am Waterloo–Salisbury they had a much easier job: only four coaches, and 31 minutes allowed, fast line to Hampton Court Junction and slow line thence to Woking. Even so, they could still get into trouble, and I can remember one morning when 30850 *Lord Nelson* distinguished himself by achieving 47mph at Vauxhall, and speed fell away for the rest of the journey! Another, much harder job dominated by the 'Nellies' was the 10.35pm Waterloo–Weymouth news and mail, comprising about fifteen coaches and mail vans. It started from two platforms, the loco drawing out the mail portion from platform 11 and backing onto the passenger coaches at platform 10 a few minutes before departure. Progress was usually pedestrian, but I can recall one night when 30851 *Sir Francis Drake* was worked really hard and produced a spectacular fireworks display that must have been visible over the whole of Surrey, and in Berrylands Cutting our coach was bombarded with red-hot coals the size of golf balls! (See Appendix, Table 5.)

My slowest-ever journey between Waterloo and Woking was on the same train with 30854 *Howard of Effingham*. It clearly ran out of steam, and by Weybridge speed had dropped to 28mph; by West Byfleet we were creeping through the station at 8mph, and we finally expired halfway up Woking's platform 4, with all the passenger vehicles off the platform. We had to wait twenty-five minutes for 30854 to raise enough steam to drag us into the station before we could alight. It eventually woofled out of Woking a staggering 89 minutes late, in a shroud of leaking steam and with 80% of its journey still to be completed. (For my 'disaster' runs see Appendix Tables 4 and 5.)

Despite my predilection for 'King Arthurs', which meant I chose a train likely to be hauled by one of those 'knights' whenever possible, I of course had many more runs behind Bulleid Pacifics, 'Nelsons', 'Schools' and the Standard Class 4 and 5 4 6-0s. I kept a meticulous record of these runs, although I timed only some of them in detail, and find that over the four years of commuting (three to University and one to Paddington) the following were locomotives behind which I travelled most frequently:

30453	(55)	30853	(26)	34053	(21)	34048	(17)
30777	(53)	30857	(26)	34093	(21)	35004	(17)
30451	(44)	30859	(26)	35007	(21)	73111	(17)
30798	(39)	30861	(26)	73081	(21)	75079	(17)
35013	(39)	75078	(26)	73086	(21)	30491	(16)
30457	(36)	30856	(25)	73087	(21)	30852	(16)
35009	(35)	35006	(25)	73114	(21)	30865	(16)
30763	(32)	73117	(25)	75077	(21)	34051	(16)
34052	(32)	30765	(24)	30863	(20)	34055	(16)
35008	(31)	34049	(24)	35023	(20)	35011	(16)
35010	(30)	34059	(24)	73089	(20)	35019	(16)
30850	(30)	73110	(24)	73112	(20)	35022	(16)
30855	(30)	73113	(24)	73115	(20)	73082	(16)
30858	(30)	73116	(24)	73119	(20)	73084	(16)
30905	(30)	75076	(24)	30799	(19)	30794	(15)
30450	(29)	30851	(23)	30904	(19)	34006	(15)
30455	(28)	34004	(23)	73088	(19)	34020	(15)
30796	(28)	34050	(23)	30860	(17)	34028	(15)
73118	(28)	34054	(23)	30864	(17)	30489	(14)
30854	(27)	73083	(23)	30908	(17)	30456	(14)
30862	(27)	30907	(22)	30918	(17)	30773	(14)
34022	(27)	34009	(22)	34003	(17)	34010	(14)
35003	(27)	34025	(21)	34034	(17)	34090	(14)

30450 *Sir Kay* between Woking and Brookwood with the 2.54pm Waterloo–Salisbury, September 1959.

A one-time St Leonards 'Schools' now transferred to Nine Elms, 30903 *Charterhouse*, calls at Woking with the 12.54pm Waterloo–Salisbury in 1960.

During those years of commuting (1957-61) I travelled behind all the 'Merchant Navies', all the 'West Countries' and 'Battle of Britains' except for 34035, all the 'Lord Nelsons', all the 'Scotch' and Eastleigh 'King Arthurs' except for a handful that were on the Eastern Section at that time and would be withdrawn after the Kent Coast electrification without ever being transferred to the Western Section (30766, 30769, 30776, 30792 and 30801) and most of the 'Schools', including 30903, which was named after the school I had attended and which frequently graced the 12.54pm Waterloo–Basingstoke following its reallocation to Nine Elms and before its eventual transfer to Guildford to spend its last days on the 'Rattler'. The most frequent representatives of the other types behind which I travelled over the route during this period are listed below.

'H15' (Urie)	30489	(14)
	30491	(16)
'S15' (Maunsell)	30827	(8)
'H15' (Maunsell)	30478	(6)
	30521	(6)
'S15' (Urie)	30499	(4)
'U' (2-6-0)	31630	(4)
	31635	(4)
	31798	(4)
'L1' (4-4-0)	31786	(2)
	31788	(2)

Tableau 5
Hungerford Bridge, March 1958

I've got a free morning today — my first tutorial is after lunch. However, I need to buy some new books which my professor has indicated to be required reading next term — plays by Schiller and Kleist. The best bookseller is in a small cul-de-sac parallel to Villiers Street by Embankment tube station — the previous year's students have tipped us off to get our paperbacks here rather than at Foyles or one of the bigger expensive bookshops. I've caught my usual train to London, therefore, the 6.45 Salisbury, with 34055 *Fighter Pilot*, in my view Salisbury's best 'Light Pacific', and we've arrived at Waterloo on time at 9.16am. I could walk over Hungerford Bridge or even use my Underground season ticket to take me to Embankment, but as I've got plenty of time I decide to purchase a single ticket from Waterloo East to Charing Cross and cross Hungerford Bridge in style!

I stand on the deserted main-line platform — everyone else is on the middle platform awaiting down expresses or on the far platform for one of the myriad electrics to Lewisham or Orpington. A couple of local electrics use this platform and disgorge a few passengers, then a 'Battle of Britain', 34083 *605 Squadron*, ambles in with an express from Ramsgate. I'm tempted to take it, but I really want to get a 'Schools' on a train from Hastings, so I let it go. Patience is rewarded, for less than ten minutes later a large-diameter-chimney 'Schools', 30901 *Winchester*, appears from around the corner with a train of narrow-bodied coaches used specifically on the Hastings route. 30901 looks to have been recently outshopped from Ashford, for it's a very clean Brunswick green with the latest BR emblem on the tender. A fair number of passengers alight, and I slip unobtrusively into the first coach, immediately behind the engine. I stand in the corridor on the upstream side of the Thames, and *Winchester* strains on the curve to start the train, then slips violently on the oily track, polluted by many engines (especially the oil-leaking Bulleids) that have stopped at this very spot. The engine sets back, buffering up to its train, then tries again, and suffers another bout of slipping; then, very slowly and softly, it grips the rails and starts to pull away, with barely a sound from the chimney.

We pass under the bridge to the main Waterloo station, looking down at the fine entrance, and roll onto the girders of Hungerford Bridge past the South Bank site of the 1951 Festival of Britain and the exhibition of railway locomotives — 70004 *William Shakespeare*, brand-new and straight from Crewe Works, an electric locomotive (26020) for the newly electrified Woodhead route, Southern diesel-electric 10201 and an Indian Railways 'WG' 2-8-2 representing British

Class L 4-4-0 31760 pilots 'Schools' 30929 *Malvern* in 1959. The train was a semi-fast from Charing Cross to Ashford, which the author took to London Bridge.

manufacturers' locomotives for the export market. The site is now cleared, and the main edifice is the towering Shell building. The 'Schools' is coasting now, and as we rumble onto the main girders spanning the river the only noise comes from our wheels as they reverberate on the heavy steel. I recollect that it was here during the Second World War that 934 *St Lawrence* suffered a direct hit from a German bomb that ripped a hole in the bridge as well as crippling the locomotive. We roll on at a steady 15mph, and we are now over the centre of the river, with views across to Big Ben and the Houses of Parliament, seen between the side girders and a squall of rain that suddenly splashes against the corridor windows, then stops as quickly as it started. We are already entering the platform at Charing Cross opposite 34083's empty train and draw slowly to the buffer-stops, having taken barely three minutes for my minuscule journey. I mingle with the crowd and hand in my ticket surreptitiously, in the hope that the ticket collector will not notice and be suspicious that I've actually travelled from much further afield, requiring me to explain that I'm not mad in seeking to travel by steam train over such a short distance. Once through the ticket barrier I relax and stare for several minutes at *Winchester* resting at the buffer-stops, all its passengers having long since departed for Trafalgar Square or the Underground.

My shopping does not take long. I purchase three plays in the preposterously cheap (9d) East German editions and climb the steps by Embankment station to the footpath that runs over Hungerford Bridge on the Festival Hall side. I don't pluck up sufficient courage to purchase a ticket back to Waterloo East and have to show it to a ticket collector on the main-line platforms 5 and 6, who would, I'm sure, have attempted to direct me to one of the suburban electrics on the other platforms. I would perhaps have done this if I'd decided to go out to London Bridge, but today I'm going back to Waterloo to catch the 10.54am back to Woking, as I saw an Eastleigh-based 'King Arthur', 30788 *Sir Urre of the Mount*, as we passed Nine Elms this morning, and I suspect (and hope) that it might have come off the 6.4 Southampton Terminus instead of the usual 'Nelson' and therefore be on the 10.54. I can still get back in plenty of time for lunch in the college refectory before my tutorial.

Anyway, I decide to walk across Hungerford Bridge, although I risk getting caught in another squall. The footpath vibrates as electric units rumble past, and I look out at the famous skyline dominated by St Paul's. As I near the Festival Hall I hear something starting out of Waterloo East and peer between the girders and electrics passing in both directions at another 'Schools', Ashford's 30924 *Haileybury*, which has a string of parcel vans behind its passenger vehicles. I find myself wishing I'd had a run behind that as well — perhaps it will be on the semi-fast to Ashford via the Otford loop, which I know runs sometime mid-morning. But enough is enough. I'll chance getting 30788 to Woking — a decent run, and free; my season ticket from home to college will cover that.

Chapter 7
The wider horizon

Chapelon Pacific No 231E 34 on the 'Blue Train' from Belgium at Gare du Nord, April 1956.

Like many other schoolchildren I really had no idea what career I wanted to follow and just carried on studying what I happened to be best at, through 'O' and 'A' levels to university degree. In my case, through a number of chance encounters and a particularly conscientious and persuasive schoolmaster, this happened to be modern languages, and I suppose I might have become a teacher myself but for a work-experience course with British Railways which opened my eyes to possibilities with my real interest. In the meantime, and before finally deciding for a management career with BR, I enrolled for an honours degree course in German at University College London, with French as a subsidiary subject. I subsequently opted to specialise in stylistic analysis of mediaeval German poetry, which would appear to have even less relevance to a railway career, other than making me an expert on Arthurian legends and allowing me access to the source of some of the more abstruse Southern Region 'King Arthur' names!

However, this choice of study opened up a number of reasons for visiting railways overseas. My first venture was in the spring of 1956 when I was in the Modern

Languages Sixth at Charterhouse and somehow got myself enrolled to do a three-week vacation course at the Sorbonne in Paris. To this day I can remember nothing about the content of the course itself, although the travels and accommodation stay vividly in my mind. There were around 1,000 sixth-formers on the course, and we left Victoria on two special boat trains, with 30915 *Brighton* on our train and 30918 *Hurstpierpoint* on the other. The Newhaven–Dieppe crossing was vile; a shallow-bottomed ferry called *Lisieux* seemed to list permanently to starboard as the strong easterly wind swept up the channel, and there was no room for us below deck, so we huddled like penguins on the sloping deck, ducking whenever a nearby pupil succumbed to seasickness and the warning cry came in time.

On arrival at Dieppe I managed to escape the schoolmarm attempts to marshal us in crocodiles onto the awaiting trains and got to the front to obtain my first sight of foreign locomotives, both État Pacifics, '231D' 710 on our train and '231H' 740 on the relief. I can remember little more than being crammed into our compartment, four on each side, and watching the smoke billowing over French meadows bathed in sunshine and wild flowers. We were lodged in primitive accommodation at the Lycée St Germain, near Montparnasse, and quickly became expert at negotiating the garlic-smelling Métro (all the tunnels seemed to advertise Dubonnet ... Dubonnet ... Dubonnet ...) and looking for alternative snacks to cover for the leathery horsemeat smothered in garlic that in those days seemed to pass for French school meals.

Luckily there was one other like-minded railway enthusiast in our small party from Charterhouse, and the main educational benefit of our stay seems to have been our ability to fend for ourselves around the SNCF and Métro systems. How many lectures we cut I cannot remember, but Martyn and I spent many happy hours at Gare du Nord and Gare de l'Est with notebook and camera and a few French coins to relieve the slot machines of bars of chocolate.

At Gare du Nord we saw '241P' Mountains and a couple of the '232R'/'232S' Baltics on trains from Lille, '231E' and 'K' Pacifics from the Belgian border and Calais and several ex-Nord Super-Pacifics ('231Cs') on semi-fast services, as well as the de Glehn '230D' 4-6-0s. The Nord de Caso '141TCs' dominated the local suburban service, although some huge '242TA' ex-PLM tank engines were running out on the line through Aulnaye-sous-Bois and beyond. Someone had told us that in France you could walk across the tracks from platform to platform (maybe I learned that from the classic 78rpm record by Reginald Gardiner about his experience of French trains). Martyn and I put it to the test at the business end of Gare du Nord, and in hindsight I think this was not the wisest decision by a future Head of Safety Policy for BR. We got away with it but received a good ticking-off from a French railwayman, which improved our language ability no end!

Gare de l'Est was equally exciting, with plenty of those splendid Est '241A' Mountains and a large number of PLM Pacifics transferred on electrification of the Paris–Marseilles main line. There were also a number of the Chapelon '141Ps' and some ancient Est '230Bs' and '230Ks', which managed to look more antiquarian than they actually were. Everywhere the fussy suburban '141TBs' rushed in and out like the 'N7s' at Liverpool Street.

We paid a few visits to St Lazare terminus, but it was pretty quiet there, with usually at best a couple of État Pacifics and perhaps one or two of the ungainly ex-Ouest '141TD' tank engines on push-pull suburban trains. Our one visit to Montparnasse was a big disappointment, yielding only one steam engine, a ghostly '141C' 111 from the non-electrified route from Granville and Argentan, amid the silent electrics. It seemed more like a cathedral than a busy railway station.

Our return to Britain was fairly uneventful — the boat train from St Lazare had an État Pacific modified by Chapelon, '231G' 772, the crossing was calm, and the BR boat-train locomotive was a Bulleid Pacific, 34068 *Kenley*. The one bit of excitement was at the British Customs, as one of our party was David Dimbleby, son of the then-famous Richard Dimbleby, who had shopped to excess in Paris and now required assistance to carry his haul from the boat. I got separated from him and ran into dire trouble when I tried to explain to a curious and increasingly suspicious Customs official that the large wooden box I was carrying housed a bust of Beethoven, that I was carrying it for someone else who had disappeared and that I did not know what it was made of, or its value, or where it had been purchased. In the end the official decided that if I had really been smuggling something I would have concocted a better story than that, and he sent me packing, box unopened. I'd dearly love to know if David remembers that — I guess not, as he was already boarding the boat train at the time.

My next 'official' student trip was a couple of years later, in April 1958, with a party of first-year students from UCL's German Department under the much less watchful eye of a couple of our eccentric tutors. (I can't remember which ones, but they were all eccentric and exceedingly good fun.) We were bound for Bad Harzburg in the Harz Mountains, only a few miles from the border of the German Democratic Republic (East Germany), to attend a language and literature course. I really had no idea what (if any) railway interest there would be apart from the Hook '*Day Continental*' boat train from Liverpool Street ('B1' 61046), and the long sea crossing was followed by a series of electric runs across Holland to Bentheim, where in pitch darkness the shape of DB Pacific 03 091 backed onto our train for the run through Rheine to Osnabrück.

At Osnabrück we changed and we went downstairs to a connecting train for the junction of Löhne on the line from the Ruhr to Hanover and Berlin. My first impression of the waiting locomotive ('P8' 4-6-0 38 2219) was that we had come across a real veteran — the sight of the tall chimney and generally antiquated appearance misled me — but we piled into a coach reserved for our party and were duly dumped in the middle of Löhne Yard for upwards of three hours. Attempting sleep in our crowded quarters was pretty hard anyway, but Standard 2-10-0 50 921 was attached and kept whisking us off to the other end of the yard with a great jerk every time sleep seemed imminent. I finally cottoned on to the fact that our coach was to be attached to a D-Zug to Berlin, and it suddenly swept past us when I was hardly ready, just noting that the smokebox-door numberplate of the locomotive had lots of 0s and 1s in it. On arrival at Hanover, where we had to change at 06.00, I hurried to the front (our coach had been attached at the rear), but as we seemed to

Ex-PLM 4-8-4 tank 242TA 35 with a suburban train at Gare du Nord, April 1956.

have about seventeen coaches on I managed only to see No 01 1087 backing down for the trip to the GDR border. At the time I wrote 01 010 in my notebook, but I later suspected that we'd had an '01.10' three-cylinder Pacific, probably 01 1001, 01 1100 or 01 1101. (Since first drafting this book I've become a member and contributor to a 'Railways of Germany' website forum and posed the question of the possible identity of this locomotive. I was astounded to get a flurry of answers from erudite British and German enthusiasts, and two members of German club DSO, Ronald Krug and '03.1008', advised me that D119, calling at Löhne at 02.56 to pick up through coaches from the Hook of Holland, was diagrammed for a Hanover-based '01' — rather than an '01.10' — through to Hanover and the engine change. As 01 010 was a Hanover engine at that time it is 99% certain that my loco that night was indeed 01 010 and not one of the three '01.10s' that I thought subsequently might have been our motive power.)

The connecting Eilzug from Hanover to Bad Harzburg was conveyed efficiently enough by 03 131, which became one of the last two '03s' to survive in far-off Allgäu (Ulm) in the early 1970s. This visit was definitely cultural and had little room for railway tours, especially as I knew little about my surroundings. I did spend a few

DB Pacific 03.131 at Hanover with the 6am Eilzug–Bad Harzburg, April 1958.

hours around the railway station at Goslar while others went visiting the town's castle and other sights, and I have a vague memory of seeing a huge narrow-gauge 2-10-2 tank emerge from the forest when we had the obligatory coach visit to the Iron Curtain border to stare at the barbed wire and guard posts on the Brocken Mountain. I cannot think that we got close enough to the border to see a train from the DR Harzquerbahn, but I believe we must have seen a train on the Süd Harz system between Walkenried and Braunlage, which closed in 1963 (more information gleaned from the 'Railways of Germany' website forum).

Our return journey to the UK was a little better remembered, as I was now prepared on what to look out for. Our first leg was completed behind 03 086, and the run to Löhne was behind a DB standard '01' (definitely this time), No 01 161. (I have a somewhat fuzzy photo to prove it.) At Löhne we managed to get shunted by both 2-10-0 50 816 and Prussian 'G8' 0-8-0 55 5449. Another 'P8', 38 1988, took us back to Osnabrück, and the '*Nord Express*' (from Flensburg) to the Hook of Holland had 03 169, still with its original large smoke-deflectors, as far as the Dutch border at Bentheim. A 'B1', 61311, on the '*Day Continental*' from Harwich completed the experience.

These first forays into foreign parts had whetted my appetite, and I determined to be a little more prepared whenever such opportunities next presented themselves.

Prussian 'P8' 4-6-0 38.3473 at Goslar with a local passenger train from Brunswick, April 1958.

Chapter 8

Old Oak Vacation

In August 2000 I was involved at the Old Oak Common Open Weekend in the naming of EWS electric locomotive 90 031 *The Railway Children Partnership* and, in support of that event, was present during the two days with a stand and display about the international street children's charity after which the locomotive was named. Coincidentally that stand was on the ground floor of the old train-crew accommodation — where forty-two years previously, immediately above, on the first floor, I had spent several weeks, just before the building's completion, copying out the new winter timetable train-crew rosters in isolation, as the Chief Clerk feared I might be subject to some animosity. I was apparently doing some clerk out of overtime he had been expecting in order to complete the same task! As a result I found myself unsupervised with a grandstand view of all the main-line locomotives going on and off shed — 'Kings', 'Castles', 'Britannias', '47xx' 2-8-0s, the lot! So my banishment was hardly an ordeal.

So how did I arrive at this happy situation? Back in the summer of 1956 I'd enrolled in what was termed 'a short works course' with British Railways — a scheme to show sixth-formers career opportunities. I'd always believed that I'd need an engineering degree to turn my hobby into a railway career, but this course seemed to advertise other potential opportunities. I was instructed to make my way on a Sunday evening to a hotel in Bath and duly caught the 4.15pm from Paddington behind one of the WR's derided 'Britannias', 70019 *Lightning*, which did not live up to its name, enduring a lot of slow-line running because of engineering work. Seven fellow students joined me there, and we spent the week under the tutelage of the Bristol District Assistant Operating Superintendent, Rodney Meadows, a former Traffic Apprentice, who was to show us the opportunities such a scheme offered.

The week was a joy for train enthusiasts (and most of us were), although I gathered later that I was the only one of the eight that actually joined BR. We had a tour of Bristol Docks in a brake van behind pannier tank 3623, spent an afternoon at Severn Tunnel Junction marshalling yard, spent time in a new signalbox at Bathampton (and caught a local back to Bath behind 6027 *King Richard I*, running-in after a Swindon overhaul) and had a most fruitful day at Swindon Works, where we were permitted to view *Lode Star* and a row of stored Dean Goods 0-6-0s and 'Dukedogs' in the works 'stock shed'. I returned home via a visit to Wickwar (on the Bristol–Gloucester former Midland route) to see relatives, travelling behind Saltley's Compound 41073, and then caught the Saturday 12.0 from Bristol with Old Oak's current 'Bristolian' engine, 7036 *Taunton Castle*, which was in a decided hurry. Subsequently I kept in touch with Rodney Meadows, who became the agent by which I got the opportunity to work at Old Oak Common.

Having nothing better to do during my 'half gap year' between school and college during the first half of 1957, I applied, with a reference from Rodney, to the London Divisional Office of the Western Region for temporary employment, knowing by then that I wished to pursue a railway career. (I duly became a management trainee — or 'Traffic Apprentice', as it was known — in 1961 and had a further three months at Old Oak Common as part of my footplate training in 1962, as described in Chapter 15). During my first summer vacation from London University in 1958 I repeated the experience, but the summer vacation of 1959 was spent brushing up my German at Munich University and discovering the delights of Bavarian Compound Pacifics on the Munich–Lindau route.

Old Oak was always short-staffed during the holiday periods, so for most of my time there I was employed in various clerical jobs, which involved spending time in different sections of the shed. Initially I spent a few (rather boring) weeks doling out thick green engine-lubricating oil to drivers and enjoying the atmosphere of the depot. At that time Old Oak Common's allocation included 170 steam locomotives — about half of the 'Kings' and 43 'Castles', amongst others — and 20 diesel shunters. I lived at East Molesey, near Hampton Court, during the first spell and used to travel to Waterloo via a change at Surbiton onto an early-morning Basingstoke semi-fast, almost always hauled by a Urie 'H15' of the 30482-91 series. On weekdays I reached Willesden Junction via the Bakerloo Line, but on Saturday mornings there was a Rugby semi-fast from Euston that stopped at Willesden Junction and was hauled by a Crewe 'Royal Scot' or 'Jubilee', as well as an occasional ex-works engine running-in, like Blackpool's 'Jubilee' 45580 *Burma* on my first memorable attempt.

Every morning, as I walked down the long slope from Old Oak Common Lane into the depot, I was greeted by the sight of at least two '47xx' 2-8-0s simmering at the stop-blocks by the carriage shed after arrival on overnight fast freights; indeed one particular siding there was known to all as the '4700 road'. I would then cut through the side entrance of the shed, across one of the four electric turntables, glancing at the 'Kings' and 'Castles' on display, searching for a rare visitor. I would need to be careful at this point because the turntable, being fully covered in and electrically operated, would often start off with little warning and at quite a lick.

On my first day I was given a tour of the shed, which included a trip in the cab of 5074 *Hampden* being prepared for the 'Torbay Express' down to the coaling plant and shed-exit signal. The depot was a very cosmopolitan place, and although work seemed to be allocated along racial lines there seemed to me to be only good-natured banter between the various groups — perhaps I was just a little naïve at the time. The shed labourers working the coaling plant and emptying the ashes from smokeboxes and dropping fires near the coaling plant were all Irish. The cleaners employed in the shed itself were all of West Indian origin, and a gang would be seen cheerfully smothering an engine with oil until it gleamed, and if it was still there after the gang had gone around one of the roundhouses cleaning the other locomotives it would get another dose. Was there a method in this madness? Perhaps they were on piece rate and no-one scrutinised the numbers of the engines cleaned too closely! We had many Welsh firemen, and I learned that they had come on promotion to get a foot on the driver's promotional ladder, as there was little hope of becoming a driver in the Welsh Valley depots before reaching one's mid-50s.

The 'Stores', where I was initially employed, adjoined the 'Factory', where facilities existed for the repair of several steam locomotives, which usually included two or three undergoing the three monthly valves-and-piston renewals and a couple of 'hot box' repairs involving lifting the engine from the bogie, which seemed the location of most problems. When a locomotive had been repaired here it was despatched under the eyes of Billy Gibbs, the Maintenance Foreman, for a high-speed trip around the Old Oak–Greenford–Ealing triangle to see that all was well. As well as driver and fireman, Billy Gibbs and a fitter from the Factory, it was practice to allow one of the apprentices to make the trip. I got a turn too, and my loco was 6024 *King Edward I* after a bogie hot-box repair. I remember sitting on the tender toolbox, head above the cab roof (any railway inspectors please shut your eyes — although I did wear a pair of motor-cycle goggles) as we accelerated hard from Old Oak West after a signal check, so we only got up to around 65mph instead of the 80 hoped for to test the bearing. A sedate run on the branch, pauses to feel the offending bearing, and then another burst of speed back from West Ealing to Acton saw all successfully concluded, and 6024 was on the 'Limited' the next day.

By this time I was getting used to the smell of the place. Although it can't be true, I remember the shed always baking in a heat wave, and everywhere was bathed in a peculiar pungent odour of hot oil, sulphur and a faint whiff of stale urine, which seemed especially strong around the dead locos awaiting repair outside the Factory. Once I was working on clerical rather than Stores duties I used to wear a white shirt (why? — I only had white shirts), and my poor mother had a dreadful time trying to get it clean after one day's wear in that atmosphere.

By the early spring of 1957 I had graduated to the Central Office at Old Oak, so named because it was located exactly in the centre of the engine shed, the bullseye between the four turntables that made up the main depot. But it was central in another way, because it was from here that all the maintenance work of the shed's allocation was organised. The clerk who was in charge of engine histories was on long-term sick leave, and Billy Gibbs put me to work covering his post. This was a delight, because my role involved recording the oil and coal consumption of each locomotive from dockets issued by the Stores or coaling plant, compiling mileage records from the loco rosters operated for Old Oak engines and preparing routine maintenance plans (boiler washouts and valves-and-piston exams) as well as shopping proposals for heavy and intermediate repairs at Swindon Works.

Some memories stand out from this period. 4090 *Dorchester Castle*, the second 'Castle' to be fitted with a double chimney and the first at our depot, was regular on the down 'Bristolian' from May onwards, and it was so highly regarded that after the three-month valves-and-pistons exam it went straight back onto the 'Bristolian' roster — an almost unprecedented move. I believe this was at the request of a number of the drivers who swore by this engine.

Left: The author on the footplate of 6024 *King Edward III* during its pause on the Greenford–Ealing branch on its post-repair test run, 29 July 1957.

Below: One of four Old Oak Common roundhouses, with 4900 *Saint Martin* and a '28xx' 2-8-0, 3 August 1957.

Some of the 'Castles' from the postwar build attained some incredibly high mileages between visits to Swindon Works — I recall 5099 and 7020 in particular, the latter still on South Wales main-line work with 116,000 miles on the clock since its previous shopping; by this time its paintwork was nearly black from the regular oily cleaning, but it was a very shiny, rather rich greeny-browny-black! Most 'Castles' ran about 82,000-86,000 miles between works visits, (even some of the early '40xx' engines), and 'Kings' were shopped after about 78,000-80,000 miles, which they acquired very quickly, as they averaged about 2,000-2,500 miles a week, there being no such thing as a light turn for a 'King'.

Other memories are less pleasant. Whilst the location of the Central Office was ideal in one respect, it was hard on the senses. The noise around meant that phone calls were a strain, and at the end of the day a sore throat and headache were quite commonplace. One day 6019 *King Henry V* failed before going off shed after the fireman had prepared a big fire for its duty, and the loco stood inside the shed on one of the roads adjoining our offices blowing off steam furiously for what seemed like hours. On another occasion a 'Britannia' whistle got stuck, and the loud chime lost its attraction long before until it eventually diminished to a feeble cracked note.

Around this time one of the shed's regulars was *City of Truro*, which for several weeks came up to town on a commuter train and returned home on either the 5.20 or 6.20pm Paddington–Reading (I can't remember which). I travelled on it one day to the first stop, West Drayton, with its eight non-corridor coaches, in a fine drizzle — a most unsuitable duty, as the driver had great difficulty in controlling its slipping. I did record that we just managed to touch 60mph before the stop, and we lost only about a minute on schedule, but it must have been hard going thereafter, as the train was then all-stations to Reading. Following this stint 3440 returned to Didcot and was used on the Didcot–Newbury–Winchester service, a much more suitable assignment.

Another veteran much in evidence in the summer of 1957 was the last 'Star', 4056 *Princess Margaret*, then at Bath Road shed. She was by now in very poor condition, and one Saturday in September she was pressed into service on the Plymouth–Paddington non-stop leg of a Saturdays-only train from Newquay. Apparently the driver stopped at virtually every location with a depot to request a fresh locomotive, but there was nothing to be had, so he had to 'blow up' a head of steam and continue to the next point. When 4056 came on depot the driver had to make out two repair cards, as he couldn't get all the engine's failings onto one card — and I subsequently got hauled before the Divisional Motive Power Officer to be dressed down for reporting this fact to *Trains Illustrated*! 'Washing our dirty linen in public' was his description of my offence. Despite this 4056 was booked on the Monday to return to Bristol on the 8.5pm Paddington fast freight, and when 7018, booked for the 7.15pm passenger to Bristol, failed on shed she was substituted. I took a photo of 4056 about to go off shed in the failing light, and I'm sorry to say she got no further than Southall, where she was abandoned in favour of a filthy 'Hall'. That was 4056's last run, as she went straight to Swindon for cutting-up, which was a shame.

One morning I was asked to do a small job which meant walking down to the throat of the depot, where, on the line leading out of the depot that all engines took

The 1957 '*Bristolian*' engine, 4090 *Dorchester Castle* (with extended smokebox), under repair at Old Oak Common in July 1958.

3440 *City of Truro* resting at Old Oak Common between commuter runs, 18 May 1957.

'Star' 4056 *Princess Margaret* at Old Oak Common on 9 September 1957, two days after its laborious run from Plymouth.

Princess Margaret leaving Paddington later the same day to work the 7.15pm Bristol, its last working before failure at Southall and condemnation.

en route to Paddington, there was an Automatic Train Control (ATC) ramp for drivers to test the equipment on their locomotive before going off shed. There had been problems requiring a fitter's attention, and now they wanted a test before drivers were reminded once more to check their ATC. This was no hardship for me — it just meant climbing onto the footplate of the next four locos going off shed and asking their drivers to check the correct working of the apparatus. I therefore carried out the instruction on 6012 *King Edward VI*, 0-6-0 2222, 6868 *Penrhos Grange* and 2-6-2T 6101. They all worked, and I reported a clean bill of health for the equipment.

An event of interest during my time in the Central Office was the decision by the WR Motive Power Department to review the allocations of all top-link engines in order to equalise mileages, so that no depot had all the low- or high-mileage locos — this applied mainly to the 'Castles'. It was a golden opportunity to get rid of any 'black sheep', and much effort was made to hang on to the favourites. (The 'Castles' had a reputation of having a wide range of superb and weaker locomotives — more than any other class I knew.) About 33% of our allocation changed — I can remember we got locos like 5005, 5008, 5027 and 5029 and somehow didn't manage to lose 4091, which was known then as the only three-cylinder 'Castle' (one beat being entirely missing); everything was tried to cure it, without any conspicuous success, and I was not surprised when, early in 1959, it became the first true 'Castle' to be withdrawn. We, did, however, manage to hold on to 4090, 5034, 5035, 5040, 5056, 5099, 7001, 7027, 7030, 7032, 7033 and 7036, which were our star performers.

My presence at Old Oak did cause some consternation. Clerical work was jealously guarded, and local staff did everything in their power to ensure no excuse could be made for staff cuts. Besides the embarrassment of doing a clerk out of his overtime in copying out the 1958/9 winter rosters, I completed my day's duties in the Mechanical Foreman's office by around 11am on most days. This flummoxed the other clerks, and I was told to take an early and long lunch break in Old Oak's hostel canteen and, as they knew I was interested, spend the afternoon with a different fitter each week. I remember vividly spending one week with Joe Parrott (then 72 years of age), who was the ATC fitter, and going out to North Acton, to knock out the ATC shoes of GW locos coming from the Midlands and heading across to the Southern. Another week was spent with the boilersmith, enduring the usual ritual of being sent into the firebox of a loco whose fire had only just been dropped. On one occasion I came across one rather rotund Traffic Apprentice who had actually got stuck in the firehole door after such an initiation, and we all had to haul him out, much to his embarrassment.

My first attempt at carrying out any maintenance work by myself was a total disaster. I was told to dismantle the clack box of one of 81A's many pannier tanks, and I found the nuts so worn that I managed to break two substantial monkey spanners and dismantle half the engine before I prised off the offending part. However, I can't have been completely useless, as the locomotive concerned, 5764, survives to this day on the Severn Valley Railway!

In the summer of 1958 I spent more time acting as the Running Foreman's assistant in the main office block (before my banishment to the new train-crew depot). I was actually in charge of booking the engines out to their jobs as well as receiving other

'Castle' 5043 *Earl of Mount Edgcumbe* at Old Oak Common after working the Down 'Bristolian' diagram, September 1958.

'57xx' 0-6-0PT 5764, now on the Severn Valley Railway, seen at Highley, 2010.

6018 *King Henry VI*, the last 'King' to retain its single chimney, at Old Oak Common, 26 June 1957.

depot messages about incoming locos turning around at Ranelagh Bridge. Although I tried to manipulate some turns my scope was in fact very limited. We had the practice of keeping the best locos on the same turns for weeks (as opposed to the ER method of allocating regular engines to crews). The top-link engines got best Welsh coal — Oakdale or Markham — whilst the second-link engines went to the other side of the coaling stage and got briquettes or worse. I could choose which 'Castle' to banish to act as Ranelagh Bridge standby — one of my predecessors, I was told, had regularly despatched 4037 when it was at Old Oak (c1955/6) to stand there, in the knowledge that it looked superb with its huge polished nameplate, but such was its reputation for rough riding that no foreign crew would think of taking it unless their steed was a total failure! (I had a footplate run with 4037 on the Plymouth–Shrewsbury through working in 1961 after it had had a front-end frame renewal, and it was a lion of an engine — see Chapter 13.)

Our star engines that summer were 5043, working the '*Bristolian*', 7013 (the erstwhile 4082), on the out-and-return '*Cambrian Coast Express*', and 5093, alternating with a Newton Abbot 'Castle' on the '*Torbay*'. The first two were among the increasing number of double-chimney 'Castles'. 5057 had at length replaced 7018 on the up '*Bristolian*', a Bath Road turn, and 4087 (my favourite) and 4097 were much in evidence on Laira and Landore turns respectively. By this time all of the 'Kings' with the exception of Old Oak's 6018 had double chimneys, and that loco was fitted during my time there, maintaining its reputation (along with 6022 and 6024) of being one of the best.

One of the jobs I had been given in 1957 was to fetch the strongbox of pay packets from the HQ paybill office in Paddington and escort it back to Old Oak — I don't think that at the time I realised either the responsibility I had or the real security risk I ran. The heavy safe was delivered to me on the platform at Paddington on a Wednesday evening, ready for payday on the Thursday. I had to transport it on the footplate of a locomotive going to Old Oak — I guess this was thought safer than sending it by road. I could hardly run off with it; the safe was securely padlocked, and we were unlikely to be stopped by armed raiders between Paddington and Old Oak Common — access to the line was hardly as easy as the location of the Great Train Robbery. I can remember heaving it into the cabs of 4098, which had arrived with the up 'Torbay Express', and 5082, which had arrived on the 'Cambrian Coast Express'. On another occasion 7030 was my taxi, and I recall on another payday hauling it into the confined space of 1504's cab.

Whilst at Old Oak I was given the opportunity for my first 'official' footplate ride by a very generous and sympathetic Shedmaster, Ray Sims. Earlier experiences on 69654 at Shenfield and an even earlier ride on the Guildford shed pilot, 0-4-0ST 30458 *Ironside*, did not really count. The Shedmaster had obtained an official pass for me to ride the 11.5am Paddington–Gloucester and return diagram, and he put one of Old Oak's best 'Castles', 7001 *Sir James Milne*, on the turn for my initiation, knowing that I would have a very comfortable journey in which to learn the art of firing, which he guessed would be offered to me.

After Swindon my rite of passage began in earnest as I was handed the shovel and expected to keep steam up as we climbed to Sapperton — a feat accomplished, although I have to say not all the coal found its way into the firebox at the first attempt. I had expected to have a clean-up and eat my sandwiches during the Gloucester break, but Locomotive Inspector George Price, my mentor on this occasion, had other ideas and took me around Gloucester Cathedral, where the sight of two boiler-suited men, one still filthy from the enforced exercise, must have seemed a little odd to the other tourists and pilgrims!

A couple of months later Ray Sims, the Shedmaster, hinted that I might like to apply for a second pass, and I duly received one for a return trip to Wolverhampton, out on the 9 o'clock Paddington. I joined 6015 *King Richard III* (the first 'King' fitted with a double chimney) on the turntable at Old Oak and went up with it to Paddington, where we awaited the inspector. Departure time came, and there was no sign of him; the train crew said not to worry (they were happier without), so off we went.

A good punctual run ensued, but I was left to my own devices at Wolverhampton. As I was wondering what to do — I still had a return footplate pass, but no particular train was specified — I saw 5032 *Usk Castle* of Stafford Road backing onto an up express. Although I'd really finished train-spotting by this time, 5032 was in fact the only '50xx' I'd not seen, so I introduced myself to Driver Bert Griffiths and Fireman Forrester of Wolverhampton Stafford Road and was made most welcome. Until Banbury we were hampered by the presence of a horse-box marshalled behind the engine, restricting us to 60mph (why was this permitted?), but after Banbury we went to town and whirled our 13-coach load to 84mph after Ardley and through Gerrards Cross. When I got back to Old Oak I found that everyone was searching for me — the inspector had turned up at Paddington for the 9.10 with the last single-chimney 'King', 6018, and had waited for me. I was deemed to be in trouble until they examined my pass, which was clearly made out for the 9 o'clock and not the slower 9.10!

'Castle' 7001 *Sir James Milne* at Swindon on the occasion of the author's first official footplate trip on the 11.5am Paddington–Gloucester, 19 June 1957.

6015 *King Richard III* on arrival at Wolverhampton with the 9am Paddington '*Inter City*' express on the occasion of the author's footplate trip, 21 August 1957.

Midland Compound 41113 arriving at Willesden Junction, 1 August 1957.

5032 *Usk Castle* on arrival at Paddington with the 11.35am Wolverhampton, 21 August 1957.

Opposite page: Driver Bert Griffiths and Fireman Forrester of Stafford Road on the occasion of the author's footplate trip from Wolverhampton, 21 August 1957.

It wasn't always undiluted pleasure. Emboldened by my experiences I applied to the Southern and was granted a footplate pass for the 9am Waterloo as far as Salisbury. Unrebuilt 'West Country' 34026 *Yes Tor* backed on in good time, but for the first and only time I was made less than welcome by the footplate crew. The driver (Cross by name, and cross by nature) complained bitterly that he didn't want a passenger; I made to dismount but was stopped by the inspector. However, the driver was an absolute misery and kept muttering under his breath all the way, until after Andover the inspector suddenly asked me what my highest speed on the footplate had been, and when I said 84 he persuaded the driver to let 34026 run down Porton Bank until we touched 87. I think the inspector felt sorry for me, and I had a lingering hope he might take me back to Waterloo on the footplate of 35009 *Shaw Savill* on the up '*ACE*', on which I returned to the capital, but no such luck.

At the end of each day I would walk back to Willesden Junction and wait for a Rugby–Euston semi-fast instead of using the Bakerloo Line, which I should have done. The Euston train waited for ten minutes in the station at Willesden to let ticket collectors go through the train (at Euston it drew into an open platform), and I used to hang around and board at the last moment to avoid tedious explanations about why I wanted to travel via Euston instead of the quicker direct Bakerloo route to Waterloo. The attraction was the motive power on this train. Although in winter it was a Rugby 'Black Five' (44715, 44716, 44860 and 44862 most frequently), for the summer timetable Rugby returned its stored Compounds to traffic, and 41093, 41105, 41113, 41122, 41162 and 41172 were regulars, even if their timekeeping was a little shaky. Occasionally, after the failure of one of them, we would get the Camden stand-by engine (a 'Jubilee') or a 'Crab'.

At the time, for an enthusiast 'in heaven', it was the locomotives that made the deepest impression, but in later years it was the interaction with the people I met

at Old Oak that stood me in good stead in my railway-management career — Ray Sims, Norman Willis, the Chief Clerk, Billy Gibbs, the fitters who humoured me, the character who realised after a few hours that I did not swear and apologised profusely for calling a spade a spade. (He didn't — he called it a [expletive deleted] shovel; when he was telling me what to do I almost had to stand, notebook in hand, extracting the odd word that meant something from the string of obscenities preceding and succeeding it!) Then there was George Price, the kindly inspector who took me on my first footplate trip on 7001 and guided me around Gloucester Cathedral in filthy overalls during our turnaround and managed to lose me on my second footplate trip!

Tableau 6

Old Oak Common Shed, July 1957

4087 *Cardigan Castle* prepares to leave Old Oak Common for Paddington prior to taking out the 9.30am Plymouth, April 1957.

It always seems to be hot here. I'm sure it's an illusion, but today seems the same as every other day this summer, and, much as I love this place, I'll be tired and probably suffering from a headache before the day is out. I saunter down the long driveway from the gates to the shed — no hurry, my work will not keep me occupied all morning, so no-one will complain if I'm after half past eight, the official time for day-shift clerical workers to start. I pause at the side entrance to the shed and go forward to gaze at the two Churchward 2-8-0s, 4701 and 4708, still warm from their overnight freights from Birkenhead and Plymouth, stabled on the siding where at least one of this small band of fast freight locomotives stands every morning. Then I turn back and enter the shed, stepping over the exit rail and glancing at the bevy of 'Kings' and 'Castles' that have arrived during the night and are even now being prepared for their day's work.

The shafts of sunlight are picking out a couple of Old Oak 'Kings', 6015 *King Richard III*, with 'Cornish Riviera' headboard already in place, and 6028 *King George VI*, rostered for a later Wolverhampton turn. There's also a Landore 'Castle', 4074 *Caldicot Castle*, amid the Old Oak engines, probably for the 'Pembroke Coast Express' at 10.55 from Paddington. Despite being one of the oldest 'Castles' still in service it looks in fine condition — it stands out immediately, for its buffers and smokebox-door hinges are painted silver, as Landore does for all its top-link engines. It's surrounded by three of our own 'Castles', 4089, 5052 and 5082, and Bath Road's 5085. I walk over to the huge blackboard by the enginemen's lobby, where today's allocations have been chalked up by the Running Foreman. My guesses are correct; as well as 4074 for the 10.55 it's showing 6028 for the 11.10 Wolverhampton, just ex-works 5082 for the 10.10 'Cambrian Coast Express', 5052 for the 11.5 to Gloucester and, a surprise, Laira's 4087 for the 11.30 to Plymouth.

I go in search of my old favourite, 4087 *Cardigan Castle*, pleased that it's working a top-link job today. It must be on No 2 turntable, whose outlet via the side of the shed I've just crossed. I spot it immediately, sandwiched between Old Oak's 5035 and a 'Modified Hall', 6979. Smoke is curling from its chimney, and I peer into its cab to see if anyone is already tending the fire. There's no-one there, so I haul myself up onto the footplate and sit for a moment on the driver's tip-up seat and peer down the length of the boiler, noticing the mechanical lubricator positioned high on the side of the smokebox on this engine, one of the experiments noted on the engine-history cards that I maintain as part of my new role — our 5084 has a similar experimental lubrication arrangement. The fire door is open, the blower is on, and I note that there is already 120lb indicated on the steam-pressure gauge, ample time to get to the full 225 before it's due off shed around 10.40. I take a handful of waste, lean out of the cab and polish the numberplate — it's just a bit dusty. The engine looks in pretty good condition, although, according to the tiny painted date on the back of the tender, it was last outshopped from Swindon Works on 5 July 1956, just over a year ago, and must have run a fair mileage since then, so I'm surprised it's still booked to a job like the 11.30. A quick phone call to my opposite number at Laira later establishes that it has already clocked up 70,000 miles since its last 'Heavy General' repair at Swindon in the spring of 1956. I'm happy to lounge here, but I ought to get to my desk fairly soon, so I dismount, giving the engine an affectionate pat on the cabside, telling myself that I'll keep an eye on the clock and make an excuse to see her go off shed.

I enter the office of the Mechanical Foreman, Billy Gibbs, a forthright Londoner well respected by the fitting staff here. He's on the phone and just waves an acknowledgement to me as I slide into my desk and look at the various dockets and notes left for me. I've got dockets from the Stores on the amount of oil issued to the various engines, dockets from the coal stage on the tonnage of coal dropped to each tender or bunker, and yesterday's engine-roster sheets, from which I can calculate engine mileage to add to the individual engine-record cards. I go methodically through each engine card, searching the dockets for details appropriate to that engine — it's quicker that way rather than keep looking for the cards in a haphazard order, for I've about 150 cards to complete, minus those engines that are stopped on depot or in works — about 30 today. At roughly a minute a card I'll have finished the basic job by 11 o'clock. Billy Gibbs knows this, so he makes no objection when I absent myself to wander over to the shed outlet road off No 2 turntable and find, as I'd hoped, 4087 standing half in, half out of the shed, blowing off steam furiously, while the fireman is stoking up further. I look up at the driver. 'Can I come up?' He nods, and I scramble up onto the footplate. The driver is obviously curious as to why I want to come up, and I explain my enthusiasm for this engine going back to my childhood memories of it. He grunts and then opines that he's not so enamoured of it, though he doesn't put it quite like that! He complains that 'they' shouldn't put an old '40' like this on a fast Plymouth train; she's too rough. She seems to have got plenty of steam though — and, I note, a four-row superheater boiler, new to the engine at its last overhaul. (I've found this out from the various engine records.) Despite the grumbles it's time for them to go, and I scramble down to watch 4087 move off, coal stacked high on the tender, still blowing off, steam tight at the front end.

I complete the records by 11.15. I'm quick because I know the mileages of each diagram by heart and the records kept for the Prairie and pannier tanks are pretty sparse — no-one seems to bother with recording fully their oil and coal consumption. Our 'Kings' are knocking up 2,000-2,500 miles a week, especially if they're used mainly on the Plymouth road, and most 'Castles' between 1,500 and 2,000, although 5082 on the 'Cambrian Coast Express' is doing well over 2,000 regularly to Shrewsbury and back plus light running, six days a week. She'll have done 25,000 miles before she's due for her first valves-and-pistons examination in the Factory in the autumn and we have to select a new 'Castle' for that turn. Billy Gibbs wants me to check which engines are due for a weekly boiler washout; those with Afloc water treatment, mainly the '70xx' 'Castles' and engines on the Wolverhampton run, can run a few days longer. They'll get tube-cleaning at the same time, essential if they're to steam well, for we can't guarantee all our engines will get the best Welsh Markham or Oakdale Colliery coal which we keep for our top-link turns. And then — it's still not lunchtime yet — he wants me to plan the likely shopping dates for our 'Kings' and 'Castles', looking carefully at when we're due to get engines back from Swindon Works to replace them.

One of our problems is that we've currently six 'Castles' in works (5029, 5065, 5066, 7010, 7030 and 7033) and a seventh (7036) stopped waiting to go, plus a couple of 'Kings'. Two of them — 5029 and 7030 — have been there nearly five months now. That means we've got only thirty-three of our allocation theoretically available, and we'd normally have two or three stopped for boiler washout and possibly a couple in the Factory, one with a planned valves-and-pistons exam and another on casual repair. On summer Saturdays we've forty-three Old Oak diagrams for 'Castles'. We'll obviously ensure we book none for boiler washouts on a Saturday, but that still means we'll have to find ten and possibly more substitutes — our 'Modified Halls' will be first in line, with 'Halls' and 'Granges' from Southall (81C), Reading (81D) and Oxford (81F) making up the rest. Billy therefore impresses upon me that we should line up engines for our shopping proposals immediately at the end of the summer timetable, and he'll get the fitters to concentrate on keeping the high-mileage engines going for another couple of months. After half an hour of digging through the records I produce the following, in order of priority:

5014 ex works 2/56, mileage now 95,000, due Heavy General
4089 ex works 2/56, mileage now 79,000, due Heavy General
7024 ex works 2/56, mileage now 101,000, due Heavy Intermediate
5055 ex works 3/56, mileage now 88,000, due Heavy Intermediate
5060 ex works 3/56, mileage now 104,000, due Heavy Intermediate
5099 ex works 5/55 but with an unplanned works repair in 11/56, mileage since last Heavy Intermediate 106,000, due Heavy General
5044 ex works 2/56, mileage now 89,000, due Heavy Intermediate

I add that 7020 has also clocked up well over 100,000 miles since its last Heavy General in March 1956 but that it has had a couple of light repairs in Swindon in the meantime. Billy sits down with me and instructs me to prepare shopping proposals for 5014 and 4089 immediately — 4089 has been reported by drivers for rough riding and is on what we call 'restricted working', meaning it must not be diagrammed to fast passenger turns. Although 5060, 5099, 7020 and 7024 have over 100,000 miles he knows that they are all running without any major complaints or heavy casual repairs, so he marks them off to wait for the autumn. He asks me to check through the record cards for 5044 and 5055 and scrutinise their repair cards, which have been filed separately, and when I show him the cards, which give little apparent cause for concern, he decides that both these engines can also wait, unless we have a major failure with either in the next month. I then tell him that 4082, 4090 and 7032 are due for a valves-and-pistons exam. He pulls a face and says that 4090 will have to come in, as it's been our regular '*Bristolian*' engine since April, but that 4082 and 7032 will have to wait another month, until the end of August.

I make out the shopping-proposal forms for Nos 4089 and 5014, and Billy rings the Running Foreman to tell him that 4090 should be marked off to the Factory the week after next and that 5029 has been advised as due off Swindon Works and could be available to replace 4090, if its running-in is successful. He asks me to look at the 'Kings' and 'Halls' tomorrow, but he doesn't think the situation there is so critical, as the number of 'Kings' we have balances our diagrams, and the Summer Saturday requirement is the same as that for a normal weekday.

'Time you went to lunch,' says Billy just after midday, and I wander between turntables 1 and 2, glancing at any newcomers that have arrived. Most foreign engines arriving at Paddington in the morning — engines from Stafford Road, Worcester, Gloucester and South Wales — are serviced and turned at Ranelagh Bridge, but 'King' 6016 *King Edward V* has arrived from the West of England, and there's 5002 *Ludlow Castle* of Swindon and our own 5008 *Raglan Castle*, which has just returned from overhaul at Swindon. There's 4706 of Bristol St Philips Marsh, along with a couple of 'Modified Halls' that have appeared on turntable 2, and

Reading's 4085 *Berkeley Castle*. The canteen is at the top of the drive by the main gate, and I take a leisurely lunch — traditional British meat, potatoes and two veg plus apple pie (for me, no custard) but no cup of tea — for 1/6d. I don't like tea anyway and certainly not the Old Oak variety, made for strong stomachs. And I haven't yet learned the coffee habit — college will teach me that.

I reappear in the Central Office around 2pm, having had another good wander around the shed and outside to see what's in and waiting for the Factory, and Billy suggests I spend a couple of hours with the boilersmith, as I've completed everything he needed me to do in the office. The fitter is quite happy to take me on — I'll be useful handing tools and holding things, I suppose. He's another over-age fitter (I didn't catch his full name, he was just introduced as Bert) who proudly tells me that he's one of the younger fitters — 67! 'We've got to sort out 4900, she's been reported with leaking superheater units,' he informs me.

We find the prototype 'Hall', 4900 *Saint Martin*, the original 1924 convert of the 1907-built 'Saint' with 6ft 0in wheels, on No. 3 turntable, surrounded by '9Fs', a couple of '28xx' 2-8-0s, another 'Hall' and a couple of '61xx' Prairie tanks. She's still black with the old BR lion-and-wheel, quite clean, no doubt following a recent going-over by the cleaning gang, as she seems to have an oily sheen over the layers of grime beneath. Bert opens the smokebox door, and I spend twenty minutes handing him up tools while he tinkers, hammers and eventually expresses himself satisfied. 'We'd better have a look at the stays,' he says, looking at me meaningfully; now we're up on the footplate, and he's opening the firehole door, laying a piece of

Midland Compound 41113 at Willesden with the evening semi-fast train from Rugby to Euston, 1 August 1957.

sacking over it and expecting me to crawl through. Luckily I'm slim, but the heat nearly overpowers me as I get into the confined space. It's pitch black, and I see nothing until Bert passes his lamp through to me and follows with more dexterity, even though he's a larger man. He's obviously well used to it.

'Too hot for you, sonny?' murmurs Bert, and I try to make light of it. 'The fire's been dropped on this one for over three hours now — you should try one which needs urgent attention and whose fire has only just been dropped!' He casts the light over the tubeplate and instinctively starts hammering some tube ends, deafening me in this confined, echoing space. I'm left holding the lamp for him, bending nearly double at first, then finding it more comfortable to get down on one knee, until he decides it's time to finish. When we finally stagger out he looks at me, brushing the dust and ash from my trousers. 'You should get them to issue you some overalls from the Stores if you're going to come out with me again. Go back and tell the foreman that he should authorise some proper clothing for you. I've got a job to do on a pannier tank on turntable 4, but I should go home if I were you. Come out with me tomorrow afternoon, and we'll do a couple of boiler washouts.'

I take the hint and tell Billy, who instructs me to call into the Stores in the morning and then suggests I go home. I go and wash the dirt off as best I can, collect my belongings and dawdle through the shed once more, as I want to catch the Rugby semi-fast from Willesden Junction at just after 5.30pm rather than hurry to catch an earlier Bakerloo Line train. I spy 4073 *Caerphilly Castle* over on No 2 turntable and go and look at her. She's looking rough, not in Canton's usual spotless condition, and I wonder how much longer she has before withdrawal. Both she and the resplendent 4074 I saw this morning were slated for withdrawal back in 1955, but they're still going — although not for much longer in the case of 4073, by the look of her. I've got my camera with me today — I don't usually bring it to work. But I took a photo of 4087 this morning and 4900 after we'd worked on it, and I take a picture of 4073 alongside 5035 and 6979 now.

I walk slowly up the slope to the gate and along Old Oak Lane. It's still hot, and despite washing earlier I still feel grubby. I arrive at Willesden's up slow platform and find I've beaten the Rugby–Euston stopper. As I've got my camera, and the train — when it deigns to arrive — will stand for at least ten minutes while two ticket collectors go through the train, I go over to the middle platform to get the sun behind me and wait. A couple of expresses dash through the station — one with a 'Scot', the other with a re-boilered 'Patriot' — and my train is late. I hope this means we've got a Compound tonight rather than the booked 'Black Five', and, so it proves; I take a photo of 41113 as it draws into the station, already about twelve minutes down, and another as it comes to rest. I wander over and join the rear coach a couple of minutes before departure and sit back in an empty compartment to savour the ten-minute journey, during which, I estimate, we don't exceed 45mph. Then it's the Northern Line back to Waterloo and an electric all stations to Hampton Court while I just relax and realise how tired I am, with the noise of Old Oak still singing in my ears.

Chapter 9

Munich University, 1959

SNCB US-built 'S160' 2-8-0 29.045 at Liège on the Ostend–Munich express, July 1959.

It was the summer of 1959 and the end of the second year of my languages degree course at University College London. Most second-year students in the German Department qualified for the summer term to be spent at a German university, having passed appropriate exams in their subsidiary subject at the end of the first year. My French being somewhat below par (my having wasted my Sorbonne training on the platforms of the Gare du Nord), I was obliged to stay in London to sit these exams at the end of the second year and enrol in a two-month summer course at a German university to make up for my earlier absence.

I dithered as to which course to choose, desperately trying to find out which might have the most railway interest, but finally allowed myself to be persuaded to enrol for a course at Munich University, despite my meagre knowledge that this would be at the heart of the DB electrified system. I was therefore resigned to putting my studies first for once. The Kent Coast had been newly electrified, and I set off from Victoria in the late afternoon on one of the brand-new '4-CEP' units and crossed overnight to Ostend, where my through train for Munich originated. A small SNCB Bo-Bo electric (122 series) took me to Liège, where, to my surprise, an

American-built austerity 2-8-0, 29.045, backed onto the train and chirrupped through the unusually sunny summer Ardennes forest to the German border at Aachen.

An '03' Pacific duly took the train to Cologne, where the first of many reversals took place (my main recollection of this journey is the constant see-saw of direction of travel) and a 'V200' diesel-hydraulic piloted by a new 'E10' electric backed down and took us as far as Koblenz. Here the electric departed, and the 'V200' took us across the Rhine onto the right bank past the vineyards to another reversal in the dead end station of Wiesbaden. Steam appeared again in the shape of a grubby Pacific, 01 171, for the short trip to Frankfurt-am-Main, for yet another reversal and the appearance of one of the 1930s 2-BB-2 'E18' electrics, which took us through Würzburg to Nürnberg, where another 'E18' backed onto the rear of our train for the final leg through Ingolstadt and Augsburg. I arrived at Munich at bedtime and found bedlam. Although it is a Catholic city I belatedly discovered that it was hosting the Protestant Lutheran Church's annual 'Kirchentag' rally, involving thousands of delegates, and every single hotel was fully booked. My registration for the university course and fixed accommodation was not until the next day, so for the first time in my life (but not the last) I had no alternative but to find a bench on the station and try to sleep. And at midnight the pile-driving began, as the station was being rebuilt following wartime damage …

At 6am, bleary-eyed after two nights without sleep, I became aware of steam movements and an ancient 2-6-0 (a former Bavarian Class 54 Mogul) bringing in empty stock. I established this was for a local and bought a ticket to its destination, Lermoos, as I still had four hours to fill before I could register and crash out at my lodgings. A former Prussian 4-6-4 tank, 78 181, duly stopped at all stations to a somewhat rural suburb and ran round the train, returning with commuters.

Eventually I decided I could take a tram to the university and obtain details of my digs, only a five-minute walk from the college (Türkenstrasse 54 still rings a bell in my subconscious). The landlady showed me to my room, came up with a welcoming glass of very dry white wine and left me to unpack. I lay exhausted on the bed and was gone. When I woke up it was five minutes to the deadline for the course registration and language tests to allocate me to the appropriate class group, and I could not bring myself round. Head under the cold tap, self-administered slaps around the face, a dash around the block and joining the queue at the registration desk got me nowhere, and the test conducted was only a vague sort of extra-sensory experience happening to someone else. I did not graduate to the more advanced group.

Now feeling disorientated and vaguely sick, I somehow gravitated to the Hauptbahnhof (there being no formal start until the next morning), where my first sight was of this glorious, most un-German-looking locomotive, with flared chimney, bullet-shaped smokebox nose and huge cylinders, standing facing me at the buffer-stops. It was, of course, one of the thirty re-boilered four-cylinder compound locomotives of the '18.6' series, built to the Bavarian 1908 design by the Reichsbahn in 1926 while the standard '01' and '03' Pacifics were being developed. There were forty of these DR-built locomotives, originally in the series 18 509-548, and some were used in the late 1920s and 1930s on the '*Rheingold*' between the Dutch border and Mannheim. They were particularly economical locomotives and were well suited to the heavily graded lines of the former Bavarian state system. Thirty were rebuilt in the mid-1950s with new all-welded boilers, renumbered in the 18 601-630 series and allocated initially to Heidelberg, Hof and Lindau (the latter on Lake Constance — the 'Bodensee') before ultimately nearly all being housed at the Lindau depot, which was almost on the shore of the lake. I think one or two were allocated to Ulm for the Ulm–Friedrichshafen–Lindau services, but the majority monopolised the Geneva/Zürich–Munich expresses — taking over from Austrian electric power at Lindau, another dead-end station — via Kempten and Buchloe, threading the Bavarian Alps between Oberstaufen and Immenstadt. On seeing this apparition in front of me I suddenly felt that perhaps I might enjoy this vacation course after all …

A few days later, after I had got used to the college routine and was getting on well with my landlady (including acting as interpreter between her and the other lodger, a French-speaking Algerian medical student who spoke no German), I found myself at the end of the day's sessions again at the Hauptbahnhof in time to see the 4.35pm Eilzug (E826) to Kempten and Memmingen, which I had by now identified as a likely candidate for '18.6' haulage. In those days my resources were not great, so it was only a return ticket to Pasing (the Clapham Junction of Munich, a few kilometres outside the city) that I had purchased as I made my way down to the front end for a run behind my first Bavarian 'S 3/6', 18 606.

The short journey under the Hackerbrücke and past the electric and steam roundhouses was completed, I meticulously noted, in 8 minutes 10 seconds, with a top speed estimated as an unexciting 45mph. The return run was via a local train from Geltendorf, a suburban station on the Munich–Kempten–Lindau main line, about twenty-five miles distant. This service was worked almost exclusively by push-pull trains with a former Prussian 'P8' 4-6-0 tender-first at the Munich end of the set. On this first 'excursion' the train was hauled by No 38 1650, a 'P8' with 'Witte' smoke-deflectors and a tender from one of the scrapped austerity '42s'. The train itself consisted of one eight-wheeler (the push-pull control vehicle) and ten six-wheel coaches.

In between seminars on Thomas Mann's *Tod in Venedig* (Death in Venice), a novella that later spawned a well-known film, and an official course tour to Germany's highest mountain, the Zugspitze (I thought this meant 'Train Peak', but of course 'Draughty Peak' or 'Windy Peak' is a more logical translation), I found myself gravitating more and more often to the Hauptbahnhof and thence to Pasing. The 4.35 Eilzug was a good option, as classes finished at 4pm, and I noted further runs behind 18 603, 609, 611, 612, 618 (twice) and 630 on this train, the fastest being 18 618 in 7 minutes 36 seconds. The return journeys offered more variety (depending upon when I wanted to get back for an evening meal), and I tried out a number of services, the most frequent being the Geltendorf push-pull with 38 1650 or one of its numerous sisters (1748, 2407, 3824 or 4035). There were other '18.6s' if I waited for a semi-fast from Freiburg, or a Prussian 'P10' three-cylinder Class 39 2-8-2 on stopping services from Kempten, or a Class 78 4-6-4 tank or an old 'E44' electric on other Munich suburban services.

120

On another occasion I took a Class 38-hauled train to a quiet and pleasant country suburb and watched Class 50 2-10-0 freights and the lunchtime Munich–Würzburg–Ostend *'Tirol Express'* roar through behind an immaculate Treuchtlingen '01' Pacific, before joining another (No 01 102) on a returning Eilzug to Munich. Where was this rural idyll? Dachau. I was so ignorant of its hideous history that the significance only dawned on me later.

Re-boilered Bavarian four-cylinder compound Pacific 18.606 on train E826 at Munich, July 1959.

DB 2-10-0 50 147 passes Dachau at speed with a freight heading towards Munich, August 1959.

Bavarian Pacifics 18.611 and 18.481 await departure westwards at Buchloe, August 1959.

Tegernseebahn 0-8-0 No. 6 at Schaftlach, August 1959.

After a few days of this I got a little more ambitious. One weekend I purchased a Sunday excursion ticket to the Tegernsee and travelled to the Bavarian Alp foothills behind one of the oldest 'P8s', 38 1142 (there were more than 3,000 of them, numbered from 38 1000), our train being hauled around to the lakeside terminus behind a privately owned 'V65' 0-6-0 diesel-hydraulic. I discovered later that the Tegernsee Bahn owned three steam locos — No. 7, a 2-6-2 'freelance' tank engine based on Bavarian lines, No. 8 (of which I have no knowledge at all except for a reference in J. H. Price's *Railway Holiday in Bavaria*) and the oldest, No. 6, an 0-8-0 tank, Krauss works number 8315 of 1924 (DB Class 98.8), which delighted me by returning to the Schaftlach junction with our string of a dozen six- or four-wheelers, with their wooden-slatted seats. At the junction a former Prussian Railway 4-6-4 tank, 78 301, whisked us in a very sprightly (not to say bouncing) fashion back to the state capital.

I also started to venture out as far as Buchloe — about forty miles distant, on the main line to Lindau, and the first stop of the D-Zug international trains, which were normally formed of half a dozen or so light and low-slung Swiss coaches and invariably hauled by an '18.6'. If I could raise the price of the two-mark Zuschlag (D-train supplement) as well as the fare I could wait for the 5.20pm Munich–Geneva D98, and on 29 August 1959 I did just that, 18 630, hauling seven coaches, completing the non-stop 68km run in 19 seconds under the 54-minute schedule but with a modest top speed sustained at around 60mph. On a couple of earlier occasions with 18 611 and 18 618 we had more energetic runs on the E826 semi-fast, which stopped at Geltendorf and Kaufering as well as Pasing and required brisk and noisy acceleration to 60mph to keep time. (I later discovered that the section of line to Buchloe was restricted to 100km/h at that time.)

My real joy, however, started at Buchloe. On my first arrival there on a wet and dismal August evening I was standing, eyeing 18 611, which had just arrived on the Munich–Geneva D-Zug, when another totally unexpected apparition appeared smokily from the direction of Augsburg. The same bullet-nosed smokebox and huge cylinders were there, but the boiler was smaller, and the chimney taller and flared, with what seemed like a copper cap! This was No 18 481, one of the seven remaining Bavarian 'S 3/6' Pacifics of 1908 design (this one built c1923), all of which were allocated to Augsburg depot. It was hauling an Augsburg–Oberstdorf Eilzug and would follow the express westwards, giving me time to race to the booking office and purchase a ticket to its first stopping place, Kaufbeuren, about 20km away, without even checking if there was a return service! I was back in time to hear the Augsburg driver pining for the '18.6' off the Munich train before it set off, and after taking water we made our leisurely and steamy exit with our diminutive four-coach load, which we managed to hustle up to 60mph.

At the Kaufbeuren stop I alighted and was looking with some trepidation for the timetable, to see if I had a service back, when 18 603 hove into view on E892 (Oberstdorf–Augsburg) — a balancing service to the train I had just experienced. On my return to Buchloe I watched a D-Zug for Munich depart behind two '18.6s' and caught the next Eilzug with 18 616 on a heavier, 10-coach train, which ran very

18.626 on an Eilzug for Oberstdorf at Kempten, August 1959.

Bavarian 'S3/6' 18.483 at Augsburg on train E4096 to Buchloe, August 1959.

vigorously up to 65mph and gained time comfortably on each start-to-stop section, although extended station stops made us seven minutes late into the city.

I was so enamoured with this experience that I repeated it a couple of times and got two further surviving unrebuilt 'S 3/6s' from the 1926-30 series, 18 516 and 18 528, on the Augsburg Eilzug and 18 604 and 18 624 on the return journeys to Buchloe, plus other '18.6s' on the Eilzug to Munich. The other surviving unrebuilt members of the class were 18 478 (today beautifully restored as Bavarian State Railways 3673), 18 483, 18 508 (the last of the locos built by the Bavarian State Railways before nationalisation — and nicknamed the 'Saunalok' because of its propensity to fill the cab with steam) and 18 512.

Near the end of August I decided to blow my remaining Deutschmarks on an all-day trip to the railway town of Kempten, mid-way to Lindau, where there was both a steam depot and a major diesel depot for the 'V200' hydraulics used on main-line services in southern Germany. Up early to catch the 7.30 Munich–Freiburg Eilzug (E766), we had 18 617 on a light load of five coaches with which the loco played, arriving early at all points. I changed at Buchloe, picking up E880, Augsburg–Oberstdorf, which to my surprise ran in with 'P10' 39 227, built by Henschel in 1930 to the Prussian design. Departure on the seven-coach train was 4 minutes late, but a steady three-cylinder roar up the wooded and twisting climb to Günzach, topped at 45mph, ensured a punctual arrival in Kempten. This was yet another dead-end station, so I watched 18 626 back onto the train for the short run to Immenstadt, where the Oberstdorf portion would be detached for the run up the branch to the Alpine resort behind a Class 86 2-8-2T or a '64' 2-6-2T. I wanted to travel on, but by now I was broke, so I watched various '18.6' and '39' movements before returning eastwards.

I discovered that there was an avoiding line that bypassed the terminus and that the D-trains called at Kempten Hegge on this line, enabling avoidance of the reversal and allowing through locomotive working from Munich to Lindau. This meant I had to return, at least as far as Buchloe, with an Eilzug or stopping (Personenzug) service. The E689 Lindau–Augsburg duly reversed, and a recently ex-works (and nowadays preserved) 'P10', 39 184 of Kempten depot, backed onto the ten-coach train. I therefore joined the train for another noisy climb to Günzach from the other direction, but a long signal stop at the summit station made us twelve minutes late into Buchloe, where I alighted. I spent time taking photos around the station before joining a semi-fast train (E4091) behind 18 618 (yet again) to Augsburg on the electrified Stuttgart–Munich main line. The return Eilzug (E4096), with the same set of five coaches, was to my pleasure powered by yet another unrebuilt 'S 3/6', 483 (Maffei, 1923), recently outshopped from its final repairs at the end of 1958. (It would eventually be withdrawn in May 1960, although 18 481, 508 and 528 were destined to last until 1962.) The run, though punctual enough, was mainly distinguished by the alliterative effect of the wayside stations we passed at a steady 50mph — Göggingen, Inningen, Bobingen, Wehringen and Grossaitingen! After our one intermediate stop at Schwabmünchen, more 'ingens' were broken only by Dillishausen before arrival back in Buchloe.

After an afternoon spent taking more photos I joined the D195 Zürich–Munich express, hauled by 18 626, which I had seen earlier at Kempten, heading towards Lindau. The loco made light work of its train of six SBB coaches, covering the 12km to Kaufering in 9 minutes 58 seconds start to stop and the 56km run on to Munich in 12 seconds under the scheduled 44 minutes, with a top speed of 65mph.

The time now came for my return to the UK, on 30 August, and, clutching my certificate of competence in the analysis of *Tod in Venedig* (almost done to death by an over-enthusiastic German 'professoress'), I awaited the late shunting of coaches to form the D673 '*Tirol Express*', which I had chosen as the vehicle of my return after noting its progress behind steam during my short trip to Dachau. The main train had originated in Bologna at 1.44 that morning and arrived in Munich behind Bavarian electric E04 018. To my surprise not one but two steam locomotives backed onto our train (now augmented by a parcels van to make a load of eight coaches, hardly justifying the power) — 01 046, built by Henschel in 1928, and the pilot, 'P8' 38 3346, built in 1921 at Breslau, cut inside. Both were from Würzburg depot, the 'P8' presumably working home unbalanced. The '01' was one of only four fitted with an ugly feed-water heater above the smokebox; deprived also of the front running-plate down to the buffer-beam, the engine looked particularly top-heavy.

I imagine our running was hampered by the presence of the 'P8' and its restricted speed, for we laboured through the countryside, mainly in the high 50s, with a pronounced fore-and-aft rocking motion. A short dash before our first stop in Ingolstadt, just touching 70mph, was distinctly uncomfortable, and an unscheduled halt on the next section turned our seven-minute-late departure from Munich into an eleven min-late arrival in Treuchtlingen. After gaining a couple of minutes at the water stop a long, steady plod at around 60mph non-stop to Würzburg via Ansbach and Ochsenfurt saw us gain a further couple of minutes on the 104-minute schedule for the 140km and arrive at the same lateness as we had departed. No E18 25 converted this lateness into a ten min-early arrival in Frankfurt, where another 'P8', No 38 3625, backed on for the short run to Wiesbaden, from whence I had resigned myself to diesel haulage.

However, a surprise was in store for me. 03 111 backed onto our train, and I discovered that the now rear vehicle was a brown Italian corridor second-class coach with huge full-height oval windows in the vestibule to the rear. We set off into the sunset down the right bank of the Rhine, and my memory is of standing in this rear coach, watching the rails disappear rapidly behind us, a haze of brown smoke trailing, merging with the pinks and oranges of the sky reflected in the waters of the river. We stopped at Rüdesheim, where a wine festival was in full swing, and a honeymoon couple joined our train amidst much celebration, glasses of the local wine being handed to the watching passengers! The '03' joined in the mood and raced along, depositing us in Koblenz more than eleven minutes early! Quite honestly the views were too good to miss, so I just savoured the experience and gave up trying to pick out kilometre posts in the dusk, although I estimate we progressed at the maximum permitted 120km/h (75mph).

After that it was an anti-climax — an 'E10' to Cologne, a brief interlude with another '03' (211) to Aachen, a Belgian diesel (201.015 — Cockerill, 1954) through the Ardennes and SNCB electric 122.025 to Ostend, and then much-required sleep … I preferred to dream of 03 111, the wine and the sunset.

But next morning was a new day, and instead of the expected electric unit our boat train from Dover was headed by 34103 *Calstock*, and we journeyed to Victoria through the neat and pretty Kent countryside via Maidstone East, arriving on time and exhausted.

Train D673 double-headed by Wurzburg '01' 01.046 (one of four '01s' with a feedwater heater) and 'P8' 38.3346 at Munich, 30 August 1959.

Chapter 10
My first privilege tickets

Churchward 2-8-0T 5232 scurries past with an early-morning freight near Danygraig, Swansea, on 13 August 1957.

Back in 1957, after a few months at Old Oak Common, I became eligible to purchase 'privilege' quarter-rate tickets. Thus began a series of Saturday excursions to sample more exotic fare. My first sortie was down the Midland main line on a bitterly cold and snowy March day behind a filthy Kentish Town 'Jubilee', 45648 *Wemyss*, which lost a quarter of an hour unchecked to Kettering, the first stop. After a quick look around the small depot there and spying one of the last Holden Great Eastern 'E4' 2-4-0s at the back of the shed I made my way back to Wellingborough on a semi-fast behind a punctual 45655 *Keith* and spent longer in the large freight depot there, full of Standard '9Fs' and Stanier '8Fs' plus a few inevitable '4F' 0-6-0s. I was just too late to see any active Beyer-Garratts. Whilst waiting for the return semi-fast to St Pancras I watched 45573 *Newfoundland* go storming through with an express from Leeds, then joined my train, which sauntered in a few minutes later behind 'Standard 5' 73067.

A couple of weeks later, in glorious sunshine and with the longer evenings after the clocks went forward for British Summer Time, I caught the 5.10pm from Paddington with Stafford Road's 6001 *King Edward VII* as far as Banbury and was delighted on the return to get another Stafford Road engine, a burnished 4092 *Dunraven Castle*, of the 1925 batch, still going strong. I joined the rear coach and stood in the corridor, enjoying the sight of the locomotive glistening in the setting sun as we rolled our way down past the wooded hills below the infamous golden ball on West Wycombe's church.

On 22 June I paid a visit to King's Cross with the intention of making a journey north to Grantham or Doncaster. An ex-works Top Shed 'V2', No 60828, took us to Grantham non-stop on the 1.40pm train to Newcastle, and I returned behind a filthy Gateshead (52A) 'A4', 60020 *Guillemot*, to Peterborough and changed there for 'A1' 60158 *Aberdonian*. A few weeks later I tried again — I can't even remember the destination on this occasion, nor my return trip, as this was just before I started my log-book records, but I vividly recall being squashed in the middle of the first coach, four a side (it was now a peak summer Saturday), listening to the syncopated roar of 60104, still in its single-chimney state, as it erupted from Copenhagen Tunnel on the climb to Finsbury Park. I recall that this locomotive always seemed one of the more elusive of the 'A3s'; in fact I don't remember seeing it again, and *Solario* was the first 'A3' to be condemned, in 1959. A further East Coast jaunt in early August provided me with another single-chimney 'A3', 60059 *Tracery*, which made a splendid noise until stopped for an hour and a half near Tempsford while the track ahead was searched for a hoax bomb. Plans for longer runs were aborted at Grantham, and I returned in stages behind another 'A3', 60108 *Gay Crusader*, and 'A1' 60148 *Aboyeur*.

During this period I worked most Saturday mornings at Old Oak Common, and one July day I got away and caught the 1.25pm Paddington–Kingswear ahead of the 'Royal Duchy'. On Saturdays Old Oak used to put the 'King' rostered during the week for the latter on the heavy preceding 13-coach holiday train to the South Devon resorts, often providing a '47xx' 2-8-0 for the named express with its chocolate-and-cream set. Unfortunately this service was barred to holders of privilege tickets, so I took the earlier train behind double-chimney 'King' 6009 *King Charles II* as far as Taunton and waited to see what I could get back. As the 'Duchy' produced only a 'Hall' on this date I was not tempted to take it through to Exeter and instead returned to London on the last up Penzance, another heavy train, with 6013 *King Henry VIII*.

By August I'd worked at Old Oak for six months and was now eligible for my first free pass. I thought long and hard about how to use it, eventually deciding upon an overnight trip to Swansea and Carmarthen. The obvious choice would have been the 1.25am sleeper to Swansea via Gloucester, arriving at a respectable hour, but part of my purpose was to arrive early enough to get to Danygraig and Swansea East Dock sheds to see the assortment of 0-4-0 tanks shedded there before they went out for their dock-shunting duties at 6am. I therefore boarded the one passenger coach on the 12.45am newspaper and mail, train routed via the Severn Tunnel and due to arrive at Swansea High Street early enough for my purpose. The train was berthed

Churchward 2-6-0, 6329, prepares to take the *Pembroke Coast Express* on its Camarthen - Swansea leg, 13 August 1957.

1001 *County of Bucks*, on which the author was given a lift from Landore shed back to Swansea High Street, 13 August 1957.

Carmarthen shed on 13 August 1957, with ex-GC Robinson ROD 3041.

at platform 8 at Paddington to allow the newspaper vans access to the train up to the last moment, and 81A 'Castle' 5084 *Reading Abbey* backed down for a fast run through the night. Being next to the engine, I didn't sleep much and was wide awake at Cardiff to watch 5084 being replaced by Canton 'Modified Hall' 6969; 5084 would turn and return to London on the morning Fishguard boat train. I walked down the deserted Swansea streets to the dock area in the first rays of the dawn and astonished the foreman by presenting my shed permit before the 6am shift began. I was duly rewarded by finding a number of locos of the '1101' class and photographed two of the Swansea Harbour Trust saddle tanks (1140 and 1144) before capturing 5232 on a freight as I walked to Danygraig in the now rising sunlight.

Job done, it was off to Landore shed, where I noted on the chalked engine-allocation board that 5077 was booked for the 'Pullman' back to London later that day, on which I'd made a reservation. I'd seen everything there was to see and was making my way to the shed gate when I was hailed by a driver who'd been watching me. 'Want a lift back to High Street?' he called, and I found myself invited into the cab of Neyland's 1001 *County of Bucks*.

There followed a quick trip to Carmarthen, behind 5981, and another shed visit, which elicited a couple of rarities (for me anyway) — ROD 3041 and 2-6-2T 8103 — and Mogul 6329, complete with headboard for the '*Pembroke Coast Express*', on which I returned to Swansea. When, on arrival there, I saw Canton's burnished 5030 *Shirburn Castle* couple up I was tempted to get back on, but I resisted and took my reserved window seat in the luxury of the '*South Wales Pullman*', for which the promised 5077 *Fairey Battle* duly appeared. The return journey was comfortable rather than spectacular, and signal checks on the last leg into Paddington made our arrival eight minutes late.

There are some classes people consider 'hard to get'. In the latter years of steam, whilst 'Duchesses' were fairly common (though every time I made a sortie on the West

Coast I seemed to find the same few turning up for my train — 46225, 46228, 46229, 46235, 46237, 46238, 46244, 46250), 'Princess Royals' seemed to be rarer beasts. And here I was fortunate. In early June I had decided to use one of my 'priv' tickets to visit 'Mecca' — Crewe. After watching the departure of the 'Royal Scot' I joined the 10.40 Euston–Perth, with the powerful combination of 46237 *City of Bristol* and a pilot in the shape of rebuilt 'Patriot' 45540 *Sir Robert Turnbull*, the latter presumably wanted back at Crewe, as I don't think our load warranted such resources. I seem to remember spending most of the time — along with myriad 'spotters' — on the footbridge at the north end of the station, overlooking Crewe North shed (today a car park, where my 1996 VW Passat estate is even now residing as I type this sentence on a London-bound 'Pendolino'). When I saw a 'Royal Scot' backing onto a local for the North Wales coast I bought a return ticket to Beeston Castle to enjoy a short trip behind 46123 *Royal Irish Fusilier*, and after I'd had a brief glimpse of the crag on which the castle was perched opposite, 46137 *The Prince of Wales's Volunteers (South Lancashire)* rushed in on a balancing return local. Back at Crewe I began to start looking for attractive turns for my return south and watched with interest as a very clean 'Duchess', Camden's 46229 *Duchess of Hamilton*, complete with headboard, positioned itself to take over the up 'Midday Scot'. I'd just decided to take this when 46205 *Princess Victoria* swept in with the up 'Red Rose', and I made an instantaneous decision to take that instead. I'm glad I did. I've had plenty of opportunities to ride 46229 since, but I never even saw 46205 again after that splendid journey. It was long before the day when a college friend coached me in the intricacies of train timing, but I remember occupying the rear coach and standing enthralled in the empty corridor as we raced towards London. Somewhere around Hemel Hempstead I can remember being exhilarated by the sheer speed (memory tells me it was probably in the high 80s if not 90mph), and seeing the locomotive hard at work as we rounded a curve — probably Berkhamsted — was most impressive.

I decided to expand my experience of the London Midland further in early September with a triangular trip to Rugby, Nottingham (via the Great Central) and back, on the Midland main line. Camden's ex-works 46168 *The Girl Guide* got me to Rugby without any undue alarms, and one of Neasden's three 'Standard 5s', 73157, appeared on the 10 o'clock from Marylebone, which I took through to Nottingham Victoria. From here I went to Derby Friargate and then walked back to Derby Midland before returning to Nottingham behind Fowler 2-6-4 tank 42373. The up 'Waverley' was headed by a very clean Holbeck 'Jubilee', 45564 *New South Wales*, which, against the grain of most of my 'Jubilee' runs, performed admirably.

My next encounter with a 'Princess Royal' was also in 1957, on my return from a holiday at Dunoon. I chose the 'Midday Scot' and was overjoyed to see 46203 *Princess Margaret Rose* (a favourite from my early train-spotting days, when I had seen her in blue livery at Euston) backing onto the huge train at Glasgow Central, blowing off furiously from all four safety valves. Excitement turned to chagrin as we limped through the industrial suburbs, the excess steam replaced by turgid black smoke until we ground to a halt at Carluke to raise steam for thirty minutes. After a painful climb to Beattock (at an estimated 10mph at the summit) we let fly down the other side and swept through

132

Beattock station at a full 90mph. At Carlisle an unkempt 'Black Five' was hitched on as pilot, and we careered through the Lake District and the Lancashire industrial scene on a murky afternoon, regaining time in handfuls and with 46203 now blowing off steam at intervals to show the crew of 45382 that their efforts were unnecessary. At Crewe we were only twenty minutes down, and lo and behold, the pair were relieved by another 'Princess', Camden's No 46209 *Princess Beatrice*. She swept south into the darkness in fine style, and arrival in Euston was barely ten minutes late.

The 'Princess Royals' had a reputation for beautiful riding (even if they were sometimes shy for steam), and drivers were certainly prepared to let them run fast. In their latter days I was fortunate to enjoy long runs behind 46201 *Princess Elizabeth* (Carlisle–Perth), 46206 *Princess Marie Louise* (Rugby–Euston) and, right at their end, on 6 August 1962, 46208 *Princess Helena Victoria*, of Edge Hill shed, from Crewe to Euston on the '*Red Rose*', a mirror image of my 1957 run with *Princess Victoria*. This time I had my stopwatch, and we touched 85mph after Norton Bridge, 83 at Castlethorpe, 82 at Apsley and, after a Watford stop, 80 at South Kenton. We were five minutes early into Euston (Appendix Table 16).

The 1957 holiday at Dunoon, on the Firth of Clyde, gave me my first experience of Scottish steam. A return ticket from Euston to Gourock cost exactly seven pounds and tuppence (but this was two weeks' wages). I'd had a crisis of conscience — I had finished my six months at Old Oak between school and college and was tempted to buy a privilege ticket for my Scottish trip before I left. However, I did the right thing with a clear conscience, even though it nearly bankrupted me at the time, for I did not want to risk future BR employment options. It enabled me to sample the summer non-stop '*Royal Scot*' (well, not quite — we stopped to change crews at Carlisle Kingmoor) behind Camden's blue 'Duchess' 46244 *King George VI*.

Summer drizzle over the Clyde kept the foghorns going for three days on end and encouraged me to seek items of railway interest away from the coast. A day in Edinburgh was very fruitful. I crossed to Craigendoran on the steamer and caught a precursor of the 'Blue Trains' behind a 'V1' tank to Glasgow, where I luxuriated in the 11am '*Queen of Scots*' Pullman from Queen Street behind Haymarket's 60004 *William Whitelaw*. The sun emerged briefly, and I spent an hour or two taking photos at Waverley and from Princes Street Gardens of 'V2s', 'A2s', 'B1s' and 'D49s'. Then the clouds returned, so I went out to Longniddry to see a row of Scottish 'Directors' (Class D11/2) and 'C16' 4-4-2Ts stored in the soaking rain. The next day it was still pouring, so I explored the GSW line from Glasgow St Enoch and went out to Kilmarnock behind one of Holbeck's 'Scots' (46108 *Seaforth Highlander*). There were plenty of LMS '2Ps' everywhere, so I hardly gave them a second glance, but on my return I spied a Pickersgill 4-4-0, 54506, on a local (4.12pm to Greenock Princes Pier). I dashed to the booking office and got myself aboard, alighting at Paisley Gilmour Street to connect with a Gourock train, a ferry across the Clyde and evening dinner.

I had seen enough of Scotland through the clouds to be tempted to return, and the following year I was blessed with a fortnight's heatwave. This time I went via East Coast route, taking the Saturday '*Elizabethan*', with my old favourite 60033 *Seagull* at the business end, and a Haymarket (64B) 'A3', 60087 *Blenheim*, on to Glasgow Queen Street.

Gresley 'V1' three-cylinder 2-6-2T 67601 at Glasgow Queen Street with a stopping train along the Clyde coast from Craigendoran, 19 September 1957.

'A2' 60535 *Hornet's Beauty* threads Princes Street Gardens with a local from the Fife coast, 19 September 1957.

LMS '2P' 4-4-0 40667 at Glasgow St Enoch with a train for the Ayrshire coast, 20 September 1957.

Pickersgill 'Dunalastair' 4-4-0 54506 at Paisley Gilmour Street with the 4.12pm Glasgow St Enoch–Greenock Princes Pier, 20 September 1957.

'Top Shed' favourite 60033 *Seagull* on the Saturday '*Elizabethan*' at King's Cross, 5 July 1958.

Although most of the holiday was spent hiking the glens with other students, using the Craigendoran–Arrochar push-pull with a 'C15' (67460 or 67474) to get into the hills, I could not resist a further foray to Edinburgh. This time 'A1' 60159 *Bonnie Dundee* was motive power for the '*Queen of Scots*' Pullman. I returned to Waverley to see what was up, and, 'Ah!' — there was a 'D34', all ready to leave for the Fife coast. Another dash to the booking office, and, clutching my return to Inverkeithing, I joined the LNER non-corridor coach behind 62487 *Glen Arklet*. I released the window droplight for the crossing of the Forth Bridge, and my 'Ah!' became an 'Aaaaagh!' as the wind knocked all the breath from my body! I had scarcely crossed the platform at Inverkeithing when 62488 *Glen Aladale* swept in with a following northbound local.

I returned to Edinburgh almost immediately behind a Class D49/1 'Shire', 62708 *Argyllshire*, and was so pleased with myself that I decided to repeat the experience. Another local was standing ready with 'V2' 60969, but as we left Waverley I saw a 'Director' backing onto coaches at an adjoining platform. The 'V2' stopped at Dalmeny, at the southern approach to the Forth Bridge, and I decided to get out and chance my luck. Sure enough, it was my day. Some twenty minutes later 62677 *Edie Ochiltree* hove into view, and, joy of joys, it slowed down and stopped. So, for

NBR 'D34' 4-4-0 *62487 Glen Arklet* at Inverkeithing with a semi-fast from Edinburgh to the Fife coast, 9 July 1958.

'C15' 4-4-2T *67474* at Craigendoran with the push-pull train to Arrochar & Tarbert, 8 July 1958.

Edinburgh Waverley on 5 July 1958, with Haymarket 'A3' 60043 *Brown Jack* arriving a few minutes behind the *'Elizabethan'* with the 8.40am King's Cross.

the second time that day, I lowered the window high above the Forth and gulped in the air as we clanked over the famous bridge behind a pre-Grouping-design 4-4-0. I was reminded of another well-remembered passage from *Trains Illustrated* (possibly a witticism from someone like Hamilton Ellis), in which the caption to a photo of 62678 remarked that its name, *Lucky Mucklebackit*, sounded like the engine's motion when in a run-down condition. I got back to base courtesy of another Haymarket 'A3', 60037 *Hyperion*, on a semi-fast Edinburgh–Glasgow Queen Street train.

I returned to London a fortnight later, surprisingly bronzed from the unaccustomed sunshine, and decided to start off on the 'Queen of Scots' Pullman again, but disappointingly it produced only an Eastfield 'Standard 5', 73105, although we were banked up to Cowlairs by North British 'N15' 0-6-2T 69181. *Bonnie Dundee* was on the 'Heart of Midlothian', so I chose its relief behind 'A2' 60530 *Sayajirao* to Newcastle, 'A1' 60122 *Curlew* to Grantham (an engine that I subsequently had several runs behind) and, disappointingly, a 'V2', 60874, on to King's Cross.

I'd left August and September free for a further spell of working at Old Oak, so I was again able to enjoy free tickets, which I utilised to the full with further Saturday trips to Grantham (60112 out, 60115 back) and to Newport (70027 out, 5004 back). I also had an unofficial footplate ride to Swindon behind the current 'Bristolian' engine, 5043 *Earl of Mount Edgcumbe*, invited by a driver who'd seen my disappointment when my request for an official cab ride had been turned down by the authorities (who'd put a black mark against me after 'losing' the inspector on the Wolverhampton run the previous year).

Soon enough it was time to give up my 'priv' tickets and go back to college again. However, I interrupted my studies and my daily see-saws between Woking and Waterloo, as I was determined to get a run on the weekday 'Bristolian', and 'dieselisation' of the route was looming. In March 1959, therefore, accompanied by college friend Alistair Wood, who helped me log the journey, I travelled down to Bristol behind the now double-chimney 5084 *Reading Abbey* (which ran punctually, achieving a top speed of 94mph at Dauntsey), returning on the up 'Bristolian' with Bath Road's 5054 *Earl of Ducie*, which struggled against a severe side wind and, despite speeds in the upper 80s, was unable to recover time lost by permanent-way slacks and arrived eight minutes late.

'D11/2' ('Large Director') 4-4-0 62677 *Edie Ochiltree* at Inverkeithing with a stopping train from Edinburgh to Dundee, 9 July 1958.

Chapter 11

Weekly season ticket to Reading, 1959/60

In Chapter 8 I described my experiences as a student undertaking work in my university vacations at Old Oak Common depot during 1957 and 1958. Having lived among the locomotives and men there I was keen to experience them 'on the road' and decided to celebrate the end of my second-year exams in June 1959 and Finals the following year by purchasing a weekly season ticket from Paddington to Reading and spending most days travelling to and fro, timing the trains and keeping records — an interesting comparison with my experiences from Woking to Waterloo and not unlike the 'free days' I spent going backwards and forwards as described in Chapter 6.

On Monday 15 June 1959, therefore, I came up to London on the 7.51 from Woking, 'Lord Nelson'-hauled as usual, and quickly purchased my weekly season, the cost of which I cannot now exactly recall, but I have a feeling it was about 15/- (75p). I was just in time to dash up to the front of platform 2 at Paddington to ascertain that a Landore 'Castle' was at the head of the heavy (13 coach) 8.55 to Swansea and West Wales and find myself a corner seat in the front BSK when whistles blew, and 7009 *Athelney Castle* gave its first few emphatic exhaust beats and drew the long train steadily out past Ranelagh Bridge sidings and on towards Old Oak Common. I knew from my Old Oak experience that there were three Landore turns going down from London in the morning — the 8.50 '*South Wales Pullman*', the 8.55, which was the back working of the 'Castle' on the previous evening's '*Pembroke Coast Express*', and the 10.55 down '*Pembroke Coast Express*', with the engine off the up 'Pullman'.

I soon learned that there was a severe speed restriction to 15mph at Hayes because of a bridge rebuilding, and this caused late running in both directions for most of the week, especially in the down direction, as there was no recovery time built into the schedules until Swindon or Westbury was reached. This slowing caught the down trains just as they should have been reaching a reasonable speed to maintain on the level track, and it meant that drivers had either to work their engines hard immediately — and risk damage to the fire before it had properly burned through — or take it easy and lose time. The majority of drivers, I found, took it quietly and relied on time recovery later. We had made a slow start to Southall anyway, taking a little over 14 minutes, and had just reached 61mph when we got signal checks from the 'Pullman' as it slowed for the Hayes slack and then ourselves crawled over the suspect bridge at the required 15mph. We got back up to 64mph by Slough but only maintained this speed thereafter and took a full 44 minutes to the Reading stop, against a 40-minute schedule.

By this time I had long since ceased collecting locomotive numbers, but I did keep records of engines behind which I'd travelled and sought where possible to experience 'new' ones. I tended during this week to let some trains go, in the hope of a new loco on the following train, a hope not always fulfilled. I therefore had a fifty-minute wait before I decided on my return, which was with an up Weymouth train regularly hauled by a Westbury 'Hall'. 6955 *Lydcott Hall* was the motive power that morning and ran with energy when the signalman allowed. We were checked even before we cleared the platform but reached a rousing 75mph by Taplow before Slough brought us down to 15mph, then just reached 63mph again before the Hayes slack. Another acceleration to 66 was cut short at Acton, and a dead stand outside Paddington was the coup de grâce, making us ten minutes late in. Although difficult to calculate, net time was well under schedule — I estimate around 37 minutes for the 36 miles.

My records show that I did not return to Reading until the 1.18pm Paddington–Bristol. I often used the 11.30 West of England train that week, but the Weymouth would not have pulled in until 11.25, and unless there was a particularly attractive engine on the 11.30 I would have let it go, without a charge across the station. The 11.45 to Worcester did not then stop at Reading, and I'm not sure if the 11.55 South Wales express stopped either that year; it certainly did in 1962, when I did my management training at Old Oak, but I can't understand why I didn't take it if so. Of course, there were DMUs to Reading and Oxford, but main-line steam services were not so frequent in those days, and they certainly didn't stop as often as diesel and electric trains today because of the additional fuel cost and time penalties in stopping heavily loaded trains hauled by steam traction. Anyway, the 1.18 it was. A Bristol engine, 5062 *Earl of Shaftesbury*, backed onto ten coaches at platform 1, and it looked in good nick, well polished and steam tight. A fine run ensued. We made a fast start, passing Southall in under 12½ minutes at 65mph, and accelerated after the Hayes slack to 72 at Slough and a top speed of 75mph before a punctual Reading stop in under 40 minutes (just over 36 minutes net) — which, I have to say, was one of the few punctual down runs that week.

I completed at least three return trips each day that week and have a full performance log of each. As stated above, much of the running was spoiled by the Hayes bridge-rebuilding slack, just at the point where down trains would have been accelerating nicely, and many drivers did not bother to try to keep schedule to Reading, presumably in the knowledge that could take advantage of recovery time in the schedule approaching Swindon and before their destination. (At that time most WR expresses had two batches of four minutes' recovery in schedules to Taunton, Bristol, Cardiff, Gloucester, Worcester and Birmingham.) I shall therefore limit myself to describing some of the best runs, the others being documented in tabular form, for the record.

Last train for the day for me on Tuesday 16 June was the up '*Merchant Venturer*' from Bristol, with Bath Road depot's 5085 *Evesham Abbey* on nine coaches, 302/330 tons tare/gross. After a very mediocre day we at last had some vigour: a rousing acceleration to 80mph at Maidenhead (passed in 12 minutes 42 seconds), and passing

Slough in even time (17 minutes 42 seconds) and a clear run after the bridge slack saw us arrive almost punctually at Paddington in a net time of 36 minutes for the 36 miles, just two minutes late, having picked up four minutes of previously lost time. The next day started with a very similar run with a 'County', with one coach less. Swindon's 1019 *County of Merioneth* achieved my fastest start of the week from Reading, clearing Twyford in 6 minutes 48 seconds and already doing 68mph; 77 was reached at Maidenhead, and Slough (17.5 miles) was passed in 17 minutes 14 seconds, but an early arrival was prevented by a signal stand at Acton and further checks into the terminus, arrival being again two minutes late.

The up trains were definitely performing better than the down. Later that same afternoon the Hereford train, due Paddington at 4.47pm, drew in behind a 1925-built 'Castle' in its original state, Worcester's 4089 *Donnington Castle*, a loco due for heavy overhaul at Swindon Works, and I feared the worst. However, the driver was game, whisking his light load (eight coaches, 262/290 tons) up to 83mph at Ruscombe and reaching 70 after a check to 48 at Slough and 72 again after Hayes, and we actually arrived at our destination two minutes early, in 35 minutes net.

On the Thursday I eventually achieved one more punctual down run, with, surprisingly, another 1925-built veteran, albeit this time just ex works. I'd seen the up '*Cheltenham Spa Express*' belt through the middle road at Reading while we waited for the road that morning on the Fishguard boat train, so I was interested to get

4089 Donnington Castle approaches Reading with a Worcester train, 17 June 1959.

4085 *Berkeley Castle* ready to leave Paddington with the 2.15pm to Gloucester and Cheltenham, 18 June 1959.

Gloucester's 4085 *Berkeley Castle* on its return working, the 2.15pm Paddington–Gloucester, with ten coaches (342/360 tons). A very vigorous start was made to clear Southall in under 12 minutes at 64mph, and after the bridge check speed was maintained at 72mph all the way from Slough to Twyford, Reading being reached on time, in 37 minutes net. A wait of three quarters of an hour culminated in the arrival of Landore's No 5091 *Cleeve Abbey* on a South Wales express, running 12 minutes late on account of the failure of gas-turbine 18000 ahead of it just before Reading. Progress on the ten-coach train was steady but unspectacular, with a 10mph signal check at Taplow as well as the Hayes check, and arrival at Paddington was seventeen minutes late.

After a quiet day on the Friday — nothing spectacular, good or bad — I hoped perhaps for something unusual on a summer Saturday. I was expecting a 'Britannia' on the 1.55pm to South Wales, but 'County' 1012 *County of Denbigh* of Swindon was a last-minute replacement for one of the pacifics, which had failed on the up journey. The loco seemed ill prepared and performed erratically, unable to sustain more than 56mph with its twelve-coach load after the Hayes check. It took nearly 50 minutes to reach Reading, having dropped eight minutes, only half of which was attributable to engineering work. Another long wait ensued without a '47xx' or '63xx' or any other rare locomotive, so I took a ten-coach train from Bristol which arrived behind Old Oak's 5035 *Coity Castle*, a loco often picked for royal trains. Surprisingly we were unchecked apart from the bridge slack, running steadily at 80mph before Slough, and approached Paddington at 35mph behind the signalbox to platform 11, very early. I was in the packed corridor when suddenly the standing passengers were catapulted into each other like falling dominoes as an emergency brake application was made. We ground to a halt just as 5056 appeared tender-first from under the station canopy and stopped about two engine lengths short of a collision. Apparently 5056's ECS had been drawn out to Old Oak, leaving 5056 on the stop-blocks while its fireman went in search of tea for his billycan. The signalman assumed the platform was clear, as 5056 was standing on track so heavily contaminated by oil that it failed to operate the track circuit, and our train was admitted under clear signals. Thank heavens for an alert driver and very effective brakes. So our net time of just under 36 minutes was only up to a train's length from the stop-block!

Full details of the week's running are as follows:

Record of runs from Paddington to Reading, 15-20 June 1959

Train	Load	Locomotive	Actual time	Net time	Punctuality
Monday 15 June					
08.55 WestWales	13	7009 *Athelney Castle* (87E)	44.10	40.00	4min late
13.18 Bristol	10	5062 *Earl of Shaftesbury* (82A)	39.48	36.45	on time
17.05 Bristol	10	5958 *Knolton Hall* (81A)	48.55	40.30	16min late (departed 7min late)
Tuesday 16 June					
10.05 Bristol/Gloucester	9	5064 *Bishop's Castle* (82C)	50.15	41.00	10¼min late
13.18 Bristol	10	5062 *Earl of Shaftesbury* (82A)	50.35	39.00	10½min late
15.18 Wolverhampton	12	6960 *Raveningham Hall* (81D)	(Semi-fast, not timed)		
18.35 Gloucester	11	5007 *Rougemont Castle* (85B)	(Not timed)		
Wednesday 17 June					
08.55 West Wales	12	4097 *Kenilworth Castle* (87E)	46.55	42.30	7min late
11.15 Gloucester	9	5052 *Earl of Radnor* (81A)	42.00	38.45	2min late
14.55 Swansea	9	5964 *Wolseley Hall* (82C)	45.03	40.00	5min late
18.35 Gloucester	11	6019 *King Henry V* (81A)	46.40	40.30	6¾min late
Thursday 18 June					
08.55 West Wales	12	5080 *Defiant* (87E)	47.31	41.30	7½min late
11.30 Plymouth	9	5058 *Earl of Clancarty* (83D)	51.25	39.45	11½ min late
14.15 Gloucester	10	4085 *Berkeley Castle* (85B)	40.35	37.00	½min late
17.05 Bristol	10	6920 *Barningham Hall* (81A)	48.24	43.30	8½min late
20.05 Bristol	10	D804 *Avenger* (83D)	38.24	36.00	1½min early
Friday 19 June					
08.55 West Wales	12	5016 *Montgomery Castle* (87E)	44.25	40.00	4½min late
11.30 Plymouth	9	5028 *Llantilio Castle* (83D)	40.57	37.45	1min late
14.15 Gloucester	9	7000 *Viscount Portal* (85B)	40.40	37.30	¾min late
Saturday 20 June					
09.15 Weston-super-Mare	14	5034 *Corfe Castle* (81A)	48.35 (SO stopped at Ealing Broadway)		
13.55 West Wales	12	1012 *County of Denbigh* (82C)	49.15	44.00	9¼min late
18.35 Gloucester	12	6019 *King Henry V* (81A)	40.57	38.00	1min late

Record of runs from Reading to Paddington, 15-20 June 1959

Train	Load	Locomotive	Actual time	Net time	Punctuality
Monday 15 June					
11.15 arr ex Weymouth	8	6955 *Lydcott Hall* (82D)	49.00	38.00	10min late
15.20 arr ex Worcester	10	5042 *Winchester Castle* (85A)	44.00	39.00	3min late
16.15 Gloucester	9	5044 *Earl of Dunraven* (81A)	42.01	37.30	on time
Tuesday 16 June					
11.45 arr ex Swansea	13	5056 *Earl of Powis* (81A)	49.15	43.00	6min late
15.00 arr ex Gloucester	11	5094 *Tretower Castle* (85B)	44.36	38.30	6min late
15.00 Bristol	9	4082 *Windsor Castle* (81A)	43.41	40.00	6min late
17.25 Bristol	9	5085 *Evesham Abbey* (82A)	40.36	36.30	2min late
Wednesday 17 June					
10.30 arr ex Swindon	8	1019 *County of Merioneth* (82C)	42.36	36.15	2min late
14.15 arr ex Oxford	9	7008 *Swansea Castle* (81F)	45.38	39.00	14½min late
16.47 arr ex Worcester	8	4089 *Donnington Castle* (85A)	40.49	35.00	2min early
Thursday 18 June					
10.40 arr ex Fishguard	9	4093 *Dunster Castle* (87E)	51.23	36.30	10min late
13.00 arr ex Swansea	13	70024 *Vulcan* (86C)	45.18	42.30	8min late
16.47 arr ex Worcester	8	4088 *Dartmouth Castle* (85A)	43.22	37.30	½min early
19.20 arr ex Swansea	10	5091 *Cleeve Abbey* (87E)	46.47	39.45	17min late
21.25 arr ex Bristol	8	5090 *Neath Abbey* (82A)	43.36	38.15	on time
Friday 19 June					
10.30 arr ex Swindon	9	5008 *Raglan Castle* (81A)	43.26	38.30	7min late
13.00 arr ex Swansea	13	70029 *Shooting Star* (86C)	43.48	41.15	10½min late
16.47 arr ex Worcester	7	5958 *Knolton Hall* (81A)	44.10	40.00	5min late
Saturday 20 June					
08.20 Penzance	13	4078 *Pembroke Castle* (82A)	55.50	40.00 (7min early at Reading)	13min late
15.00 Bristol	10	5035 *Coity Castle* (81A)	39.25	35.30	4min early
21.30 arr ex Bristol	11	7006 *Lydford Castle* (83D)	50.30	38.30	13min late

So what was I to make of the week? How did it compare with commuting from Woking? Well, for a start, punctuality was poor, the bridge rebuilding at Hayes affecting all trains, and signalling problems — both technical and operational — delayed many runs. There was a huge contrast between those drivers who attempted to maintain time despite the checks and those who accepted them as reasons for lateness and appeared to make little effort, although their engines — apart from a few exceptions — seemed to be in no difficulty. Of the forty-four runs I timed, only eighteen ran with vigour and arrived at Reading or Paddington more or less on time. Two were delayed by earlier loco failures (gas-turbine 18000 and a Canton 'Britannia'), and eleven tried hard but were thwarted by operational problems, signal failures and congestion. That leaves three trips on which time was dropped because the locos (1012, 6920 and 70029) were obviously below par and ten where the driver, despite having a good loco with plenty of steam, made no real attempt to recover time lost by the planned engineering work.

Newly ex-works from Swindon following overhaul, 5008 *Raglan Castle* draws into Reading on 19 June 1959 with a train from Swindon booked to arrived at Paddington at 10.30am.

7025 *Sudeley Castle* enters Reading with a Paddington–Worcester train in June 1960.

It is interesting to make comparisons with the SR performance (described in Chapter 6 and in the Appendix logs) during the New Malden bridge repairs, when nearly all down runs worked hard to eliminate the arrears before the Woking stop. Speeds on the level between Slough and Reading were not dissimilar to those of SR locomotives between Hampton Court Junction and Walton, but the couple of miles of gentle descent from Weybridge past Brooklands encouraged the highest speeds in the mid- to upper 80s. The best speed on the WR was 83mph by 4089 on the level, which was equal to the best of the 'Merchant Navies' on my SR journeys. Overall, timekeeping by SR drivers was more consistent; WR punctuality was affected by a culture that condoned the acceptance by some drivers of engineering delays without any attempt at time recovery, in contrast to the best, who made every effort to keep time despite, at times, very long odds.

I needed an antidote to this surfeit of Western-concentrated experience, a little over the top despite my Western bias. A few weeks before buying the weekly season I'd joined my first enthusiasts' special train, the *Potteries Express*, which started from Paddington with 'Royal Scot' 46154 *The Hussar* and took a tortuous route to reach the Midland main line, travelling via the Greenford–Ealing branch and over the the North London line from Acton through Willesden Upper and Brent before joining the St Pancras route at Welsh Harp Junction. Attaining a maximum of 84mph at Ampthill and managing 44mph at Sharnbrook Summit, we proceeded competently enough but without any real fireworks to Derby, whence we were due to be double-headed by two '2P' 4-4-0s to Rudyard Lake en route to Macclesfield. In the event our motive power was a single Horwich 'Crab' 2-6-0, 42922, and after a walk around the lake we were hauled by two Fowler 2-6-4 tanks, 42346 and 42398, over the long-closed 'Potteries' line from Macclesfield to Stoke, bringing a game of cricket to a complete standstill as the white-clad fielders turned and observed a sight that had not been seen there before. A 'Black Five' took us from Stoke to Wolverhampton Low Level, where 'King' 6008 *King James II* took over the nine coach special and ran well within itself until opened out finally on the descent through Denham, touching 93mph.

I then decided to try the East Coast main line for an invigorating breath of more bracing air. On Saturday 25 June I caught the 9.40am King's Cross–Newcastle behind Grantham double-chimney 'A3' 60105 *Victor Wild*, which was energetic, with a top speed of 83mph after Sandy and 88 at Connington, but p-way slacks at Arlesey and Werrington Junction and diversion to the slow line half way up Stoke Bank caused us to drop ten minutes on the mile-a-minute schedule. Finding a local at Grantham, in from Nottingham behind GC 'A5' tank 69827, I decided to go to Derby Friargate. I was surprised to get a GNR 'J6' 0-6-0, 64235, but at Nottingham it was changed for a more prosaic 'L1', 67800, and, disappointingly, I returned from Derby Friargate to Grantham behind a filthy and run-down 'B1', No 61209. The next London-bound train ran in behind a dirty 'V2', 60909; given its light load of eight coaches I decided to give it a go and was rewarded with a swift descent of Stoke Bank, reaching 88mph; then there was a sound of grating metal, and we screeched to a halt opposite Lolham 'box, our mechanical lubricator

147

'Crab' 42922 pauses at Rudyard Lake en route from Derby to Macclesfield with the 'Potteries Express', 9 May 1959.

now in bits several miles behind us. We limped into Peterborough, where the 'V2' station pilot (60821) took over and left twenty minutes late, while I decided to wait for something better. Sure enough, double-chimney 'A3' 60044 *Melton* of Top Shed followed straight in, having been delayed by the disintegration of the 'V2', on the up eleven-coach '*Northumbrian*'. We left fifteen minutes late, and 60044 whisked us to London in fine style, reaching 81 at Huntingdon, 81 at Sandy, and with a net time of 69 minutes from Peterborough, despite three signal checks and the p-way slack at Arlesey, we regained six of the lost minutes.

.   Five days later I was tempted to have another go but was intending to resist and simply watch, as my finances were running low. However, when double-chimney 'A3' 60111 *Enterprise* backed onto the 12.30pm King's Cross–Newcastle '*Northumbrian*' my good intentions collapsed, and I screwed up my nerves and forked out for a day return to Grantham. The load was a heavy thirteen coaches (460 tons gross), and we ran very steadily, with maxima of 84 after the Arlesey slack and 88 at Connington South and a clear run this time up Stoke Bank, sustaining a minimum of 57 with this load, cutting the 111-minute schedule by thirty seconds. I had now become attracted to the double-chimney 'A3s' (the performance of which compared very favourably with that of the same locomotives in original condition) and, heading south again, gladly took Grantham's 60049 *Galtee More*, complete with a set of the new German 'elephant ear'-style smoke-deflectors. The train was the twelve-coach, 450-ton-gross '*Heart of Midlothian*', which arrived and left ten minutes late, touched 91mph at Little Bytham and maintained the upper 70s from Huntingdon to the Arlesey slack, but then progress was ruined by a series of signal checks in from Hitchin, and we arrived sixteen minutes late. Perhaps the Western punctuality was not so bad after all! I rounded off the evening by finding a 'new' 'King Arthur', 30786 *Sir Lionel*, waiting for me on the 11.15pm Waterloo–Basingstoke, so I peddled home and crawled into bed, satisfied but with my annual student grant all but exhausted.

In July I crept out to King's Cross again, looked at pacifics going north but counted the change left in my pocket at the end of the college year, before the next grant came through, and had to satisfy myself with a couple of runs through the tunnels and up the bank to Finsbury Park to take a few unsuccessful photos of engines working hard at the top of the bank; most were already going too fast for my 1/25sec shutter speed. 'A3' 60047 *Donovan* graced one Peterborough slow train I caught, and I returned to the terminus on an express behind 'A4' 60029 *Woodcock*, which, along

Headed by 'Royal Scot' 46154 *The Hussar*, the Ian Allan *'Potteries Express'* special waits to depart Paddington for Derby and Stoke-on-Trent, 9 May 1959.

with other terminating expresses, joined the queue at Finsbury Park awaiting a King's Cross platform. A few days later I tried again and was pleased to sample one of the Thompson rebuilds of the Gresley 'P2' 2-8-2s, 60506 *Wolf of Badenoch*, and returned south on a train hauled by 'B1' 61027 *Madoqua*, which surprised me by turning left and finishing up at Broad Street — a real mystery tour as far as I was concerned, with, luckily, no ticket collector at the Broad Street barrier!

The summer of 1959 was spent on a compulsory course at a German university (see Chapter 9). Then it was back to my final year at University College London and the daily routine of steam trains to Waterloo. In December Rodney Meadows, with whom I'd kept in touch after my 'short works' course in Bath and was now Passenger Marketing Officer of the King's Cross Division, persuaded me to join him on a run down to Grantham on the 16th to take a first trip behind the blue Deltic prototype, which was at that time running a regular Hull–King's Cross service from Doncaster. 60111 *Enterprise* was on the 9 o'clock to Newcastle, which we took as far as Grantham; it kept time exactly, unchecked on the 104-minute schedule for the 105 miles, with a top speed of 85mph at Biggleswade. I hadn't been really sure I wanted to waste my precious money (I had no 'privs' now) on a diesel run, albeit with Deltic, and I was therefore particularly pleased to get ex-works Heaton 'A3' 60084 *Trigo* instead of the diesel, which had failed — much to Rodney's chagrin. The train was the 12.20 Hull and left Grantham with nine coaches (350 tons gross) twelve minutes late, but it picked up four minutes, achieving 84mph at Little Bytham, 84 at Huntingdon and 84 again (was 'A3' 84 fixated on that number?) on the slightly rising gradient at Sandy, before a 30mph p-way slack at Hitchin, completing the 76 miles from Peterborough in a net time of 73 minutes. I was happy. It was the end of term, and Christmas loomed.

My table-tennis partner, Gordon, invited me to his home in Bradford in the New Year, and I travelled north on a chilly and dull January day on the 9 o'clock King's Cross–Newcastle as far as Doncaster. I was pleased to get a 'new' Grantham 'A3', 60065 *Knight of Thistle*, on a lightly filled nine-coach train (325 tons gross), and after a slow start and much slipping through the murky tunnels, taking nearly seven minutes to Finsbury Park, we got going. After 55 at Potters Bar we were just beginning to motor when signals brought us right down to a slow walking pace at Hitchin — apparently a signal failure, as there was a man beside the track, waving us past the red signal. Now late, we accelerated hard over the traditional racing stretch, making 82 at Sandy, 80 at the St Neots hump, 87 at Offord and 84 at Connington. We passed Peterborough in 77 minutes 38 seconds and held 72mph for miles around Essendine before gradually trailing away to precisely 60 at Stoke Summit. We arrived at Grantham just over two minutes late, in 106 minutes 13 seconds — 99 minutes net. We changed engines to a second 35B 'A3', 60056 *Centenary*, another new one for me, and were doing well, managing 80 at Newark, when we got caught by another signal failure — this time coming to a complete stand for more than five minutes. Two p-way slacks to 15mph after that, at Retford and Bawtry, meant that we were seventeen minutes late into Doncaster, through no fault of engine or crew.

After a pleasant couple of days with Gordon and his parents we were both due to visit Sue, another of our college year, who lived near Manchester, at Ashton-under-Lyne. However, I'd come down with a bug (caught, no doubt, as a result of a very wintry visit to the Brontë country at Haworth, before the days of the K&WVR) and had to be dosed up with brandy before I was fit to risk a Sunday journey on a train across the Pennines from Bradford Forster Square to Manchester Victoria — behind a 'Black Five', 44694. I survived that but nearly came to grief on a long and very jerky trolleybus ride to Ashton. (Is trolley-sickness a recognised condition?) Some thirty-six hours later I was deemed fit enough to return with Gordon via the Diggle route to Leeds, joining a Liverpool–Newcastle express at Stalybridge, which appeared behind Longsight's 46114 *Coldstream Guardsman*. In semi-darkness and still not 100% fit, I took little note, though I do remember spectacular pyrotechnics in Diggle Tunnel as we slogged up the grade.

After further night to recuperate at Gordon's I set out alone on 12 January 1960, picking up the 11am Leeds–St Pancras, a mere six-coach load as far as Sheffield, headed by a filthy 'Royal Scot' transferred from Crewe to Kentish Town, 46123 *Royal Irish Fusilier*, which I'd had a few years before to Beeston Castle on my first visit to Crewe. We picked our way between slowings for mining subsidences but arrived on time at Sheffield, where the restaurant car and other vehicles were attached, our load on departure being now ten coaches (360 tons gross). We dropped a couple of minutes to Chesterfield but recovered them with a 75 down through Langley Mill and left Nottingham on time. 46123 was not in good condition and slipped badly departing Nottingham; then the weather deteriorated, and we ran into heavy drifting snow in the Oakham area. With just two slight p-way slowings we'd dropped 14 minutes to Kettering and then tried hard but lost time steadily on a tight schedule. We climbed Sharnbrook at 48 minimum and touched 80 on the descent, but a p-way check to 10mph at Bedford knocked the stuffing out of us, and we couldn't make 60mph before a special stop at Luton to rescue passengers from a failed DMU. Then we struggled on in a fog of steam at the front end, arriving at St Pancras a full 36 minutes late, having dropped twenty-two minutes from Kettering on an admittedly tough mile-a-minute schedule in poor visibility.

In March I decided to spend a day in Birmingham and sample briefly the former Midland line to Bristol. 6018 *King Henry VI* got me to Snow Hill on the 8.30am Paddington–Wolverhampton, running non-stop to Birmingham in 124 minutes (113 minutes net) — four minutes late, after signals forced us through the platform lines at Beaconsfield and High Wycombe and a prolonged p-way check to walking pace at Aynho Junction; we attained no higher speed than 78mph anywhere but managed 53 at Saunderton and 50 minimum at Hatton.

I walked across the city to New Street and caught a Bradford–Bristol train leaving Birmingham at 11.24 with Bristol Barrow Road 'Jubilee' 45662 *Kempenfelt*. With a light load of eight coaches (270 tons gross) the rather dirty 'Jubilee', unchecked, just made the scheduled 54 minutes to Cheltenham, a very slow start being offset by sustained running in the high 70s after Abbotswood Junction, with a maximum of 80 at Depford. With a quick change at Cheltenham I was able to sample the northbound

'*Devonian*', with No 45576 *Bombay* of Sheffield Millhouses on nine coaches (315 tons gross). We left two minutes late, and *Bombay* failed to distinguish itself, with no speed higher than 65mph. We were banked up the Lickey Incline by a pair of Hawksworth panniers, 8403 and 8405, accelerating to 25mph while the 'Jubilee' took a breather. On arrival at New Street we were four minutes late after a check through the tunnels, but we had barely held schedule even on net time. Then it was back across the city to catch the two-hour 4.45pm Birmingham–Paddington with 6027 *King Richard I*, which would have run in on time but for a signal stop for half a minute outside Paddington station. It was a good steady run, with nothing spectacular, but efficient enough, in 112 minutes net.

It was now time to do some revision during the Easter vacation, because my Finals would start in May. Have all my trips between Woking and Waterloo reading poetry and plays paid off? Have my Arthurian knights helped? Will 'Sir Harry le Fise Lake' (or 'Erec fils du roi lac', as he was known in the Breton/German epic) feature? However, right in the middle of the exams I braced myself to take a day off. On 14 May I joined an Ian Allan special, the '*Severn & Wessex Express*', at Paddington, starting behind 6000 *King George V*. The load was just seven coaches, and the 'King' massacred the schedule, arriving at Severn Tunnel Junction more than twenty minutes early, in 116 minutes (103 minutes net) for the 123 miles, the high-spots being 82 on the level at Maidenhead, 87 at Cholsey, 87 at Little Somerford, a minimum of 76 at Badminton Summit and another 80+ down through Winterbourne. We coasted through the Severn Tunnel, still doing 54 as we emerged, before an unsurprising signal stop outside the station. Ex-works Churchward Mogul 6384 took us to Bath Green Park via the other Severn Bridge at Sharpness, but a Somerset & Dorset 2-8-0, 53807, struggled, stalling on the climb to Masbury Summit, stopping at Chilcompton to raise steam and finally clambering over the top at 14mph, arriving at Evercreech Junction eighteen minutes late. We recovered five minutes at this stop and managed to lose no more time to Bournemouth West, whence 35008 *Orient Line* made an easy run to Waterloo, with nothing over 80mph, arriving a minute early.

Despite this indulgence my revision and my mediaeval Arthurian studies paid off — nothing too distinguished, but I got my 2.2 and graduated at the Albert Hall with 1,400 other successful students, filing in line to touch (not squeeze!) the proffered hand of the Chancellor, the Queen Mother. Finals were over, a letter had been received from the MoD indicating the end of National Service (which I'd framed and hung on my bedroom wall), and I was in negotiation with BR (Western Region) to start work at Paddington Passenger Train Office in August, pending an application to become a Traffic Apprentice (Management Trainee) the following year. In other words, at least until the results of my degree examinations were received, all was well in my world.

There were the more conventional celebrations with colleagues in UCL's German Department, but I owed myself some relaxation and decided to purchase a weekly season from Paddington to Reading again, to see if I would fare any better than the previous year and to fill the gaps of Western locomotives behind which I'd travelled. So it was 'Nelson' time once more via the 7.51 Woking–Waterloo (they had a few more months — not many — before withdrawal), and I was at Paddington in time to buy my ticket and find I had a choice between the 8.55 to South Wales and the 9.5am to Bristol. Both locos were normally attached in good time, and they ran from adjacent platforms, so I could reflect on my choice. On Monday 20 June 1960 I rejected the Landore 'Castle' on the 8.55 in favour of a Penzance 'County', no less, on the 9.5 — 1008 *County of Cardigan*, with eleven coaches (378/405 tons). At least this year there were no engineering speed restrictions on the down line, although on the Monday and Tuesday there was a 15mph temporary speed restriction on the up fast at Iver after re-laying over the previous weekend. However, we got no further than Old Oak Common West before we were checked to 25mph, and with no higher speed than 64 between Slough and Maidenhead and a dead stand for signals at Ruscombe sidings, resulting in an eight min-late arrival at Reading, the omens were not good.

The Weymouth express due Paddington at 11.15am duly arrived on time with Westbury's 5974 *Wallsworth Hall* on eight coaches (264/285 tons) and started vigorously, although the engine began to prime. It was in good nick, however, and flew, hitting a maximum of 76mph before Slough and then a resounding 80 at Ealing and 81 at Acton, after the Iver p-way check. Unfortunately a two-minute stop outside the terminus made us a minute late in, but net net time was a praiseworthy 36 minutes. The 11.30am Paddington–Plymouth was one of the few West of England diagrams still booked for steam haulage, and an Old Oak 'King' seemed to be alternating with the two 'Kings' (6002 and 6016) remaining at Laira. 6002 *King William IV* was in charge that Monday on nine coaches (312/325 tons) and ran very steadily, with a top speed of 70mph and a signal check (outside Reading) to walking pace, which failed to prevent a punctual arrival.

Another Weymouth express due Paddington at 1.15pm was now booked for a Reading 'Castle' and duly appeared behind double-chimney 4074 *Caldicot Castle*. This engine, together with 4073, had been slated for withdrawal in 1955, but here it was fitted with all 'mod cons' and still going strong. It arrived at Reading three minutes early with eight coaches plus three bogie vans (366/390 tons) and reached 74mph before being checked at Slough in advance of the Iver p-way slowing. A speed of 64 was again reached at Hanwell, but signal checks from Westbourne Park made us a disappointing ten minutes late into Paddington.

After a couple of steady runs with 'Castles' I decided to see if the 5.5pm Paddington–Weston-super-Mare was any better this year than last and found 6019 *King Henry V* once again in charge. The load was a modest ten coaches (342/370 tons), and we started reasonably enough, achieving 63 by Southall; however, we were checked by signals at Hayes, and all went horribly wrong thereafter; the recovery was almost non-existent, culminating in a six-minute stop just after Slough to raise steam and a further ten-minute stand at Ruscombe sidings for a similar purpose. We eventually dragged our way forty minutes late into Reading, where 6019 was removed and replaced by Reading's down-line pilot.

On the Tuesday I discovered a 'fun' train. The 2.55pm Paddington–Swansea, with a Gloucester portion, was booked for the rostered Landore engine to be double-headed by the Swindon loco off the 10.30am arrival. On this occasion it was 5080

153

6002 *King William IV* accelerates through Reading's middle road with an up West of England express in June 1960.

5003 *Lulworth Castle* ready to depart Paddington on the 9.5am to Bristol, 22 June 1960.

Defiant with 5000 *Launceston Castle*, and the two romped away with the heavy, thirteen-coach train (458/480 tons), passing Southall in 11 minutes 49 seconds and arriving at a dead stand in Reading in 37 minutes, after 70-72 all the way from Hayes to Twyford. On the whole I did not suffer many really bad runs or failures, notwithstanding 6019's spectacular collapse the previous day, but I didn't do too well on Tuesday afternoon. The 12.30 Cardiff (3.10pm arrival in London) was announced as ten minutes late at Reading and ran in fourteen minutes late behind Old Oak's No 5093 *Upton Castle*, which looked to be in difficulty: it was emitting dirty brown smoke, and the blower appeared to be on as it arrived. The tender was full of the ovoids heartily detested by most crews, and we struggled up to 60 at Ruscombe before being brought to a complete stand for three minutes before Slough. This finished us off; the 'Castle' was clearly in dire trouble for steam thereafter, just making 50mph at Ealing, and we were thirty minutes late into the terminus. The driver said that, in addition to the poor coal, the boiler tubes were overdue for cleaning.

On my next 'up' opportunity a very late-running train from the West of England appeared around the Reading West curve headed by a 'Warship' diesel-hydraulic, with, intriguingly, a steam locomotive coupled inside. It drew to a stand in the up main platform, and I dithered for some time as to whether I should join D832 *Onslaught* and the Taunton standby pilot, 4904 *Binnegar Hall*. Curiosity got the better of me, and I embarked for the experience. It being mid-June, the inability of the diesel to provide steam heating was clearly not the reason for 4904's presence, and it quickly became apparent that the well-groomed 'Hall' had been added at Taunton because one of D832's engines had failed. The 'Hall' gave vigorous assistance in accelerating the heavy (twelve-coach) train to the low 70s by Ruscombe sidings and then eased, allowing *Onslaught's* sole functioning engine to maintain this speed until the Iver 40mph slack, when the 'Hall' exhibited more energy until 70mph was again reached. Signal checks into the terminus turned an already very late train into a forty min-late arrival, the net time being about 38 minutes.

One of the fastest runs of the week was on Thursday 23 June on the 11.30am West of England train, which produced an 81A 'Castle' rather than the booked 'King'. No 5065 *Newport Castle*, looking in good condition, had a light, eight-coach load (266/290 tons), and a very fast run followed, with 80mph reached by Slough and a top speed of 82 at Ruscombe. Unchecked, we drew to a stand exactly 36 minutes after leaving London — 4 minutes early. The driver was an Old Oak man I knew — Driver Beak.

Next day I again caught the 11.30 West of England train, which had a burnished Old Oak 'King', 6025 *King Henry III*, and an easy, nine-coach load (312/330 tons). We started with great energy but caught out the signalman at Southall, who had allowed a tardy freight to cross our path into the sidings at Hayes, and ground to a halt there for four minutes. Once we got the road the driver really pushed the 'King', and we roared through Slough at a full 80mph, reaching a maximum of 83 between Maidenhead and Twyford. Although we took 47 minutes, dropping seven minutes, our net time was only 36 minutes — identical to that set by 5065 the day before.

Now for the week's tour de force. There was a Fridays-only Bristol–Paddington train, due to reach its destination at 5.43pm. This arrived at Reading just over three minutes late, Old Oak rebuilt 'Star' 5087 *Tintern Abbey* being in charge of a very heavy load — a packed thirteen coaches (451/505 tons). My experience so far had been that 'Castles' ran exceedingly well with up to ten coaches but that twelve-thirteen coaches taxed them on the level, and speeds higher than the upper 60s with this load on the Reading–Paddington section were rare. This 'Castle' made mincemeat of that notion. A comparatively slow start to Twyford (although we'd reached 62mph by then) was followed by a steady, roaring acceleration to 77mph by Maidenhead and 81 by Slough and subsequent running between 78 and 80 all the way to Acton. An unusually clear road into Paddington meant that, having left Reading late, we drew to a triumphant stand three minutes early, in 37 minutes start-to-stop. It rounded off a very satisfactory day.

I was going to have a hard job to repeat that success on the following day, a summer Saturday (25 June). The 9.5am to Weston-super-Mare had fourteen coaches (480/525 tons) and Old Oak 'King' 6010 *King Charles I*, which ran unchecked to Reading in 42 minutes, with nothing higher than 68mph (just before Slough). However, this was sufficient for timekeeping on the Saturday schedule. I returned with the Westbury 'Hall' turn on the up Weymouth, which arrived at Reading punctually behind a 'Modified Hall', Westbury's 7917 *North Aston Hall*. The load was nine coaches (304/325 tons), and the locomotive accelerated vigorously, sustaining 80mph on the level between Maidenhead and Slough, then easing to avoid getting too far ahead of time but still running in the low 70s until the inevitable signal checks between Acton and Paddington, but we still managed an on-time arrival (net time 36½ minutes). A long delay in the afternoon, exacerbated when, eventually, a run-down Canton 'Hall' turned up instead of the booked 'Britannia', was followed by a vigorous evening run behind a 'County' (1009) on the up '*Merchant Venturer*', which brought my week to a close.

Full details of the entire week's running are given below.

Record of runs from Paddington to Reading, 20-25 June 1960

Train	Load	Locomotive(s)	Actual time	Net time	Punctuality
Monday 20 June					
09.05 Bristol	11	1008 *County of Cardigan* (83G)	49.08	42.00	9min late
11.30 Plymouth	9	6002 *King William IV* (83D)	39.39	39.00	½min early
13.40 Bristol	11	5078 *Beaufort* (82A)	40.02	38.00	on time
17.05 Bristol	10	6019 *King Henry V* (81A)	80.45 (loco failed)		41min late
Tuesday 21 June					
08.55 West Wales	11	4076 *Carmarthen Castle* (87E)	42.39	39.00	2½min late
11.15 Gloucester	8	5037 *Monmouth Castle* (81A)	42.58	42.58	3min late
14.55 Swansea	13	5080 *Defiant* (87E)	37.28	37.28	1½min early
		5000 *Launceston Castle* (82C)			
Wednesday 22 June					
09.05 Bristol	11	5003 *Lulworth Castle* (83A)	39.34	39.34	½min early
12.45 Worcester	9	7007 *Great Western* (85A)	46.29	40.30	6½min late
16.38 Wolverhampton	10	7914 *Lleweni Hall* (81D)	45.02	41.30	½min early

Thursday 23 June

09.15 Worcester	8	5042 *Winchester Castle* (81A)	38.06	37.45	2min early
11.15 Gloucester	8	5065 *Newport Castle* (81A)	36.17	36.00	4min early
13.40 Bristol	11	5073 *Blenheim* (82A)	41.33	38.00	1½min late
17.05 Bristol	10	5082 *Swordfish* (81A)	44.42	41.30	4¾min late

Friday 24 June

09.05 Bristol	11	7022 *Hereford Castle* (83D)	43.08	40.00	3min late
11.30 Plymouth	9	6025 *King Henry III* (81A)	47.53	36.15	8min late
14.55 Swansea	14	4094 *Dynevor Castle* (87E)	41.18	38.15	1¼min late
		5009 *Shrewsbury Castle* (82C)			

Saturday 25 June

09.05 Bristol	14	6010 *King Charles I* (81A)	42.40	42.40	1½min early
12.45 Worcester	9	5014 *Goodrich Castle* (81A)	40.31	40.31	½min late
17.20 Reading	9	5018 *St Mawes Castle* (81D)	(stopping train)		on time

Record of runs from Reading to Paddington, 20-25 June 1960

Train	Load	Locomotive(s)	Actual time	Net time	Punctuality
Monday 20 June					
11.15 arr ex Weymouth	8	5974 *Wallsworth Hall* (82D)	44.21	36.00	2½min late
13.15 arr ex Weymouth	11	4074 *Caldicot Castle* (81D)	52.14	40.15	10min late
					(3min early at Reading)
15.10 arr ex Swansea	12	5057 *Earl Waldegrave* (81A)	42.24	38.15	1min late
19.20 arr ex Swansea	10	5030 *Shirburn Castle* (87E)	49.08	41.00	6min late
Tuesday 21 June					
10.30 arr ex Swindon	11	5000 *Launceston Castle* (82C)	43.08	36.45	6min late
13.30 arr ex Worcs	8	7002 *Devizes Castle* (85A)	46.02	37.00	7¾min late
17.35 arr ex Bristol	10	6028 *King George VI* (81A)	41.45	37.15	11½min late
Wednesday 22 June					
10.30 arr ex Swindon	10	5023 *Brecon Castle* (82C)	41.10	37.15	1min late
15.10 arr ex Swansea	12	5093 *Upton Castle* (81A)	60.17 (loco failing)		31min late
(Up West of England)	12	D832 *Onslaught* (83D)	44.22	38.00	40min late
		4904 *Binnegar Hall* (83B)	(D832 on one engine)		
Thursday 23 June					
10.30 arr ex Swindon	10	5068 *Beverston Castle* (82C)	42.37	37.30	10min late
Local from Reading		7016 *Chester Castle* (86C)	(Not timed)		on time
15.00 arr ex Gloucester	11	5081 *Lockheed Hudson* (85A)	43.04	37.15	10½min late
19.45 arr ex West Wales	9	4099 *Kilgerran Castle* (87E)	41.58	38.45	15min late
Friday 24 June					
10.30 arr ex Swindon	10	5009 *Shrewsbury Castle* (82C)	39.38	38.30	4min late
13.15 arr ex Weymouth	11	5036 *Lyonshall Castle* (81D)	48.35	41.45	15¾min late
					(2min late at Reading)
17.43FO arr ex Bristol	13	5087 *Tintern Abbey* (81A)	37.02	37.02	3min early
Saturday 25 June					
11.15 arr ex Weymouth	9	7917 *North Aston Hall* (82D)	41.43	36.30	on time
15.20 arr ex Swansea	12	6943 *Farnley Hall* (86C)	53.52	41.30	54min late
20.05 arr ex Bristol	12	1009 *County of Carmarthen* (82A)	39.10	38.30	2min late

Landore's 5004 *Llanstephan Castle* at the buffer stops of Paddington's No.10 platform with an arrival from West Wales during the author's weekly season ticket escapade, June 1960

5023 *Brecon Castle* enters Paddington with a local train from Oxford and Reading, 12 February 1958.

Thus ended my second week. So how did it compare with the previous year? For a start, general punctuality was much improved. There were no engineering works on the down line, and the re-laying check on the up at Iver was eased mid-week and lifted towards the end. There were some excellent performances, especially from 'King' 6025, 'Castles' 4076, 5000, 5003, 5023, 5065, 5081 and 5087, 'Halls' 5974 and 7917 and 'County' 1009. There were three instances of real locomotive problems (6019, which was a failure, D832 and 5093) and one where there had been presumably a failure earlier, necessitating a replacement (6943). Of the other thirty-six runs timed, nineteen were on time or early, and a further nine recovered time from late starts or tried desperately hard to regain time or minimise the impact of delays. That leaves eight runs on which time was lost by signal or p-way checks without any real attempt to recover time. Over the two weeks in the two years I had five 'Kings' (6002, 6010, 6019 [three times], 6025 and 6028), fifty-five 'Castles' (4074, 4076, 4078, 4082, 4085, 4088, 4089, 4093, 4094, 4097, 4099, 5000 [twice], 5003, 5007, 5008, 5009 [twice], 5014, 5016, 5018, 5023, 5028, 5030, 5034, 5035, 5036, 5037, 5042 [twice], 5044, 5052, 5056, 5057, 5058, 5062 [twice], 5064, 5065, 5068, 5073, 5078, 5080 [twice], 5081, 5082, 5085, 5087, 5090, 5091, 5093, 5094, 7000, 7002, 7006, 7007, 7008, 7009, 7016, 7022), four 'Counties' (1008, 1009, 1012, 1019), two 'Britannias' (70024, 70029), ten 'Halls' (4904, 5958 [twice], 5964, 5974, 6920, 6943, 6955, 6960, 7914, 7917) and two 'Warships' (D804, D832). This demonstrates the dominance of 'Castles' on all bar the diesel-hauled West of England trains passing through Reading, the Wolverhampton route being at this time the main stronghold of the Stafford Road and Old Oak 'Kings'.

Chapter 12

Working for British Railways, the first year

'43xx' Mogul 5369 leaves Barmouth for Dolgelly and Ruabon in July 1960.

After a hectic week using my Paddington–Reading season ticket to the maximum I gave myself a fortnight's break from trains before my annual holiday at one of the Methodist Guild resorts much frequented by teenagers and students from the Methodist Association of Youth Clubs, a youth organisation that had more than 50,000 members in the 1950s and '60s. That year, 1960, I'd chosen the Barmouth centre and travelled down from London on 16 July on the heavy, thirteen-coach 9.10am Paddington–Wolverhampton with 6024 *King Edward I* of Old Oak, which ran well, early at all calling-points, the highlights with this load being the 53mph minimum at Saunderton Summit and 41mph at Hatton, although there was nothing over 77mph.

We arrived nearly two minutes early at Snow Hill, where I alighted to see what was of interest, as I had all day to get to Barmouth. There was a Tyseley 'Manor', 7824 *Iford Manor*, on a relief train to Aberystwyth, so I took that to Wolverhampton and then decided to await the '*Cambrian Coast Express*', which arrived twenty-three minutes late

160

behind 6000 *King George V*. Two locos then backed onto the thirteen-coach, 500-ton-gross train — 7811 *Dunley Manor*, of Shrewsbury depot, and Churchward Mogul No 6340, of Stourbridge Junction. A bright start, passing Albrighton at 73mph, was then spoiled by continuous signal checks behind a local DMU and a p-way slack to 15mph at Shifnal before we recovered to 38mph at Hollinswood Sidings 'box; then more signal checks made us forty-six minutes late as we took the southern leg of the triangle avoiding Shrewsbury station and made for Welshpool. Running in the mid-50s between slowings to get the single-line token recovered some time, and we were only thirty-five minutes late when we arrived at Welshpool and exchanged our pair for Machynlleth's resplendent 7818 *Granville Manor* and the same depot's 'Standard 4' No 75026, with which we touched 65mph descending Talerddig Bank, and, despite more signal stops, as we were way out of our path, we arrived just thirty-two late at Machynlleth, whence 7818 went off to Aberystwyth, leaving the Standard to take our six coaches to Barmouth, where we arrived forty-three minutes late.

The fortnight was spent on a challenging hike to the top of Cader Idris and easier walks along the Mawddach estuary, with me 'escaping' to Aberystwyth and the Vale of Rheidol — runs with 'Manors' 7807, 7817 and 7822, Moguls 5369, 6333 and 6371 and 0-6-0 2217, plus VoR Nos. 8 and 9. I had to suffer some mild teasing that I preferred the company of steam engines to that of the many teenage girls staying at the house, although I believe I balanced it fairly well! One evening I thought I'd managed to catch one of the last 'Dukedogs' as I spied 9014 and 5399 crossing Barmouth Bridge, and I ran to the station and bought a ticket to Harlech only to find that the pair had unhooked and been replaced by a couple of '78xxx' Standard Class 2 2-6-0s.

At the end of the holiday I decided to return via Dolgellau and Bala and caught the 7.20am Pwllheli–Paddington with a pair of Collett 0-6-0s, 2202 and 2286, which left six minutes late and took their ten-coach, 365-ton train up the nine miles of gradients averaging 1 in 58 past Pontnewydd and Drws-y-Nant to the summit at Garneddwyn at a painful 14mph but sustainted 57mph on the descent. I got out at Corwen, where the pair stopped for water, to see what was on the next train and caught 7310 on the 9.20am Barmouth–Birmingham, which departed Llangollen twenty-four minutes late, awaiting a down train, then managed to cut six minutes on the run to Ruabon, where Tyseley's 6879 *Overton Grange* took over and bustled the eight-coach train to Wolverhampton, where we arrived a minute early!

I hung around at Wolverhampton and eventually caught the 2.35pm to Paddington with Old Oak's 6003 *King George IV*, which left two minutes late with ten coaches (385 tons gross). After a punctual run to High Wycombe, with a maximum of 90mph at Blackthorn, we caught up a late-running Marylebone-bound local after Seer Green and crawled behind it all the way to Denham, then roared away to reach 80mph at Greenford, arriving at Paddington a disappointing eleven minutes late.

It was now time to start work and join the railway. However, by the time I left college in June 1960 I had missed that year's intake into the Traffic Apprenticeship scheme and therefore, with the help of contacts made earlier, joined the Western Region London Division's Passenger Train Office as a 'Class 4 clerk' — the junior

A pair of Collett '2251' 0-6-0s, 2202 and 2286, head the Barmouth–Paddington via Ruabon express onto Barmouth Bridge and over the Mawddach estuary, July 1960.

grade. Perhaps as an omen of things to come, I was made redundant within two weeks of my induction and filled the post of an office junior without any apparent change in my pay or role — which was sorting Guards' Journals. The Guard's Journal was a record of each journey, indicating the locomotive number, train formation, number of passengers and time gained and lost by the engine, signal checks, speed restrictions, station overtime etc. Part of my job was to refer any significant signal delays to the District Signalling Inspectors for explanation — an activity that was not well received by experienced time-served inspectors from the hands of enthusiastic young new entrants to the service!

After three months I regained my status as a Class 4 clerk, being put in charge of the production of the 'Daily Manuscript Notice' — a document that was compiled, Roneo-ed and distributed each day to stations and depots in the Division, indicating last-minute changes to the timetable, the schedule for specials and relief trains and formation strengthening to accommodate surges in traffic and special parties — a need I would identify through scrutiny of train loadings from the Guards' Journal records and the details of bookings from the Party Section. The culture of the day can best be illustrated by one incident I remember vividly — I was summoned one day before an angry General Manager (Keith Grand) to explain why, during his morning promenade along Paddington's platform 1, he had seen the chocolate-and-cream formation of the 'Cornish Riviera' despoiled by one maroon coach at the back. Apparently I should have required Old Oak depot, in my Notice, to attach a suitably liveried vehicle or leave the train short-formed! When I rang his secretary to arrange for the interview in which I was to be dressed down she suggested I should come in the early afternoon. When I duly arrived, quaking at the prospect, she told me to go back to work, as he was never fit enough in the early afternoon to see anyone after his usual alcoholic lunch. She would tell him that I'd fulfilled the appointment and that I'd hear no more about it. I didn't.

My first day at the office had been 1 August 1960, and by September I was eligible once more for 25%-rate 'privilege' tickets, so I began to resume my journeys on evenings and Saturdays to experience the swansong of main-line steam, before the diesels made major inroads. In fact, with a routine clerical job during the day and few commitments in the evenings (I was several years away from a romantic engagement) I went over the top in my efforts to experience the last couple of years when steam was still to the forefront on British main lines. The only constraint was whether I had enough cash — even at 'priv' ticket rates — as I was chasing steam on one of the key routes out of London at least once every week.

Already the English Electric Type 4s (Class 40s) were taking the cream of East and West Coast services, and the 'Warships' had assumed the majority of West of England and Bristol-route trains. My first opportunity was on Saturday 3 September — we still worked Saturday mornings in 1960. I got away at the first opportunity and caught the 12.5pm Paddington–Plymouth. Expecting a 'Castle' (or even a '47xx'), I was disappointed to find only a 'Modified Hall', Exeter's 6965 *Thirlestaine Hall*, which actually performed very competently — drivers at Old Oak certainly rated them highly, as I knew from my months there. With an eleven-coach load, 420 tons gross,

6004 *King George III* at Paddington on the last booked steam-hauled 'Cornish Riviera Express', 11 June 1958.

we ran steadily to Reading in just under 40 minutes but left Newbury five minutes late after a signal stand outside the station and overtime awaiting 'line clear'. We then passed Savernake Summit at 49mph, in 22 minutes 24 seconds from the standing start, and let fly down past Patney, reaching a maximum of 86mph at Lavington. After a signal stand at Heywood Road Junction we climbed to Brewham Summit at 46mph, touched 77 before Somerton and, after a signal check outside Taunton, were six late in. The climb to Whiteball was a bit painful — only 18mph at the top — and a long 5mph p-way slowing at Silverton made us nine late into Exeter, where another 'Modified Hall', Laira's 6988 *Swithland Hall*, was attached as pilot, to reduce the amount of Summer Saturday engine-changing at Newton Abbot.

I returned to Exeter along the sea wall for novelty's sake behind one of the short-lived North British A1A-A1A diesel-hydraulics, D604 *Cossack*, which — with ten coaches and three vans on the 12.0 Penzance mail to Manchester — just held the scheduled time, although running late, without exceeding 62mph after Starcross. By Exeter I'd had enough and picked up the 1.20pm Penzance–Paddington, with No 6003. This lost four minutes to Taunton — explained by a 15mph p-way slack at Stoke Canon. I might have gone through to Paddington with it on its thirteen-coach load, but I alighted at Taunton in the hope of something better on the 4.35pm Kingswear — the last up West of England–Paddington service. However, I was disappointed to get a Reading 'Hall', 5993 *Kirby Hall*, which left Taunton eight minutes late and ran well enough to Newbury before hitting trouble. For a start we were apparently right behind 6003 on the Penzance (perhaps I was better off on the Kingswear after all) and found no water in the troughs at Aldermaston, so we stopped at Theale to request a special stop at Reading to take water there. I guess 6003 was doing the same, as we crawled behind it, stopping at Reading West Junction and outside the station, and could see 6003's train at the platform. We eventually got away, and after a steady run with a 74 maximum at Taplow we ground to a halt outside Paddington, as a DMU had suffered an ATC failure and needed to be routed into the main-line platforms because of a problem with the equipment on the suburban platforms. We eventually rolled in fifty-four minutes late.

I'd noted that a newly ex-works 'Castle' now equipped with a double chimney, 5088 *Llanthony Abbey*, was prominent in the Guards' Journals I was scrutinising daily and was being credited with substantial time recovery on some of the 'King'-diagrammed Wolverhampton turns, so I grabbed the chance of riding the evening relief to the 6.10pm Paddington, the 6.23, when I saw 5088 was rostered. Sure enough, it romped away with its eleven-coach, 415-ton-gross load, arriving more than seven minutes early at Bicester despite a 15mph p-way slowing at Haddenham with 57mph at Seer Green, 45 minimum at Saunderton and 81 after Brill. I returned from Banbury with 6029 *King Edward VIII* on the last up Wolverhampton (the 4.30pm Birkenhead), which arrived eight minutes late, explained by two p-way slacks. The following Friday I saw that one of the Laira 'Kings' transferred to Canton to replace the 'Britannias', 6004 *King George III*, was motive power for the 5.55pm '*Red Dragon*', a heavy, thirteen-coach train (505 tons gross), and decided to take it to its first stop — Swindon. On a Friday the train was timed to leave at 5.58pm, behind the retimed 5.53 '*Mayflower*', but we left in front of it, as its loco, D809, had failed at the platform. We therefore got a clear road and set off with gusto, reaching 76mph by Iver before a 5mph p-way restriction at Slough. After Reading speeds resumed in the upper 60s/low 70s, and we arrived at Swindon a minute early. I returned on a train I was to catch frequently over the next few months — the 2.30pm Neyland, due Paddington at 10.10pm (just right for me to catch the 11.15pm Waterloo home). Landore's burnished 5074 *Hampden* looked fully fit for the job, but our rapid acceleration to 73mph was cut short by severe signalling problems all the way from Challow to Didcot, and we were sixteen minutes late into Paddington.

I had been invited to spend a weekend in Wallasey, near Birkenhead, visiting friends I'd made at Barmouth, so I set off from Paddington that night on the 12.5am from Paddington without going home. I was a bit put out to find that I was to be crammed into a four-a-side compartment all night in a train that was full and standing behind another 'Modified Hall', Old Oak's 6961 *Stedham Hall*, which was routed via Oxford; then, at Wolverhampton, 4918 *Dartington Hall* took over for the next leg of the journey, to Chester. I didn't get much sleep, as the fore-and-aft motion in the front coach was not very soothing! We left Chester twenty-three minutes late behind a Stanier 2-6-4 tank, No 42459, which recovered sixteen minutes of lost time on the half hour run — all recovery time, I guess, as we didn't exceed 54mph. My return on the Monday night was on the 8.55pm Birkenhead behind another 'Hall', 5989, to Wolverhampton, and then I was delighted to see 5011 *Tintagel Castle* of Reading backing onto our eleven-coaches train, in which — this time — I had a decent corner seat. We ran well enough to Reading but then crawled up the relief line from Slough, arriving at Paddington twenty-six minutes late, although few of my fellow-pasengers were worried by a later-than-booked arrival in the early hours of the morning.

I gave things a miss for a month or so, then decided that a trip down to Kemble on the 5pm Paddington–Gloucester 'Cheltenham Spa Express' behind its regular Gloucester double-chimney 'Castle', 7035 *Ogmore Castle*, was too good to miss. A steady run to Maidenhead was then marred by prolonged signal checks around a p-way slowing at Ruscombe sidings, so performance was upped after Reading, and we ran from Didcot to Swindon in the 73-76mph range, arriving at Kemble on time. There followed a 'quickie' back to Swindon behind 'Modified Hall' 6986, and then it was Landore's 5006 *Tregenna Castle* on the 2.30pm Neyland. It was a cold, frosty night, and I stood at an open window in the first coach, listening to the glorious full-throated roar of the engine as we accelerated to 71mph before Shrivenham and then again after a p-way slack. Although the train had been twenty-five minutes late after delays in South Wales we continued with great energy despite another couple of p-way slacks, and after a final 75mph at Ealing Broadway, after the Slough stop, were twenty minutes late into Paddington.

I paid what must have been my last 'steam' trip to Liverpool Street on 12 November. The 'Sandringhams' and even all the 'B1s' from the Great Eastern section had gone by then, but I wanted to travel on the 'Jazz' from Liverpool Street to Chingford and back on the last day before electrification. I went out behind 'N7' 69636, which was in excellent nick and looking smart, but the return was behind a rather less fetching 69674, which looked and sounded distinctly tired. During the turnaround at Chingford I observed Liverpool Street's GE blue pilot 'J69', 68619, arriving on a last-day RCTS special.

A week later, on 17 November, I undertook the first of several successful triangular trips to Bristol, then up the North & West to Shrewsbury and back to London via Birmingham. The 7.30am Paddington–Paignton via Bristol was one of the West of England trains still rostered for steam, and 7018 *Dryslwyn Castle*, by now transferred from Bath Road to Old Oak, was the motive power. Driver Green of Old Oak set off with energy, and by Slough 7018 was whisking its ten-coach, 355-ton train along at a full 80mph, although a p-way slack and signal checks made us six minutes late away from Reading. Speeds of 76mph before the Didcot stop and a steady 72 all the way up the Vale of the White Horse had reduced the deficit to two minutes by Swindon, but we then changed drivers, and the Swindon man appeared to lose interest, as we dropped five minutes on the run to Bristol, with only one signal check on the Bath–Bristol section to justify the loss. The rain was now pouring steadily as the 8 o'clock Plymouth–Liverpool, the Newton Abbot/Shrewsbury double-home job, came steaming around the curve into platform 4 at Temple Meads behind a gleaming Shrewsbury engine, 5095 *Barbury Castle*. I found an empty compartment in the first coach and prepared to enjoy myself as the 'Castle' stormed out of Bristol with no trace of a slip and thundered up the 1 in 75 to Filton with its eleven-coach, 410-ton train. A dash up to 81mph as we raced down towards the Severn Tunnel and then a steady staccato barking up the grades past Llantarnam at 44mph meant our three min-late departure from Bristol was turned into a seven min-early arrival at Pontypool Road. We continued in glorious fashion and completed the Hereford–Shrewsbury section in well under the hour, arriving at Shrewsbury more than thirteen minutes early. I calculated that we had gained forty-four minutes net on the schedule from Bristol, and the driver (G. Owen of Shrewsbury) said on arrival: 'She's on form, so we just let her run.' (See Appendix, Table 12.) The fact that the crew was on the last leg home of a two-day diagram might also have helped! From Shrewsbury 6922 *Burton Hall* of Oxford took the 4.30pm Birkenhead efficiently enough to Wolverhampton, whence 6024 — once more — took us back to London, doing its best between multiple p-way and signal checks, not to mention station overtime unloading mails, but arriving twelve minutes late. Speeds in the 80s at Knowle, Blackthorn (86), Denham and Greenford were evidence of our trying.

Another evening trip to Swindon, on 28 November, down on the '*Red Dragon*' with Canton's 5048 *Earl of Devon* and back with 7001 *Sir James Milne* (an Old Oak engine on a Landore diagram) was marred by the WR's continuing poor S&T performance, causing us to be twenty-six minutes late at Swindon and twenty late back at Paddington.

Problems in the Hayes/West Drayton area featured in many of my logs at around this time, and I therefore decided to try my luck on the East Coast. The previous year I'd gone to Peterborough two or three times to get runs behind the double-chimney 'A3s' now fitted with German-style smoke-deflectors — I'd had 60049, 60084, 60105 and 60111, which had all been impressive compared with my previous experience

166

of 'A3s' as single-chimney locomotives. On 3 December (a Saturday — we now had alternate Saturdays off) I caught the 10.20am King's Cross–Leeds train with Gateshead's 60040 *Cameronian* on thirteen coaches (480 tons gross). A minimum of 52mph with this load at Potters Bar was good, as was 89mph at Three Counties and 86 at Offord, and despite two p-way slacks and two signal checks we were three minutes early at Peterborough on the 90-minute schedule. I continued to Grantham, the train just holding 50mph at Stoke 'box and being four minutes early in. A Newcastle train now arrived with a rain- and dirt-streaked Gateshead 'A4' 60005 *Sir Charles Newton*, and we left fourteen minutes late, the engine hurling our twelve-coach 445-ton train up to 94mph at Essendine before coming to a signal stand outside Peterborough, in only 28½ minutes. We proceeded therefter at a more moderate pace and, without further fireworks, were eleven minutes late into King's Cross.

After Christmas I decided it was time I tried my hand at the Midland main line and its two-hour trains to Nottingham, so after working a Saturday morning I joined 45566 *Queensland* of Holbeck on the 2.10pm St Pancras–Nottingham. We had a manageable nine-coach load, 325 tons gross, and laboured to Elstree — 46mph there — but got going after Harlington and raced up to 85 at Flitwick, falling to 45 at Sharnbrook Summit. We passed Kettering in 75 minutes and travelled via Oakham and Melton Mowbray, but despite having plenty of steam and appearing to work hard 45566 wasn't up to it, and we were losing time; we arrived seven minutes late, having lost a net five minutes on the 126-minute schedule. On the return a Kentish Town 'Jubilee', 45561 *Saskatchewan*, appeared eight minutes late on the up '*Waverley*' from Edinburgh (6.4pm Nottingham) and made 45566 look brilliant in comparison; the fog of steam leaking from the front end was obvious, and the driver kept easing the engine. We ran for much of the way in the 50s and eventually arrived at St Pancras 37 minutes late, having dropped twenty-two minutes net on the 126-minute schedule. The driver said that the engine was not short of steam but was in an appalling condition and that he had had to keep easing in order to sight signals. Uphill it was atrocious; it was certainly not fit for the '*Waverley*'.

In February I managed to obtain footplate and brake-van passes from Western Region Headquarters, as I was intending to write a magazine article on the North & West. For various reasons I never got around to it. I did produce a draft but got told by a couple of other writers who looked at it that it was short on historical information or descriptions of the route; my piece was literary in style, full of personal impressions, which, frankly, with the benefit of hindsight, I feel might have been of more interest to some editors. After various trips, including a rough ride in an old LMS brake van on an overnight parcels train hauled by 'Standard 5' 73093, I had a most interesting and enjoyable all-day brake-van run behind 2-8-0 3837 on the 11am Alexandra Dock Junction Class H freight via the Eastern Valley to Pontypool Road and then via the North & West main line, finishing at Coton Hill, Shrewsbury, in the late afternoon. The GW 2-8-0 performed efficiently enough, but we spent long periods looped for passenger and parcel trains to overtake us.

The following day I had a superb footplate run on Newton Abbot's 4037 The *South Wales Borderers* on the double-home turn, the 8am Plymouth–Liverpool (with through

167

View from the brake van of the 11am Alexandra Dock Junction (Newport)–Coton Hill (Shrewsbury) freight ascending the bank up the Eastern Valley before Pontypool Road, hauled by Collett '2884' 2-8-0 3837, February 1961.

coach to Glasgow via the 'Midday Scot') between Pontypool Road and Shrewsbury — an experience covered more fully in the next chapter. I returned to Cardiff with one of the 1925-built 'Castles' behind which I'd not previously had a run, and despite an inordinate wait at Shrewsbury — the 12.15pm Manchester–Plymouth running ninety minutes late following a mishap at Sandbach, on the LMR just north of Crewe, where the overhead wires were down — I was pleased to get 4086 *Builth Castle*, of Canton (newly re-coded 88A). We had a 430-ton train and got no further than Bayston Hill before we were checked to walking pace on account of a freight dragging itself into the loop ahead. We recovered to 38mph at Church Stretton and with 78 at Onibury managed to hold schedule to Hereford. The fire was getting clinkered — the ninety-minute wait at Shrewsbury hadn't helped — and a special stop at Abergavenny to set down passengers extended our lateness to ninety-five minutes at Pontypool Road. I watched the Plymouth portion continue behind 4086 while pannier No 3655 picked up the three coaches bound for Cardiff. Despite the pannier's eagerness we suffered a broken signal wire at Panteg and yet another p-way slack at Maindee North Junction, which put our lateness over the magic 100 minute mark. I returned to London after another foray northwards, on the 8.55pm Birkenhead with Stafford Road double-chimney 5022 *Wigmore Castle* as far as Wolverhampton and 4075 *Cardiff Castle* (81A) thence via Oxford. I slept, exhausted, most of the way.

In April I made a Saturday trip to Stroud, but the 1.40pm Paddington produced a high-mileage and down-at-heel 5967 *Bickmarsh Hall*, which, with a load of nearly 400 tons, was wholly unable to cope with a 'three star' timing and lost twenty minutes to Swindon, where 7000 *Viscount Portal* took over the five coaches for Gloucester. The return journey was very different, 7037 *Swindon* — transferred, for its last couple of years, from Swindon to Old Oak Common — setting a rousing pace, climbing to Sapperton Summit with its 325-ton load at a minimum of 34mph and achieving 83 on the level at Wantage Road and 81 at Maidenhead after the Reading stop. Despite a six min-late departure from Stroud an on-time arrival looked probable until two p-way slacks and two signal checks on the last leg put paid to that ambition.

I took some time off main-line runs in early April; I realised that I'd ignored steam-hauled local services and decided to put that right by travelling from Paddington to Bourne End, High Wycombe and Princes Risborough via the Western and returning to Marylebone, before both commuter services were entirely converted to DMU operation. 6169 (81A), the last numerically of the Paddington suburban '61xx' class, performed on the 5.42pm Paddington–High Wycombe with eight non-corridor coaches (280 tons gross) and reached its first stop at West Drayton in 19 minutes, just nudging 60mph. At Bourne End I got out to take a branch trip on the 'Marlow Donkey' and was pleased to be invited into the cab of the push-pull trailer and return on the footplate of 0-4-2T 1453, although I was surprised at how 'rough riding' it seemed — due, most likely, to the state of the track rather than the engine, although she was fairly near her next works visit, which she survived. At High Wycombe I transferred to Neasden's Fairburn 2-6-4T 42282 for a trip to Princes Risborough — and a noisy climb (45mph minimum) to Saunderton with its six coaches — and returned to Marylebone with another Neasden LM tank, 42089, which stopped at all stations punctually until West Ruislip, then just touched 59mph at Neasden before standing outside the terminus and finishing four minutes late.

At Easter I joined other teenagers and members of our church youth club in a youth-hostelling weekend on the Isle of Wight. On the Saturday we took the train from Ryde Pier to Sandown behind 'O2' 0-4-4T W17 *Seaview* and spent the night there — my first experience of listening to a dozen men and youths snoring in unison the whole night long. On Easter Day we hiked over the cliffs to Ventnor, and on the Bank Holiday Monday we walked the closed line from Ventnor to Newport, threading our way through the disused Whitwell Tunnel. We returned from Newport to Ryde Pier behind W33 *Bembridge*. Inspired by this brief acquaintance with the Island's railway, I went back on my own a month later and just travelled from Ryde Pier Head to Shanklin and back — out with W14 *Fishbourne* and back with W16 *Ventnor*. This was the first of many solo trips I made to the Isle of Wight before the demise of steam in 1966.

Seen from the train to Sandown, hauled by W17 *Seaview*, W33 *Bembridge* arrives at Ryde Pier Head in April 1961.

Following my earlier success with the North & West triangular tour I decided to have another go on 17 April and joined the 7.30am Paddington, headed by 5043 *Earl of Mount Edgcumbe* (81A) on ten coaches (370 tons gross). In terms of punctuality this trip proved to be the reverse of that with 7018 — we managed to lose eighteen minutes to Swindon, with just one severe p-way check, at Taplow, and a minute's delay at Scours Lane, as we'd left Reading with a door open. The Bristol driver after Swindon showed us nothing was wrong with the engine, and we went out of Swindon like a bat out of hell, hitting 92mph at Dauntsey and 80 already by Box after a Corsham stop, reaching Bristol ten minutes late. On this Monday morning the 8 o'clock Plymouth had Newton Abbot's 5024 *Carew Castle* on twelve coaches (440 tons gross), and to my surprise we swung east at Filton Junction and made our way to Westerleigh Junction and up the Midland line to Gloucester, touching 77mph at Charfield before a 15mph slack at Berkeley Road. At Standish Junction we crossed to the WR line and made our way around to Gloucester Central, where we waited for half an hour on the middle road for an assisting engine, 6941 *Fillongley Hall* (85B), to help us over the speed-restricted branch to Hereford. We'd been diverted because weekend resignalling work at Maindee Junction, Newport, was overrunning badly. At Grange Court Junction we stood for twenty minutes waiting for the corresponding

Woking Methodist Church Youth Club walking the line from Ventnor to Newport,
Easter Monday 1961.

southbound train with 5095 to come off the single line, while at Mitcheldean Road
we had to wait to cross 4115 on the branch passenger service. We observed 5mph
speed restrictions at a number of places, including Ross-on-Wye and Ballingham
Tunnel, and eventually crept a full hour and a half late into Hereford, where 6941 was
detached. 5024 at last set off at a normal pace and covered the Hereford–Shrewsbury
section in 63 minutes net, with 49 minima of at Onibury, 34 at Little Stretton and 80
at Dorrington. We were still ninety minutes late into Shrewsbury. 5971 *Merevale Hall*
got me back to Wolverhampton, where 6002 *King William IV* took over, managing to
lose twenty-six minutes on the run to London, with p-way slacks and signal checks
at Tyseley, Hatton, Fenny Compton, High Wycombe, West Ruislip, South Ruislip and
Westbourne Park. How could a railway run this way?

I persuaded my college friend Alistair Wood to join me on the Saturday '*Pembroke
Coast Express*' on 22 April, and all looked good when we discovered we had one
of Landore's best 'Castles', recently ex works with double chimney, 7028 *Cadbury
Castle*. With only two extra coaches, making ten (375 tons gross), we should have had
no difficulty, but we proceeded to lose time against the advertised schedule while
dribbling along at 65mph, blowing off steam furiously, exhaust inaudible, and arrived
at Newport seventeen minutes late by the booked time but apparently on time, as the

171

smug driver told me, by the revised Saturday time adjusted (but unadvertised to the public) for the extra load. As far as the public was concerned we were late, and frankly I thought the driver's attitude disgraceful, for the engine demonstrated that it could easily have maintained the proper schedule.

Once we were in Wales it poured relentlessly with rain, and we consoled ourselves with a sprightly run behind pannier 9664 of Newport on the 3pm Newport–Brecon as far as Maesycwmmer, where we arrived two minutes early. We came back with lined-green 2236 on a similar three-coach train, just beating the point-to-point times, which appeared to leave little margin for the sharp curves around which we squealed, still in the pouring rain. I hoped we might do a bit better on the up '*Pembroke Coast Express*', and we left Newport with 5014 *Goodrich Castle* (81A) on 11 coaches — 405 tons. Two p-way slacks and signals on the Welsh side of the Severn Tunnel made us seven minutes late by Patchway, and then the Duke of Beaufort exercised his legal right to stop us specially at Badminton to pick up passengers attending the horse trials. By Wootton Bassett we were twenty-two minutes late, but now, at last, we got going, with a steady 74mph down the Vale of the White Horse, and with only one more p-way slack and two signal checks we were able to recover some time and reached Paddington fifteen minutes late.

Some reassurance on Western performance was now necessary — after all, I now worked for the outfit — and I tried again in mid-May, taking an evening trip to Banbury and back. On the outward run, on the 5.10pm Paddington, Stafford Road's 6006 *King George I*, with thirteen coaches, did well enough in the hands of Driver Priest, attaining 50 on the climb to Saunderton and 86 at Haddenham, while on the 2.35pm Birkenhead 5036 *Lyonshall Castle* (81A), with with eleven coaches and Driver Townsend of Banbury, did even better, maintaining perfect punctuality despite a p-way slack, to 20mph, at Blackthorn, where we should have been doing 80. We touched 88 through Denham, and despite a signal stand at North Acton we arrived back in London half a minute early. I tried the 5.10 again a week later, with Stafford Road's 5047 *Earl of Dartmouth* deputising for a failed 'King' (6011) and Driver Morris (who would be killed a couple of years later while driving a 'Western' diesel involved in a collision with a crane jib that was fouling the loading gauge). The 465-ton load (142 tons overloaded on a four-star timing for a 'Castle') was really too much, but it sounded as though it was being driven flat out, speed falling to 32mph at Saunderton but reaching 77 at Haddenham, a deficit of ten minutes at Princes Risborough (following a p-way slack at West Ruislip) being reduced to six minutes by Banbury. 6025 *King Henry III* (81A) was early on the return journey, despite some rather curious uneven driving by the Banbury crew.

At the end of May it was the custom for the office to enjoy a free day out, and an extra coach (along with crates of beer) was added to a 'Warship'-hauled express to Weston-super-Mare, whence we took a paddle-steamer to Cardiff. Most participants were well into their cups by the return trip, and I got some very odd looks as I tried to time the return run from Cardiff to Paddington with Landore's 5006 *Tregenna Castle* on the 2.30pm Neyland. I did manage to time it, recording a steady run with the eleven-coach train, which left Newport five minutes late after signal checks at Gaer

Junction. However, there was station overtime at every stop, and we were ten minutes late at Paddington despite a maximum of 78mph on the level at Didcot.

On Saturday 3 June I decided on an afternoon trip to Evesham and back to see how Worcester's 'Castles' were faring. 7027 *Thornbury Castle* on the 12.45pm Paddington got horribly delayed by the Ramsgate–Birkenhead (the 'Conti') at Reading and Oxford and left the latter station fifteen minutes late, but thereafter we made mincemeat of the easy schedule, and, with 82 down Chipping Campden Bank, we were only three minutes late into Evesham. No 7006 *Lydford Castle* was on the 1.50pm Hereford with just eight coaches and, after leaving Evesham five minutes late, ran hard to Oxford, accelerating from a 25mph slack at Honeybourne to 42 before the summit at Chipping Campden Tunnel, then 80 after Charlbury. The run was non-stop from Oxford in 68 minutes (63 minutes net), and arrival precisely on time.

The 1961 Summer Timetable was now in operation, and my thoughts turned to what could well be the last steam services to the West of England via the Berks & Hants. On Saturday 10 June I joined the 9.18am Paddington–Paignton — No 4078 *Pembroke Castle* (81A) with eleven coaches (380 tons) and Driver Harris of Exeter. We left a couple of minutes late and took things easily until a 15mph p-way slowing at Slough, but the driver seemed reluctant to take the loco much over 65mph — he complained it was roughriding and due for shopping. We climbed energetically to Brewham at 53mph, but 70mph at Charlton Mackrell was our highest speed, and the usual Summer Saturday checks put us eighteen minutes behind time at Clink Road Junction. A 43mph minimum at Whiteball was good after a slowing through Taunton to 12mph, and we lost no further time to Paignton, despite severe p-way slacks at Cowley Bridge and Teignmouth.

After a cold and drizzly reunion with the Paignton station remembered from my teenage years I found that the 1.50pm Kingswear–Exeter local was being extended through to London as a relief, so I joined 2-6-2T 4165 (83C) on ten coaches to Exeter which took a '41xx' banker at Torre and achieved a creditable 66mph at Exminster. At St Davids we swapped 4165 for 4930 *Hagley Hall* (83C) and an Exeter driver, Gater, and set off enthusiastically, managing a minimum of 47mph at Whiteball and 83 down the bank at Wellington. After gaining three minutes to Taunton we left there eleven minutes late and ran steadily through the now glorious sunny afternoon, gradually picking up time. Recovery time approaching Reading reduced the deficit to four minutes, although a p-way slack at Slough and a signal check at Iver prevented us from regaining any more time.

On 17 June I had a last try at experiencing a 'Nelson' achieving 80mph and nearly made it — 30861 *Lord Anson* on the Saturdays-only 12.22pm Waterloo–Bournemouth even raced the 'Belle' around Fleet, when we surged to 73mph as we tried to hold it as it passed us on the main. Leaving Basingstoke was painfully slow, but once past Wootton 'box things looked up, as we kept steam on down the gradient and touched 78 — my highest in 383 runs with the class — at Shawford. We arrived on time at Southampton, so I shouldn't carp. (See Appendix, Table 6.)

On 24 June — a scorching-hot day, in contrast with the weather two weeks earlier — I decided to try another full day in the West Country and arrived at Paddington in time to catch the thirteen-coach 8.25am to Penzance, headed by Old Oak double-chimney 'Castle' 5056 *Earl of Powis*. Driver Webber of Laira got the heavy load (500 tons gross) on the move after a signal check had slowed us to walking pace before we'd even passed Subway Junction, and we sustained the low 70s all the way from West Drayton to Reading, where we were brought to a stand by a tardy DMU entering the diesel depot. A nasty p-way slowing at Hungerford interrupted our climb to Savernake, which we passed at a hard-working 51mph, and we had just reached 79 after Patney when we were brought to a halt at Heywood Road Junction, where we stood for nearly ten minutes. We then crawled around the Westbury cut-off before stopping at Brewham to take water. We had clearly joined a queue of trains. After an eight-minute stand whatever was in front gave us space to stretch our legs, and 5056 got the heavy load going well, achieving a maximum of 83mph at Langport before we caught up with more trains, which had doubtless joined us at Cogload Junction en route from Bristol and Birmingham. We sailed through Taunton at 60 but got an awkward 20mph signal check at Wellington, and we did well to accelerate from this, topping the summit at Whiteball Tunnel at 31mph. Having free-wheeled down through Tiverton Junction in the low 70s, we were checked through Exeter and had another signal stand on the sea wall approaching Teignmouth, as we were obviously following something that was stopping there. At Newton Abbot, now four and a half hours from London, we acquired as pilot North British B-B diesel D6327, which didn't seem of much help on Dainton or Rattery, as 5056 appeared to be doing most of the work. Speed fell to 16mph at Dainton and 20 at Tigley 'box before we stopped at Brent for the Kingsbridge branch. The coup de grâce was a six-minute signal stop at the bottom of Hemerdon Bank, and we drew into Plymouth North Road just over half an hour late.

As there was no obvious steam train back on the Western route I took the three-coach 2.33pm Plymouth–Waterloo via Okehampton behind unrebuilt 'West Country' 34030 *Watersmeet*. This was driven surprisingly hard with — according to my notes — a lot of noise and soot, producing a surprising 80mph at North Tawton, but a p-way slack after Crediton made us five minutes late into Exeter St Davids. There I joined a Paignton–Wolverhampton train with 5075 *Wellington* (83C), leaving twenty-five minutes late and suffering signal checks at Cullompton, Tiverton Junction, Wellington and a dead stand at Poole sidings, so we were twenty-nine late at Taunton, where I alighted. I now awaited the last up Kingswear with trepidation — it was appearing quite often with a 'Warship' now — and was delighted to get a 'new' 'Castle', 4077 *Chepstow Castle* (82B) on an eleven-coach rake (390 tons) and driven by Driver Weekes of Exeter. We left Taunton nine minutes late and ran steadily without any fireworks or high speeds (upper 60s most of the way) and were surprisingly unchecked until the Reading area and then a signal failure at Southall. We arrived in London eleven minutes late. It could have been a lot worse.

A week later I tried the 12.0 Paddington–Plymouth with 7037 *Swindon* (81A), twelve coaches (430 tons) and Driver Watts of Old Oak. A p-way slowing and four signal checks before Reading made us twelve minutes late there, and I feared the worst. Reading station staff recovered a couple of minutes, and then we set off down the Berks & Hants, gradually recovering more time despite the quantity of black smoke and smuts (the coal was slack and ovoids). With a 48mph minimum at Savernake and 50 at Brewham — but nothing over 76 elsewhere — our lateness was down to four minutes at Castle Cary, and at Taunton we were actually nearly two minutes early by the public timetable. I went through to Exeter and returned to Taunton behind a Tyseley engine, 6855 *Saighton Grange*, on the 3.5pm Paignton–Wolverhampton and then got 'Warship' D801 on the last up Kingswear. That left Taunton fifteen late and got to Paddington, virtually unchecked, four minutes late, but my feeling was that it could have done a lot better — most of the running was indistinguishable from 4077's the previous week. The highest speed achieved was 75mph (momentarily) at Athelney and again after Witham; the rest of the time we cruised in the 60s. Apparently one engine had failed the previous day, and I suspect we were running on one engine throughout.

Ten days later I went for an evening trip to Peterborough and caught the 6.12pm Leeds express behind Copley Hill 'A1' 60133 *Pommern*. We took exactly the 80 minutes scheduled, without any fireworks or any undue alarms, and it was surprising not to get an '80' on the East Coast racing stretch after Hitchin. At Peterborough the last up Hull turned up with Grantham double-chimney 'A3' 60105 *Victor Wild*, which gave a super run with its nine-coach, 318-ton train. A 66mph minimum at Leys Summit was followed by a rousing acceleration to 89mph on the slightly rising gradients through Biggleswade and Arlesey, a minimum of 72 at Stevenage and another 83 at Welwyn North before we caught something up and took it easy for the remainder of the run to King's Cross, where we arrived four minutes early, in a net time of 69 minutes for the 76 miles.

I spent my 1961 summer holiday at the Lindors Methodist Guild House near St Briavels, in late July tramping the Forest of Dean with many fellow students. I'd gone down to Gloucester on the 11.15am with a pair of 'Halls' to Reading, where 5987 left us, leaving 6960 *Raveningham Hall* (81D) to struggle to Swindon, reached seventeen minutes late. Here we dropped three coaches for Bristol and continued with nine coaches, just about maintaining the booked schedule and arriving sixteen minutes late at Gloucester, where I found a Llanelli engine, 6843 *Poulton Grange*, surprisingly on the local to Lydney. 6843 reappeared the following week to take me back to Gloucester, and that city's beloved 'Castle', 5017 *The Gloucestershire Regiment 28th 61st*, took me back to London very efficiently — early at every single stop and a maximum speed 75mph at Steventon with our eleven-coach, 405-ton train.

On 26 July I went down to Peterborough again — on the 6.26pm King's Cross–Hull this time, behind Grantham 'A3' 60046 *Diamond Jubilee*. Speeds of 81-85mph between Hitchin and Biggleswade ensured a three min-early arrival at Huntingdon, and another 80 at Connington gave us a two min-early arrival in Peterborough. The last up Hull had another Grantham double-chimney 'A3', 60064 *Tagalie*, which, unchecked, arrived seven minutes early at King's Cross on an easy 87-minute schedule. We displayed some energy as far as Hitchin, touching 83 at Sandy, then took it very easily, drifting to around 60-65mph the rest of the way.

175

The following Saturday I decided to experiment with a day on the Great Central main line and joined the seven-coach 12.25pm Marylebone–Nottingham behind 73053 of Neasden. It was a pretty undistinguished effort, managing only the low 30s on the climb to Amersham and nothing over 68 on the rest of the journey. I gave up at Rugby, having decided to chance my arm on one of the Saturday holiday services, and picked up Darnall 'B1' 61138 on the Saturdays-only 10.14am Hastings–Sheffield Victoria —a well-filled eleven-coach train, 385 tons gross — which was much more enterprising and touched 75mph between the Lutterworth and Leicester stops. At Loughborough I decided to try another, similar holiday train and got another 'B1', 61265, on the 11.38am Brighton–Sheffield. My return, on the 5.15pm Nottingham, was with another filthy Neasden Standard, 73158, on a light (six-coach) train, which largely recovered from a ten min-late departure from Aylesbury, after various signal and p-way checks, to reach Marylebone just two minutes late.

Being a glutton for punishment, I determined to try the Berks & Hants on a summer Saturday again, especially when I saw that one of my favourite 'Castles', 5008 *Raglan Castle* (81A), was booked to the 12.0 to Plymouth. It was a heavy, thirteen-coach train weighing 485 tons gross, and we started inauspiciously, ten minutes late. Once we got going it became clear that 5008 was in fine fettle, and we picked up a couple of minutes to Reading, managing 72 on the level through Slough, and the deficit had been reduced to six minutes by the time we passed Bedwyn, before braking at Savernake to 52mph. A p-way slack to 30mph at Lavington prevented anything above 72 there, and we caught up the Summer Saturday queue at Brewham 'box after a splendid climb (minimum 54mph). Unfortunately further signal checks meant we were twenty-five minutes late into Taunton. Rather than go through to Exeter I decided to take a very late-running Wolverhampton–Ilfracombe service, onto which backed an attractive lined-green Mogul, 6372, of Taunton. It left forty-six minutes late and recovered three minutes before Dulverton after a lively 64mph at Morebath. I had to return immediately and picked up a four-coach local with Collett 0-6-0 2240, which left Dulverton eight minutes late (awaiting 1468 on the Exe Valley train) and arrived at Taunton fifteen seconds before time, with a suprising 60mph between the Venn Cross and Wiveliscombe stops. Then it was another drab run home with No D843 *Sharpshooter*, which proved anything but sharp, leaving Taunton ten minutes late and arriving at Paddington thirteen late, a two-minute stand at Newbury Racecourse and a p-way slack to 25mph at Slough being the only excuses. Most of the way we were travelling at 60-65mph, and I strongly suspect we were running on one engine again.

Yet another trip to Peterborough followed on 2 August, 'A1' 60118 *Archibald Sturrock* (56C) losing five minutes on the 80-minute schedule, with just one p-way slack to 20mph at Oakleigh Park. The return, with another double-chimney 'A3,' was much better. 60077 *The White Knight* (56C) had twelve coaches (435 tons) on a Bradford–London express and followed a late-running '*Heart of Midlothian*' out of Peterborough. After a 20mph p-way slack at Yaxley the 'A3' was opened up, and, having slowed to 72mph around the Offord curve, we built up speed against the collar, hitting 82 at Biggleswade. We were then stopped and asked by the signalman to examine the down line and drew into Hitchin five minutes late in consequence. A brisk run onward to London picked up three minutes, and on arrival the driver described the 'A3' as 'a real clipper'.

I'd gone down to Swindon on the Friday before the 1961 August Bank Holiday, travelling behind 5066 *Sir Felix Pole* a relief South Wales express. I was hanging around the station to see what might be about on the up road when one of the huge Churchward 2-8-0s, 4708, came off shed and ran through the station, coming to a stand on the London side of the up platform. I assumed it was going for a freight, but I just wondered with a glimmer of hope … A few minutes later a relief from the Gloucester line appeared behind one of the spanking-new 'Hymeks', D7003. I was about to ignore it when I noticed a shunter drop down between loco and train and begin to uncouple the 'Hymek'. Surely not, I could scarce believe it … was 4708 going to replace the 'Hymek'? I watched with bated breath as D7003 cut away and ran briskly into the distance and saw with growing excitement that 4708 was stirring into life and was beginning to back down onto the eight-coach train.

My mind was made up — I had longed for a run behind one of these superb locos, trying to get one on a Saturday West of England relief but always in vain. The previous year I'd gone to Taunton on the 1.25pm Paddington–Kingswear and had seen No 4706 back onto the following '*Royal Duchy*', but unfortunately that service was barred to staff with privilege tickets. However, nothing could prevent me from joining the service at Taunton and taking it as far as Exeter, where I could pick up the last London service — the 1.50pm Penzance. So I waited and waited and waited. It was indicated thirty late, then forty, then a full hour, and in the end I abandoned the wait and took a heavy Cardiff–Paignton train with 6921, only to arrive at Exeter just as the Penzance was departing with ex-works Laira 'Castle' 5058 *Earl of Clancarty*, so I had to return home via the last train on the Southern route behind 35014 *Nederland Line*.

4708 justified the wait. The lined-green monster (how suitable those projected names like *Behemoth* or *Leviathan* would have been) started slowly, then accelerated steadily until we were charging through Didcot at 75mph. After the Reading stop 4708 erupted, and we accelerated at extraordinary speed, rousing the echoes through Sonning Cutting until we were travelling at a full 80mph just beyond Ruscombe sidings. A magic moment — well … two actually: when I saw for real that 4708 was going to back onto our train at Swindon, and at Ruscombe, when I recorded 80mph, just before the driver decided that perhaps this speed was unnecessary — and illegal; I found out subsequently that the Swindon driver did not realise that these engines were restricted to 60mph! (The full log appears in the Appendix, Table 13.) Just a few weeks later, when I was commuting from Reading to Maidenhead daily, instead of the usual Didcot 'County' or 'Modified Hall' my train turned up behind Old Oak's 4701. You wait for ages, and then two come along at once …

Not content with this, I turned up on the Saturday at King's Cross and found 60014 *Silver Link* (34A) on the Saturday '*Elizabethan*' — first stop Newcastle. I looked at my meagre cash, took a deep breath and bought myself a 'priv' return to Newcastle and ensconced myself in the twelve-coach, 475-ton train. (I learned later that 60014 had been the Top Shed standby engine — we should have had Haymarket's 60031 on the '*Elizabethan*' turn, but this had failed on shed.) We left on time, and speed built up after Hitchin until I recorded a full 90mph at Three Counties. With a long p-way slack to 20mph through Holme to Yaxley we passed Peterborough in 80 minutes from London, climbed Stoke with a minimum of 56mph and passed through Grantham in 111 minutes. From Doncaster the weather deteriorated rapidly to heavy rain, and our performance similarly, as we were badly checked before York, then at Northallerton a freight was crossing in front of us, and at Darlington a DMU afficted us similarly. Running when possible in the mid-70s got us to Newcastle nine minutes late, in 311 minutes from King's Cross but just 277 minutes net.

At Newcastle the relief to the up '*Heart of Midlothian*' acquired Gateshead 'A4' 60020 *Guillemot*, and I took that to York, the filthy 'Streak' completing the 44-mile 'racing' stretch from Darlington to York in 44 minutes exactly, with a sustained 84mph after Thirsk, with the twelve-coach, 445-ton train. I decided to change at York to the '*Heart of Midlothian*' itself, for I'd seen a Kings Cross 'A4' waiting on the King Edward Bridge, and 60026 *Miles Beevor* was a new one for me. The train was thirteen coaches (485 tons gross), and we actually departed York three minutes early! After Grantham we accelerated to 48mph by Stoke Tunnel and, after touching 84 at Essendine, ran hard in the mid-70s from Huntingdon to Hitchin, then eased up considerably, as we were running very early on the Saturday schedule. We arrived at King's Cross just under ten minutes early.

I now had my first free Continental pass to enjoy, and on 15 August I took the Newhaven boat train from Victoria behind Southern electric loco 20003. From Dieppe I travelled to Paris behind a 'Chapelonised' État Pacific and continued to Lake Constance via Strasbourg and the Black Forest, steam all the way (to be described in detail in the next volume). My aim was to spend a couple of days renewing my acquaintance with the Lindau-based former Bavarian four-cylinder Compound Pacifics (the famous 'S 3/6' Pacifics that had hauled the '*Rheingold*' in the 1920s and '30s). After a highly successful trip I returned a week later and experienced an appalling Channel crossing in a Force 10 gale, when I saw even sailors being seasick. This was the only time I've ever succumbed, and I can vouch that you cease to worry about the boat going down when you actually feel suicidal. I was still hanging out of the window, feeling sick, as we returned to Victoria behind electric E5010.

I had one last major weekend tour before the next chapter of my life began. I'd had my appetite whetted by the Saturday '*Elizabethan*' and wanted to try the non-stop mid-week run. I therefore came to King's Cross on 1 September to find Haymarket's 60009 *Union of South Africa* on duty with Driver McKinley (substituting for Driver Hooper, who was ill) and Fireman Wilson as far as Alne, there exchanging, through the corridor tender, with Driver Porteous of Haymarket. The weekday load was ten coaches, 380 tons gross. We ran the 392.5 miles in 392 minutes 30 seconds exactly, arriving two and a half minutes early. Highlights were 88mph at Three Counties, 92mph at Hougham and a time of 118 minutes from Newcastle to Edinburgh, with speeds of 85mph at Christon Bank, 61 at Grantshouse and a steady 80 from Drem into the outskirts of Edinburgh. 60009 was a month ex works and in obviously good nick. Net time was 370 minutes overall.

I continued to Glasgow Queen Street behind a very run-down and filthy 'A3', 60076 *Galopin* of Darlington, which just about got its lightweight, five-coach train to Glasgow in reasonable shape (speed in the 50s most of the way), but the schedule was so easy. That evening I intended to catch the Fridays-only 8.55pm Glasgow Central sleeper service to Euston as far as Carlisle before returning to Edinburgh via the Waverley route and got Polmadie's 46232 *Duchess of Montrose* on the twelve-coach, 445-ton train. We cleared Beattock Summit at 41mph and had a curious run, our speed rising suddenly from the low 60s to the high 70s and then dropping again as the driver opened up and then shut off, and we were 3 minutes late in after a signal check outside Carlisle station. A classic engine change took place at Carlisle, 46232 being replaced by 46206 *Princess Marie Louise*. I was sorely tempted to abandon my Waverley plans, but I satisfied myself with a shot of the 'Princess' at the head of the sleeping-car train.

Carlisle as dusk fell on a Friday in summer was a fascinating and atmospheric place to be — I think only Carlisle and Crewe were more interesting by night than by day. I therefore watched the night working until the 9.10pm sleeper from St Pancras arrived behind 'Peak' D11, a poor exchange for 46206. I took this to Galashiels, where I spied a 'B1' waiting to follow it with a semi-fast for Edinburgh, so I hopped out and took my seat in an empty compartment, feeling the steam heat ooze through from 61221 *Sir Alexander Erskine-Hill* of St Margarets. Then it was back to King's Cross after the sleepless night, initially behind Haymarket 'A3' 60094 *Colorado* on the

Awaiting departure from Edinburgh Waverley on 2 September 1961, locally allocated 'A3' 60094 *Colorado* has charge of the 10.10am Edinburgh–King's Cross, which it will work as far as Newcastle.

10.10am Edinburgh–King's Cross (see Appendix Table 16). We had a heavy, thirteen-coach load (500 tons gross), and 60094 did well to hold 33mph on the climb to Grantshouse, which it followed with a maximum of 82mph at Beal after the Berwick stop. We were on time at Newcastle, where we exchanged 60094 for an ex-works Heaton 'A1', 60147 *North Eastern*, which was heavily delayed at Northallerton but then whisked the heavy train up to 83 at Tollerton. I decided to pause at York and get some food and then picked up the Saturday relief to the '*Heart of Midlothian*' (1.10pm Edinburgh), which arrived at York with the home depot's 60138 *Boswell*. This ran punctually to Grantham without any strenuous effort. 'A3' 60063 *Isinglass* (34A) was waiting for us at Grantham and whirled us down Stoke Bank at 93mph below Essendine and continued without hindrance to London, where we arrived seven minutes early.

During the spring I had duly applied for the Traffic Apprenticeship scheme and as a staff entrant, and, having taken the exam and passed the interview, I was ready to start in the autumn of 1961. However, in the interim, after nine months or so in my first clerical job, I'd applied for promotion to a Class 3 post in the Freight Train Office, where I was in charge of special and out-of-gauge loads, a subject on which I knew virtually nothing, but apparently I was the only serious applicant for the post, so I was appointed. My boss was astounded, telling me that it had taken him twenty-five years to get his first promotion from Class 5 clerk (a grade long since abolished) to a Class 4!

Although my new office was next door to the Passenger Train Office the culture was as different as could be. The practice in the Passenger Office was to work hard and play hard — when we had a lot to do we knuckled down, took short lunch breaks and worked until everything was done without claiming overtime; when things were slack we took longer breaks and went home when everything was finished for the day. There was a lot of interplay and banter between staff — including a degree of black humour when we were under pressure — and a lot of laughter.

In the Freight Office everyone watched the clock and tried to look occupied, whether or not there was work to do. Throughout the day silence reigned; you could hear the occasional rustle of papers. The phones seldom rang — in the Passenger Office they never seemed to be silent. At one minute to five o'clock everyone would rise and put on their overcoats, and at five o'clock precisely the room would be empty. One day I had a bout of hay fever or some allergy for which I was prescribed anti-histamine tablets, with a warning that they could make me drowsy. I duly turned up to work, and within half an hour my head was down and I fell into a deep sleep. I woke at midday, and no-one had noticed — or at least, if anyone had, no-one said anything. I had a desk in the corner of the room, so I was not too conspicuous, but even so … I was not happy in this atmosphere, and it was with some relief that I commenced my management training, less than three months after promotion to this section.

Tableau 7

Paddington Platform 8, July 1961

The Divisional Operating Manager is getting heavily criticised for the long delays encountered by holiday trains returning to London on summer Saturdays. After struggling up from the West Country or West Wales the coup de grâce is frequently the inordinate delay incurred within sight of Paddington station, because all the arrival platforms are occupied. This had been a feature of the 1960 summer season, when too many arrivals were recorded on the station indicator as 99 minutes late (the maximum the two-digit slats could allow). The 1961 holiday season has started badly, and in early July I'm asked by the Assistant Divisional Operating Manager if I'll be prepared to spend the afternoon, from 12 noon onwards, on overtime, recording the occupation of Paddington platforms and noting as far as possible the length of time that trains are held outside the station, awaiting a platform. I'm to join the train-spotters at the end of platform 8 and be paid for it, because of my apparent prowess at drawing graphs and generally presenting neat and readable reports. I am not only to record all this data but also to chart the platform occupation, noting all light-engine and ECS movements.

I find I am to be joined by 'Terry', the London Division DMU and local-train diagrammer, as on summer Saturdays he has to replace certain DMUs with engines and coaches — partly as a result of reduced weekend availability, as the depot staff take advantage to undertake planned maintenance outside the peak commuter weekday times, and partly because the increased passenger loadings are expected to exceed the capacity of a four-car DMU. He is nervous because he has not retimed the DMU replacements but has banked on 'Halls' pulling eight-coach non-corridor sets keeping to the diesel-unit schedules. 'They run better when we have high expectations of them' was his opinion. I certainly had found the reverse to be true on my Saturday trips on the '*Pembroke Coast Express*', when timings were eased in the Working Timetable to allow for increased loads, only for drivers to make no attempt to keep to the published timetable, despite having good engines with steam to spare.

The majority of traffic in the up direction on a summer Saturday is, of course, from the West of England, whence trains are dominated by the Maybach-engined, Swindon-built 'Warship' diesel-hydraulics. Some of the North British-built, MAN-engined, Voith-transmission locomotives are beginning to appear, but few are yet in evidence. No 'Hymeks' or 'Westerns' have yet arrived on the scene. However, only the key trains, the regular Penzance/Plymouth, Kingswear and Weston-super-

Mare/Bristol trains, are diesel-hauled. Most of the Summer Saturday extras are still steam, interspersed between the diesels, and all have to go at the speed of the slowest, as the frequency of trains on the route is intense, hampered as far as Cogload Junction by numerous holiday trains to the West and East Midlands and the Liverpool/Manchester area, nearly all steam-hauled, at least as far as Bristol.

Of course, I take an interest in the departing trains also, although I'm not required to record them, as departing trains do not interfere with arriving trains. (Not until after the complete resignalling planned for 1966 will all platforms be regularly used for arriving and departing trains.) The first train likely to be of interest (to me) is the 12noon Paddington–Kingswear, booked for an 81A 'Castle' but frequently hauled by a 'Modified Hall' and a occasionally by a '47xx' 2-8-0. Today it is indeed a 'Castle' (rather than a '47xx', which is a pity), but although I observe departures I am sufficiently occupied taking notes of just the arrivals, for I'm required to record the time of each terminating train, the platform number and whether the train is held outside the station (I can see a couple of signals out as far as Subway Junction), as well as timing the '87xx', '94xx', '15xx' pannier tanks or '61xx' Prairies attached to the ECS and noting the departure times of the ECS for Old Oak carriage sidings and of the trailing locomotive — and whether the latter goes attached to the ECS to Old Oak or reverses light-engine across to Ranelagh Bridge.

I'm kept extremely busy, for it is not long before the procession of trains approaching after morning departures from the West begins to build up. The 8am Kingswear has a 'Warship' and is reasonably punctual, and a Minehead follows it in behind a Laira double-chimney 'Castle', but the following Paignton — a heavy

5922 *Caxton Hall* on a local passenger train in the London Division, 1952.
(Gordon Coltas Trust, J. M. Bentley collection)

train with a St Philip's Marsh 'Hall' — is not doing well and is preceded by trains from Worcester and Wolverhampton and the '*Red Dragon*' from Swansea, this last with a beautifully turned-out double-chimney 'Castle', 4080 *Powderham Castle*, by now based at Canton. The gap before the 'Hall' arrives enables platforms 6-11 to be cleared ready for the rush, which soon comes. The trouble is that the trains are stacked up behind the late-runner, so, to avoid holding up following trains, the six platforms are allowed to fill before the locomotives for the ECS movements can be attached. Then, by the time the tank engines have been attached, brakes have been tested and 'right away' to Old Oak given, there are already trains waiting at both signals I can see. This continues for at least a couple of hours.

Terry has one bright spot when a '61xx' tank, with its eight non-corridor coaches, scurries amid the DMUs and Hammersmith Line tube trains into platform 13 only a couple of minutes late. Then, mid-afternoon, there is a slight lull, and Paddington signalling staff manage to clear three platfoms so that the next trains run in under clear signals or are only momentarily delayed outside whilst an ECS cuts across the the carriage line to Old Oak or the released locomotive backs out to Ranelagh Bridge. I do not record the engine numbers, only the train reporting numbers, which I will try to tie up with the scheduled services next Monday morning when I'm drawing up my magnum opus for the bosses. One memory I will retain is of the unimpeded arrival at platform 7 of 4037 *The South Wales Borderers* with what purports to be an extra from Treherbert, though I'm highly dubious, as a Newton Abbot 'Castle' on such a train seems unlikely, although on a summer Saturday almost anything is possible. I thought 4037 was still active on the North & West (see next chapter). If indeed it is the Treherbert it's early — a most unlikely scenario at this time of the day! The engine carries no reporting headcode to aid me, and I can't trace any other train that might be the relief shown in the extra weekend supplement to the Working Timetable with which I've been issued.

As the situation eases and teatime approaches, a DMU-replacement semi-fast from Reading rushes into platform 6 a minute early behind a Chester (!) 'Modified Hall', 7921 *Edstone Hall*, and Terry is chuffed, telling me that this train has a particularly tight schedule for a steam loco and eight coaches. He feels his policy is vindicated. (Incidentally, I always associate this engine with a Children's Hour radio play about a boy detective named — if I remember rightly — Norman Bones, because in the drama the boy actually talked of seeing a train leaving a station somewhere in the Midlands with an engine called '*Edstone Hall*'. Later, during my footplate training at Old Oak, described in Chapter 15, I had a run on this engine — no longer at Chester — back to my lodgings with Bob Poynter, Stationmaster at Twyford.)

Eventually 6 o'clock arrives, and I can put away my notebook and pencil. Although plenty of trains are still arriving, and I can see a train waiting patiently opposite Royal Oak tube station, it is assumed that I'll have recorded enough data by this time to serve the purpose, and the officers will pore over my graphical representation of the afternoon performance and take some positive decisions. Whether they will or not, I don't know. Probably I'll never know.

Chapter 13

No 4037 - the Western Region's highest-mileage locomotive

'Castle' 4037 *The South Wales Borderers* with the 8am Plymouth–Liverpool at
Pontypool Road on the occasion of the author's footplate trip, 15 February 1961.

Few locomotives on the Western Region achieved the two million miles mark in their career. In fact, I am only aware of three locomotives for certain that reached this mileage — the last surviving 'Saint', 2920 *Saint David*, and rebuilt 'Star'/'Castles' 4000 *North Star*, which covered 2.1 million miles, and 4037 *The South Wales Borderers* (formerly 'Queen Philippa'), which had accumulated 2.4 million miles by the time of its withdrawal from service in September 1962. Certainly they were the only 'Castles' to achieve this mileage, 4080 and 4096 just falling short of the two million mark, and most other engines in the '40xx' series clocking around 1.7-1.9 million.

During its latter days at Old Oak Common (1955/6) 4037 had a terrible reputation for rough riding. I was told during my sojourn at Old Oak in 1957 that it was most often used as the Ranelagh Bridge standby loco — always an Old Oak 'Castle' — as no incoming driver would exchange it for his own steed unless his loco were in dire straits! It underwent heavy repairs at Swindon in 1958, during which it acquired a new front end to its main frame, and again in 1960 and seems to have built a quite different reputation following reallocation to Newton Abbot. In February

1961 I obtained a number of passes for an article I intended to write on the North &
West route, and (as described in Chapter 12) these enabled me to take brake-van trip
on a freight from Newport to Shrewsbury and another on a night parcels working
from Shrewsbury to Cardiff. The highlight, however, was a footplate pass for the
Plymouth–Liverpool restaurant-car train between Pontypool Road and Shrewsbury,
which was the celebrated 'double home' through working by engine and men, shared
between Newton Abbot and Shrewsbury depots. My trip was on 15 February 1961,
and I was somewhat surprised, to put it mildly, to see Newton Abbot's 4037 run in
about ten minutes late with the 8am Plymouth. Previous recent journeys with this
train had been with the alternating Shrewsbury locos. I had seen nothing of 4037
since its removal from Old Oak and was not aware that it was now at 83A nor of its
redeemed reputation, as only the best locos were chosen for this arduous turn. 4037
looked good, and I was met by the Newton Abbot crew, Driver D. Lewis and Fireman
R. Aggett. I had been previously joined by Loco Inspector George from Newport as
we travelled to Pontypool Road behind 4086 on the 08.55 Cardiff–Manchester.

All looked in good shape on the footplate, and we accelerated rapidly to 63mph
on no more than half regulator before shutting off for a 30mph slack at Nantyderry.
A swift recovery to 59mph was followed by a slowing to 52 around the Penpergwm
curve and then a dreadful p-way restriction to 10mph just before Abergavenny
station, right at the foot of Llanvihangel Bank. With eleven coaches (410 tons gross)
behind us and the winter sunshine beaming on us and on the distant Sugar Loaf
Summit, the engine now blowing off steam, with 225psi on the clock, Driver Lewis
opened 4037 right up, full regulator and 35% cut-off. Speed crept up to 34mph past
Abergavenny Junction but fell to 28 on the steepest part as pressure dropped slightly,
to 215lb; then, as we hit the slightly easier grades, we dropped back to 30% cut-off
and accelerated initially to 36mph before storming over the summit at a full 40.

We now took things easy downhill, with a maximum of 68 before Pontrilas and
exactly 70 after yet another p-way restriction (to 15mph) before Red Hill Junction.
Firing had eased, and pressure dropped to 195lb, before the Hereford stop. I noted
that, despite her reputation, 4037 rode extremely well, although some of the cab
fittings started a rattling war-dance at speeds above 60mph. Despite the p-way slacks
we had dropped only one minute on the Working Timetable (WTT) schedule. Arrival
at Hereford was still eleven minutes late, in 49 minutes 5 seconds from Pontypool
Road, inclusive of the three severe p-way slacks and a further slight restriction to
50mph at Pandy.

We were blowing off steam before we left Hereford, having recovered a further
two minutes from the station allowance, but got a signal check to walking pace before
we got to Barrs Court Junction. Then it was full regulator to Shelwick Junction, where
we were already doing 56mph, before Lewis dropped back to the first port and 15%
cut-off, which sustained 60mph through Moreton-on-Lugg; 20% cut-off took us
over Dinmore Summit and into the tunnel at 53, and 15% thereafter kept us rolling
in the mid-60s through Leominster, in 16 minutes 45 seconds from Hereford.

By now the fire was beginning to get a bit dirty (the coal being mainly dust
and those awful chemical-compound ovoids), and Aggett was using the pricker quite

185

regularly to stop clinker forming. We swept on, 71mph at Woofferton, 60 around the Ludlow curve, 61 through Bromfield (where we failed to pick up any water from the near-empty troughs) and a minimum of 51 at the top of the 1-in-112 climb to Onibury — now 17% cut-off and still first port of the regulator, pressure 218lb.

We got up to 60 in the Craven Arms dip, the time deficit now reduced to five minutes, and were tackling the climb to Church Stretton very nicely, when we suddenly got signals on and — from 47mph at Marsh Farm Junction — ground to a complete stand on the steepest part of the climb, at Marsh Brook crossing. We stood for a couple of minutes — I suspect a gates problem — and then opened up with full regulator and 25% cut-off to the summit at Church Stretton, achieving 30mph at the top of the steepest bit and 35 at the summit, pressure now down to 195lb. With the regulator just cracked open we rolled through Leebotwood at 73mph before catching a sight of distants on before Sutton Bridge Junction.

We crawled over the English and Welsh bridges at Shrewsbury after a 5mph signal check and then a 5mph p-way slack approaching the station throat, drawing up at the platform just three minutes late by the WTT, in 66 minutes 58 seconds from Hereford — but on time according to the published timetable. I calculated the net times to be 37 minutes from Pontypool Road to Hereford and 58½ minutes from Hereford to Shrewsbury — a net gain of twenty-seven minutes on the WTT schedule over this exacting route. (For the full log see Appendix Table 12.)

The astonishing thing to me was the apparent ease with which this run was made. The engine had been pushed hard only twice (recovering from the checks uphill at Abergavenny and Church Stretton), the rest being done on the first port of the regulator and 15-20% cut-off. The working had been extremely economical. Inspector George took measurements and calculated that we had used only 1,400 gallons of water from Hereford — about 24 gallons per mile — and estimated our coal consumption at no more than 30-35lb per mile. These figures are on the same level as some of the best work recorded by the 'Castles' in their triumphant 1925 Locomotive Exchanges days — and we were not burning best Welsh coal either!

I was at Bristol about three months later and saw that 4037 was still on the southbound Shrewsbury double-home working. I saw further photos of 4037 on this working months later and concluded that she must have done at least eight months' continuous work on this diagram. It would be normal practice, after between three and four months, to stop the loco for a valves-and-piston-ring exam and change and to substitute another loco more recently out of shops, but Driver Lewis told me that 4037 had gone back onto the Shrewsbury link because she was at that time the only 83A 'Castle' fit for the work. (I understand that when 4037 was finally retired from that diagram Newton Abbot had to borrow Laira's double-chimney 4087 for its leg.)

4037 spent the last few months of her life at Exeter, although I remember seeing her quite frequently later in 1961 and the early part of 1962, and I could have sworn she had been reallocated back to Old Oak. However, it's probably just my memory playing tricks. Ultimately she became a victim of the purge of Western 'Kings' and 'Castles' at the end of the 1962 Summer Timetable.

4037 running back to shed at Shrewsbury, 15 February 1961.

Chapter 14

Commuting in the London Division

In September 1961 I was appointed as one of six Western Region Traffic Apprentices (known in later years as Management Trainees). I had an unfair advantage in the selection process. Normally around twenty young men (there was little encouragement for potential women managers in those days) would be selected throughout BR by examination and interview — but after negotiation with the clerical trade union, TSSA, it had been agreed that 50% should come from the ranks of railway staff and not be recruited directly from university. Because of my year's service I counted as a staff entrant, and therefore the railways got the bonus of an additional graduate! At that time the scheme consisted of three years' training, the first year being basic training in railway-operating activities at ground level. Managers in those days had a belief that it would be useful for managers of the future to have an understanding of what their staff were meant to do (and did do!).

After a final interview with Assistant General Manager, George Bowles, I was sent to the Headquarters Staff Officer in charge of trainees, to be allocated to a Division for Year 1 training and to receive my initial programme. For my first year I was based in the London Division, the immediate programme comprising six weeks at a passenger station (Maidenhead), six weeks at a goods depot (Slough), four weeks at a larger goods depot (South Lambeth), four weeks at a medium-sized station (Oxford), four weeks at a large station (Reading) and six weeks at a locomotive depot (Old Oak Common). After that I was to go to Margam Yard in South Wales, as the London Division was not considered to have a large enough marshalling yard for training purposes; Acton apparently did not qualify.

As Reading seemed to be the focal point of the programme (and daily commuting from Woking seemed impracticable, my personal transport being still the 1936-built pedal-cycle) I took lodgings with an elderly widow in a terraced house five minutes' walk from Reading station. The initial six weeks from late September until mid-November was spent at Maidenhead station, where I was initiated into the work of booking and parcels offices, platform staff, the small coal yard (including handling a shunting pole) and Maidenhead East signalbox. My first dose of real responsibility came during such a spell, when the signalman, closeted in the loo, shouted instructions to me to clear signals for the down '*Cornish Riviera*' (again — this train was becoming my nemesis). I accepted the train, pulled off the semaphores, watched with some trepidation as the 'Warship' roared past and remembered to give 'train out of section' and replace the pegs before my mentor emerged from his cubbyhole.

The local stationmaster agreed to my working fairly normal day shifts to begin with, which meant that I could catch the 6.45am Swindon–Paddington commuter train (Maidenhead being the first stop after Reading), returning in the late afternoon on the 4.35pm Paddington–Swindon (which stopped at Twyford also). The morning service was allowed 15 minutes start-to-stop for the 12-mile run, which required fairly smart running with the nine-coach train, a set weighing 306 tons tare and usually about 340-345 tons gross. It was booked for a Didcot (81E) locomotive, usually one of the depot's three 'Counties' (1002, 1015 and 1018) or a 'Modified Hall'. However, as the train started from Swindon, interlopers sometimes found their way onto the train, which meant that I awaited it at Reading with some anticipation. I always stood in the corridor of the first coach, as the noise from GW engines was worth hearing (unlike that of many of the soft-voiced Southern engines, with which I was more familiar).

On the first morning of my spell at Maidenhead the train ran into Reading 5 minutes late behind 1015 *County of Gloucester* and accelerated past Twyford in 7 minutes 25 seconds — about par for the course if time was to be kept. We took exactly 15 minutes 5 seconds start-to-stop, with a top speed of 64mph at Waltham 'box before shutting off steam for the Maidenhead stop. The next day we had a 'Modified Hall' but a Westbury-based engine, 6968 *Woodcock Hall*, which ran in on time and completed the short run in 14 minutes 46 seconds, with a top speed of 68mph. I did not time every journey, so despite catching this train twenty-four times (at weekends I went home to Woking, returning on the Monday morning via London) I have only seventeen logs. On most of the runs that I failed to record I had the booked 81E 'County' or 'Modified Hall'; 1002 was certainly the engine on one occasion, and I know Didcot's 6996 *Blackwell Hall* featured more often than the twice suggested by my logs, while Reading's 7919 *Runter Hall* also appeared at least once. However, I made sure to log the train when more interesting engines appeared, these including an Oxley 'Grange', 6851 *Hurst Grange*, which was the only engine recorded as reaching 70mph, thereby cutting half a minute from the schedule and having to wait time before departing Maidenhead, for any commuters who might have been caught on the hop. A Bristol SPM 'Grange' also appeared, 6831 *Bearley Grange*, although this was not quite as energetic, taking 15 minutes 16 seconds, with a top speed of 66mph. The fastest runs were with a Didcot 'Hall', 4994 *Downton Hall*, which stopped at Maidenhead in one second over 14 minutes without exceeding 68mph, and one of the journeys with the engine I had most frequently, 1018 *County of Leicester*; these were the only engines to clear Twyford in less than 7 minutes. There were two real surprises during the six weeks. A Churchward Mogul, 6364 (82B), appeared on 19 October, arriving at Reading on time but taking 16 minutes 48 seconds, mainly because of a slow start; top speed was 60mph. But even more surprising was one of the huge Churchward 2-8-0s, 4701 of Old Oak Common, which graced the train on 1 November and ran virtually to time, attaining a top speed of 63mph. A table of all the runs timed, starting with the fastest, appears overleaf.

Locomotive	Date	Time	Top speed	Punctuality
1018 *County of Leicester* (81E)	8 November	13min 57sec	68mph	on time
4994 *Downton Hall* (81E)	20 October	14min 01sec	68mph	1min early
6851 *Hurst Grange* (84B)	4 October	14min 29sec	70mph	1min early
1018 *County of Leicester*	10 November	14min 32sec	66mph	2min late
6968 *Woodcock Hall* (82D)	27 September	14min 46sec	68mph	on time
1018 *County of Leicester*	7 November	14min 47sec	68mph	on time
6996 *Blackwell Hall* (81E)	13 October	14min 52sec	63mph	8min late
1015 *County of Gloucester* (81E)	26 September	15min 05sec	64mph	5min late
1015 *County of Gloucester*	6 October	15min 12sec	69mph	on time
6831 *Bearley Grange* (82B)	3 November	15min 16sec	66mph	2min late
6996 *Blackwell Hall*	18 October	15min 25sec	62mph	3min late
4902 *Aldenham Hall* (81E)	5 October	15min 31sec	68mph	½min late
4987 *Brockley Hall* (81C)	3 October	15min 32sec	62mph	1min late
4701 (81A)	1 November	15min 34sec	63mph	1min late
5979 *Cruckton Hall* (81D)	11 October	16min 13sec	60mph	6min late
6364 (82B)	19 October	16min 48sec	60mph	2min late
1018 *County of Leicester*	9 November	17min 45sec	55mph	10min late

The final run with 1018 was the only one on which the locomotive appeared to be in difficulty — on this occasion a shortage of steam.

The evening runs back to Reading on the 4.35pm from Paddington had much more varied motive power. This was a Swindon (82C) turn, usually producing a 'Hall' though sometimes a 'Castle', but frequently Old Oak used the train to return Bristol Division engines westwards, and Swindon Works often used it as a running-in turn. Two ex-works engines are particularly remembered — Penzance 'Grange' 6808 *Beenham Grange*, which headed the train five days in a row, and former Bristol Bath Road 4079 *Pendennis Castle*, which had been reallocated to Swindon and appeared six times towards the end of my spell at Maidenhead. On a couple of occasions I went through to Didcot for the hell of it, one such being on 3 November with 4079. The train was quite heavy — eleven coaches (356/375 tons) — and ran throughout on the relief line, which was restricted to 60mph; we reached 58 before Twyford and covered the 17 miles from Reading to Didcot in 22 minutes exactly, having maintained 60 from Pangbourne to Moreton Cutting. A few weeks later — on 30 November, after I'd moved on to Slough — I took the same train from Reading to Didcot with 5035 *Coity Castle* (82C) and the same load, this run being slightly slower, taking 10 seconds short of 23 minutes, but including a maximum speed of 63mph at Cholsey. Both runs were punctual, as were all the other journeys on this train, without exception. Engines recorded during October and early November 1961, although not logged for time, were as follows:

'County':	1000
'Castles':	4074, 4079 (six runs), 5023, 5035
'Modified Halls':	6974, 6982
'Halls':	4922, 4975, 4977, 4983, 5900, 5922, 5960, 6901, 6910
'Grange':	6808 (five runs)

1924-built 4074 *Caldicot Castle* (by now with four-row superheater and double chimney but retaining its original 'joggled' frames) on arrival at Reading with the 4.35pm Paddington–Swindon in October 1961.

At the end of October I took a Saturday off to try the '*Pembroke Coast Express*' again. I really shouldn't have! 5037 *Monmouth Castle* (87E) was a good loco, making plenty of steam, but once again the driver ignored the public timetable and more than used the revised WTT timing to Newport that was applicable because he had eleven coaches on; after a Reading check he wandered down the fast line to Swindon without even touching 60mph, blowing off steam furiously — what the fireman thought of this waste of his effort I shudder to think. A belated dash through the Severn Tunnel in 3 minutes 34 seconds, touching 85mph at the bottom, could not prevent our being twenty-two minutes late into Newport by the public book.

A trip up to Maesycwmmer with 9616, returning with 2218, soothed our tempers a little, and I prayed that the return '*Pembroke Coast Express*' would not damn Western performance forever in the eyes of my colleague Alistair Wood. It turned up ten minutes late with one of the early single-chimney 'Castles', 4081 *Warwick Castle* (87F), just ex works, and ten coaches (375 tons gross). We started as I hoped we would not go on — signals to 12mph at Magor, then a special two-minute stop at Severn Tunnel Junction platform. After that things improved, with an excellent climb out of the tunnel, speed being in the 40s for most of the way, only easing to 35mph at the top,

191

before the Stoke Gifford curve. A fast descent from Badminton was curtailed by a severe p-way slowing at Hullavington, but we kept up a steady 78-79mph on the level all the way from Uffington to Pangbourne before slowing for another p-way slack at Reading. Despite this, because of the earlier delays we were still fifteen minutes late into Paddington.

Early the following month I decided to repeat my North & West triangular tour. The 7.30am Paddington was now diesel-hauled, so I waited for the Saturday '*Bristolian*' (8.45am from Paddington) with 'Warship' D828 *Magnificent*, which from Bathampton to Bath was delayed behind the 7.45am Paddington, headed by 4951 *Pendeford Hall*, the down-line pilot from Reading, its own diesel having failed there. The Shrewsbury 'Castle' on the eleven-coach 8 o'clock Plymouth was a well-burnished 5038 *Morlais Castle*, which by Pontypool Road had recovered the 5 minutes lost as a result of its delayed departure from Bristol, despite a six-minute stand for signals at East Usk and a p-way slack to 15mph at Llantarnam on the 1-in-120 gradient immediately before it steepened to 1 in 106/95 for the last four miles, over which 5038 accelerated to 31mph. It had previously touched 83mph in the four and a half mile Severn Tunnel, which it traversed in 3 minutes 50 seconds. It was promising a 58 minute run from Hereford to Shrewsbury, matching that achieved with 5095, when we ground to a halt at Bromfield because of cattle on the line. This lost us more than ten minutes, and we did well to arrive in Shrewsbury only three minutes late, after sustaining a minimum of 40mph at Church Stretton and hitting 76 on the descent through Dorrington. 'County' 1022 was on the 4.30pm from Birkenhead to Wolverhampton, where 7017

Paddington in 1958, with Oxford shed's 5025 *Chirk Castle* in charge of the 6.5pm Oxford commuter train at platform 1 and 6011 *King James I* on the 6.10pm to Wolverhampton at platform 2.

G. J. Churchward took over for an energetic run to Paddington with a 445 ton-gross load, touching 87mph at Denham — but the usual signal checks from Old Oak in made us eleven minutes late at the terminus.

My six-week stint at Slough Goods started on 13 November and lasted until the Christmas holiday. I found that the 7.30am Oxford–Paddington, on which Slough was the first stop after Reading, was a very suitable service. It was booked for an Oxford 'Castle', of which that depot then had four (5012, 5025, 5033 and 7008), and one of these was a fixture on the commuter service, with only one exception. The regular load was a very manageable nine coaches, 282/315 tons. On three days during this period I caught a later train — the 7.10am Didcot, and each time its heavy, twelve-coach load (378/425 tons) was hauled by the same recently ex-works 'Hall', 4976 *Warfield Hall* (81E). My return service in the evening, after a somewhat tedious day looking at freight-charge calculations, cartage returns and wagon demurrage, was on another non-stop Slough–Reading train shortly after 5pm that was a Reading 'Hall' turn and on which recently ex-works 4998 *Eyton Hall* was the regular engine on all but half a dozen occasions.

In the up direction 22 minutes was allowed for the 17.5-mile start-to-stop run — a hard schedule for the heavy 'Hall'-booked service. Unfortunately I did not record punctuality, but my recollection is that the Oxford service was always very prompt, as it should have been. Because of a p-way slack at Twyford immediately after a couple of weekends and because several runs experienced signal checks on the approach to Slough I've listed the runs in order of net time, as follows:

Locomotive	Date	Actual time	Net time	Top speed
5012 *Berry Pomeroy Castle*	28 November	20min 20sec	18min 45sec	74mph
5012 *Berry Pomeroy Castle*	29 November	19min 14sec	19min 00sec	74mph
5025 *Chirk Castle*	22 December	20min 49sec	19min 00sec	76mph
5025 *Chirk Castle*	6 December	26min 51sec	19min 15sec	70mph*#
5025 *Chirk Castle*	12 December	21min 19sec	19min 15sec	73mph*
5033 *Broughton Castle*	11 December	24min 13sec	19min 15sec	71mph#
5025 *Chirk Castle*	13 December	23min 03sec	19min 15sec	69mph#
5025 *Chirk Castle*	24 November	19min 22sec	19min 22sec	74mph
5025 *Chirk Castle*	23 November	20min 15sec	19min 30sec	74mph
5025 *Chirk Castle*	14 November	19min 46sec	19min 46sec	71mph
5025 *Chirk Castle*	15 November	21min 14sec	20min 00sec	72mph
5025 *Chirk Castle*	16 November	21min 17sec	20min 00sec	68mph
4976 *Warfield Hall*	1 December	20min 58sec	20min 58sec	68 mph
4976 *Warfield Hall*	4 December	24min 37sec	21min 00sec	64mph*
6942 *Eshton Hall* (81A)	19 December	21min 36sec	21min 36sec	66mph
5012 *Berry Pomeroy Castle*	30 November	21min 39sec	21min 39sec	66mph
5025 *Chirk Castle*	17 November	23min 20sec	21min 45scc	64mph
4976 *Warfield Hall*	14 December	24min 19sec	22min 00sec	63mph#

*p-way slack at Twyford
severe signal check causing at least 3 minutes' delay

It will be noted that no time was booked against the engine on any of these runs. I did not time the evening runs back to Reading — the trains were crowded, meaning that I usually had to stand, and of course it was pitch dark — but my recollection is that the trains ran punctually. In addition to ten runs behind 4998 I had four runs with 5977 *Beckford Hall*, three with 5978 *Bodinnick Hall* and one each with 5973 *Rolleston Hall* and 6913 *Levens Hall*.

In December I took a couple of evening trips out of King's Cross, to break the monotony of learning the goods-depot clerical work. On the 6th I had double-chimney 'A3' 60059 *Tracery* (34A), which got its eleven-coach, 415-ton load to the first stop at Huntingdon (59 miles) in 62 minutes (59 net), with speeds in the high 70s after Hitchin and a top speed of exactly 80 at Three Counties. A week later, on the 12th, 'A4' 60032 *Gannet* (34A), with only nine coaches (325 tons), was faster but more severely delayed, arriving at Huntingdon four minutes late after a p-way slack and four signal checks but 90 at Arlesey and 83 after the St Neots 'hump'. We were delayed there for a further twelve minutes awaiting a connection, and had a further p-way slack at Connington and a signal stand awaiting a platform at Peterborough, where we were twenty minutes late. Both return trips were with King's Cross double-chimney 'A3s' on nine coaches, 315 tons, on the last up Hull, due King's Cross at 9.44pm. 60044 *Melton* completed the non-stop run in 76 minutes (73 net) with 82 at Huntingdon and 62 minimum at Stevenage, regaining nine minutes following thirteen min-late start. 60067 *Ladas* left punctually and took it reasonably easily until it caught up with a late-running Cambridge Buffet express after Welwyn and suffered a series of signal checks behind it all the way to King's Cross, arriving three minutes late.

Over the weekend of 9/10 December I visited a girl friend I'd met at Lindors who was now at Nottingham University. I decided to go down on the Friday evening on the 4.25pm from Marylebone and was most surprised to discover our motive power was a Woodford Halse 'K3' Mogul, 61910. With a 260-ton load (six coaches and three vans) it made a spirited climb to Amersham, accelerating from 20mph around the Rickmansworth curve to 45mph at the summit of the six-mile, 1-in-105 bank — much better than a similarly loaded 'Standard 5' back in the summer. We continued on our merry way, touching 70mph between stops, and arrived punctually at Nottingham Victoria. My run home on the Sunday was rather different. I was very surprised to find Stanier 2-6-4T 42453 on the five-coach 6.15pm from Nottingham Victoria, while at Rugby Central we were all transferred to a coach, to avoid an engineering 'blockade'. At Woodford Halse there was 61910 again, on another five-coach train which took us as far as Harrow-on-the-Hill, where it was 'all change' once more, this time to the Metropolitan Line. I have no idea now of any comparison with schedule — my notes state simply that '61910 romped home with much smoke and noise'!

In the early New Year I attended the wedding of a college friend (my table-tennis partner) in Germany, involving runs on the Cologne–Hamburg main artery behind oil burning '01.10' three-cylinder Pacifics and an horrendous rough return crossing on the Ostend–Dover cross-Channel ferry. I came back to a month's training at South Lambeth goods depot, where I learned a lot (mainly how not to conduct industrial relations) but commuted from my home at Woking, as that was easier, spending such free time as I had on evening excursions to Banbury, Peterborough, Swindon and Rugby. More ambitiously, I took a couple of Western triangular trips, on the first occasion travelling behind 5092 *Tresco Abbey* (88A) on the 8.55am to Cardiff (which was actually early!), a 'Hall', 5962, across to Bristol Stapleton Road on a Cardiff–Salisbury service and 5031 *Totnes Castle* (84A) on the '*Cornishman*' to Birmingham Snow Hill via Stratford-upon-Avon, returning to London on the 4.30pm Birkenhead with 5019 *Treago Castle* (84A), which left Birmingham 20 minutes late with twelve coaches (445 tons) and arrived in Paddington 35 late despite being driven hard between innumerable checks — 87 at Blackthorn, 50 at Saunderton Summit and 85 at Greenford.

Six days later I tried the Saturday '*Pembroke Coast Express*' again, this time with a shining double-chimney 'Castle', Landore's 5078 *Beaufort*, and hoped for a different sort of run. No — it 'dribbled' all the way to Swindon without exceeding 62mph,

'A3' 60059 *Tracery* ready to depart King's Cross with the 6.26pm to Hull in the summer of 1959.

195

blowing off steam so hard that its exhaust was inaudible from the first coach. We arrived at Newport 'on time' according to the WTT's revised timings but fifteen late by the public timetable. I had a short snippet behind 'King' 6003 (now transferred to Cardiff) to Pontypool Road, as I wanted to get the Crewe 'Scot' turn on the 7.30am Penzance–Manchester. The day deteriorated further: in lieu of a 'Scot' I got, on a light load, a Bletchley 'Black Five' (45004) I'd had before, and there followed an awful run from Shrewsbury to Wolverhampton behind a badly steaming 'Hall', No 5985, replaced at Wolverhampton by a Stafford Road 'Castle', 5045 *Earl of Dudley*, which struggled with a tender full of ovoids and coal dust, depositing me at Paddington nearly an hour late, with most connections long gone. I think this day marked the nadir of Western performance as far as I was concerned.

I experimented with a different sort of triangle on 2 February, heading to Grantham on a Bradford train with 'A1' 60122 *Curlew* and catching a DMU train for Derby Friargate as far as Nottingam, whence I returned on the 5.15pm to Marylebone and was surprised to get a 'B1', 61187, instead of the more usual 'Standard 5' on this service — and got the only 80 I've ever had with a 'B1', between Brackley and Aylesbury. Timings were relatively punctual, at least in comparison with the trip described previously. Another couple of trips to Peterborough later in the month — out on the 6.26pm to Hull ('A4s' 60008 and 60025) and back on the last up Hull (both times with Doncaster 'A1' 60157 *Great Eastern*) — were reasonably punctual without being pariculary noteworthy.

On 26 February I resumed my Reading lodgings as a base from which to perform my training at Oxford — with unwary strangers I can impress by referring to 'my Oxford days'! At both Oxford and Reading I had to mix day shifts with some evenings and nights, mainly to observe the parcels working at both the platform and the cartage bays — parcels and GPO traffic was still important in the early 1960s. This gave me quite a lot of scope to 'fill in' with main-line steam workings between Reading, Oxford and Paddington, as I had little to do at my lodgings, which were B&B only, and my cooking skills were undeveloped. On 26 February 1962 I made my way from Woking to Oxford via London, using the 11.15am Paddington, as the Stationmaster did not want me until his weekly morning staff meeting was over. There was heavy snow all the way — a good start to a week when I expected to be out on the platform for most of the day. However, despite the weather 5099 *Compton Castle* managed to keep time without exceeding 67mph in the difficult visibility. It seems that the 4.5pm Hereford was initially my evening commute back to Reading — I was obviously prepared to wait well beyond my finishing time to get steam rather than go earlier on a DMU. 7920 *Coney Hall*, 7005 *Sir Edward Elgar* and 7009 *Athelney Castle*, all Worcester engines, did the honours. The first two both took things too easily, dropping a couple of minutes with their eight-coach trains, and the only energy was displayed by 7009, which had ten coaches (345/360 tons) and maintained the 34-minute schedule despite a 10mph signal check at Didcot East Junction, reaching 73mph at Pangbourne.

By the end of the first week I discovered that I could catch the 5.30pm Oxford–Paddington, non-stop in 60 minutes exactly, at a start-to-stop average speed of

63mph. This required '*Cheltenham Flyer*'- or '*Bristolian*'-style running from Didcot to London, and I worked out that I could get home to Reading nearly as quickly by catching this and the 7.5pm Paddington–Cheltenham as I could by waiting for the 4.5pm Hereford; it was certainly much more fun, and there was no cost, as I had a Divisional 'free pass' throughout my London Division training! The first two runs were on five coaches only (161/170 tons); after that I had the same Hawksworth six-coach set (189/205-210 tons). I did this for five working days, until my shift pattern changed, and then got in another four days before transferring to Reading station. The crew were Oxford men and stayed on the turn for the whole week. The train was booked for an Old Oak 'Castle', although on Saturdays Oxford had to provide the loco, usually a Hawksworth 'Modified Hall'. The two days of the first week and the first three days of the next were with men prepared to enjoy themselves and run at high speed; the last week was disappointing, as the driver was content to aim at the scheduled time without building anything in hand. Two of the runs sustained 87mph over long stretches, one touched 88, and one 86mph. Only one run lost time for loco reasons, this being on the Monday of the second week, when 5066 had been left on shed at Oxford without much attention to the fire, and clinker had formed. It set off in the usual style to Reading, but then it was winded, and speed dropped alarmingly to around 50mph between Reading and Slough before the fireman recovered the situation, following which speed rose again to the 70s by Acton. The nine runs are summarised as follows:

Locomotive	Date	Actual time	Net time	Sustained speed
7014 *Caerhays Castle*	1 March	59min 58sec	58min 00sec	83-87mph Twyford–Ealing
5060 *Earl of Berkeley*	2 March	57min 40sec	57min 40sec	82-83mph Goring–Acton
5066 *Sir Felix Pole*	7 March	71min 01sec	67min 00sec	77-78mph Goring–Reading
7021 *Haverfordwest Castle*	8 March	61min 50sec	56min 30sec	85-87mph Tilehurst–West Drayton (signals 20mph, 84mph Ealing)
5076 *Gladiator* (81D)	9 March	61min 10sec	56min 00sec	82-88mph Goring–Reading (signals 2mph, 82-86mph Maidenhead–Acton)
7018 *Drysllwyn Castle*	19 March	62min 18sec	62min 18sec	72-77mph Maidenhead–Southall
5034 *Corfe Castle*	20 March	64min 15sec	61min 00sec	75-76mph Twyford–Hayes
5036 *Lyonshall Castle*	21 March	60min 36sec	60min 36sec	74-82mph Reading–Acton
5015 *Kingswear Castle*	23 March	58min 18sec	58min 18sec	80-82mph Twyford–Acton

All locos were double-chimney 'Castles' except 5015 and 5076, two of the best performers. However, these runs were inferior to three I had a couple of months later, the second and third of which I experienced on the footplate during my training at Old Oak Common:

Locomotive	Date	Actual time	Net time	Sustained speed
5001 *Llandovery Castle*	18 April	53min 09sec#	53min 09sec	90-92mph Pangbourne–Ealing
7911 *Lady Margaret Hall*	5 May*	59min 55sec#	58min 30sec	80-84mph Reading–Acton
7030 *Cranbrook Castle*	16 May	56min 19sec#	53min 30sec	88-90mph Twyford–Southall

* SO turn, Oxford loco, poor coal (ovoids)
# see Appendix, Table 14

My other journeys, variously from Reading to Oxford and back and between Paddington and Reading, mainly behind Worcester and Old Oak 'Castles', passed efficiently enough without any particular fireworks apart from 7032 *Denbigh Castle* on the 12.5pm Hereford and 5067 *St Fagan's Castle* on the 10.5am Hereford, which both sustained 77-79mph between Maidenhead and Acton with nine-coach trains. During this period I travelled behind the following 'Castles' (most from 81A and 85A): 4081, 4082, 4096, 4099, 5002, 5008, 5011 (twice), 5014, 5015, 5016, 5017, 5032 (twice), 5042, 5067, 5084, 5087, 5097, 7005 (twice), 7009 (twice), 7011 (twice), 7016, 7018, 7021 (twice), 7028, 7031 (twice), 7033 and 7036.

Ever optimistic, I continued my evening and 'days off' excursions far and wide. On 15 March I explored the Kingham–Cheltenham line through the Cotswolds with 2-6-2T 4163 (85B), then took the '*Cornishman*' again, this time with 5019 *Treago Castle*, to Birmingham — arriving three minutes early — before returning to London on the 4.30pm Birkenhead with 6021 *King Richard II* (81A) on nine coaches (335 tons), which ran from Banbury to Paddington in 73 minutes (69 net), arriving four minutes early after top speeds of 92mph at Blackthorn, 56 at Saunderton Summit, a full 96 at Denham and still 94 at Greenford! (See Appendix Table 16.) Things were looking up.

On 27 March I tried the 4.10pm Paddington as far as Banbury with 4089 *Donnington Castle* (81A) piloted by 6997 *Bryn-Ivor Hall* (82A). I've no idea as to the reason for the pilot; my notes state that all the work was done by the 'Castle' and suggest that the 'Modified Hall' — off its beaten track — was there solely for decoration! I got out at Banbury (where we arrived three minutes early), for I'd seen 'King' 6014 waiting for the 5.10 as we passed Old Oak, and this was one of the last remaining 'Kings' behind which I needed a run (the others being 6007, 6020 and 6026). 6014 *King Henry VII* (84A) ran in on time with eleven coaches (410 tons), touched 83mph at Fosse Road and climbed Hatton Bank with a minimum of 42, arriving at Snow Hill a satisfactory half-minute early. 6019 *King Henry V* (81A), with nine coaches on the 4.30pm Birkenhead, was punctual, running hard uphill (58mph at Ardley, 57 Saunderton), with 85 at Blackthorn and 83 at Denham.

At around this time I had a few final flings on the West Coast main line. Back in September 1961 I'd been tempted to go down to Rugby on the 1.40pm Euston–Blackpool with 'Jubilee' 45703 *Thunderer*, then at Carlisle Upperby but an engine I'd noted several times in my early train-spotting days at Euston. It had a heavy, twelve-coach train (415 tons gross), which was banked up to Camden by '8F' 48623, but frankly the load was too much for the 'Jubilee', and we expended an awful lot of energy (the sounds, living up to the engine's name, were worth the trip alone) taking 102 minutes to Rugby with just two p-way slacks, managing just 44mph at Tring Summit, scrambling to 70 at Castlethorpe but then falling to 54 at Roade. I had a ticket to Crewe but alighted at Rugby to see if I could do better, but I was forced in the end to take one of a succession of English Electric Type 4 diesels to Crewe, whence I returned, thankfully, with a well-turned-out Willesden-based 'Scot', 46144 *The Honourable Artillery Company*, with ten coaches on the 3.30pm relief train from Holyhead. There was now much electrification activity south of Crewe, and we observed eight severe p-way slacks en route but still managed to arrive in Euston two minutes early on an absurdly easy 190-minute schedule. No 46144 went vigorously enough between the slacks, without exceeding 75mph.

Early in April 1962 I went out and back to Rugby on consecutive days with 46225 *Duchess of Gloucester*, both times on 450-ton trains — the 10.25am Euston–Windermere and the 1.5pm Euston–Perth. The second run was the more enterprising, clearing Tring at 58mph minimum and sustaining the mid-70s thereafter until a series of severe signal checks into Rugby extended our non-stop time to 100 minutes (83 net). On 2 April I returned with 46170 *British Legion* on the 9.5am Llandudno; this was only a seven-coach train, so timekeeping was easy, but on the 3rd 45527 *Southport* did quite well with an enormous fifteen-coach 560-ton load, regaining six minutes (after a fourteen min-late start) on a pretty easy schedule but managing nothing in excess of the 72mph reached through Wembley Central on the last leg.

46170 *British Legion* backs out of Euston with coaches from an incoming Scottish sleeper service, 20 April 1957.

On 23 April I had another go. Crewe 'Scot' 46136 *The Border Regiment* was motive power for the 11.45am Euston–Crewe semi-fast. Our nine-coach train was banked swiftly to Camden No 1 by D5134, and we then had a plod to Rugby, calling at Watford, Bletchley and Northampton, exceeding 60mph only once in the whole journey — 68 at Cheddington. I'd had enough by Rugby, so I baled out and let 46225 (on the next service north) go, in view of my two runs behind it earlier in the month. Foolish decision — another succession of diesels was my fate, but at least I got a 'new' 'Duchess' for my return to London from Crewe — 46228 *Duchess of Rutland* (5A), with a heavy, fourteen coach load (515 tons gross) on a relief Liverpool–Euston express. We left two minutes late, suffered an immediate p-way slowing to 20mph at Betley Road and cleared Whitmore at 55 before the Stafford stop. Then, in addition to the electrification slacks, we got sheep on the line at Colwich and eventually dragged ourselves into Euston twenty minutes late, in 113 minutes from Rugby, the last stop. In between slacks we got our load up to 74mph at Weedon, 76 at Wolverton (after sustaining a minimum of 63 at Roade), 61 at Tring and 78 at Hemel Hempstead.

At the end of April I started my six weeks at Old Oak Common, which I'll describe in Chapter 15. For most of the three weeks allotted for footplate experience I stayed with my trainee predecessor, Bob Poynter, who was by now Stationmaster at Twyford but also covered the Henley branch. Some days I travelled by DMU straight to Reading to pick up my workings from there; other days I caught a steam commuter train from Twyford to Paddington. Three times I travelled up on the footplate and then out to Old Oak when the engine trailed its empty coaches back to shed. Once this was with Reading 'Hall' 5982 *Harrington Hall*, but one of the suitable trains was a Stafford Road 'Castle' turn, and on the other two occasions I went up with 5019 *Treago Castle* and 5063 *Earl Baldwin*.

Then, after the excitement of my footplate training on 'Kings', 'Castles', 'Halls', a '47xx', a '97xx' condensing tank and even a few 'Warships' and 'Hymeks', on Monday 4 June I caught the 7.55am Paddington–Swansea behind 5067 *St Fagan's Castle*, to start training in Margam Yard and the Swansea District Office, with daily journeys from Swansea to Port Talbot and back and off-duty commuting to Llanelli and Carmarthen leading me to pastures new …

Tableau 8

5.30pm Oxford–Paddington, April/May 1962

During four weeks of training at Oxford I'd discovered the 5.30pm to Paddington, an odd train whose purpose I'd not really fathomed — and nor had many others, for its six coaches were never more than half full. During the winter days, when I'd used it to sashay back to my digs in Reading, I'd always been able to obtain a compartment to myself in the first coach, right behind the engine, where I could fling the window wide, despite the cold, and listen to the magnificent roar of a 'Castle' at speed — the nearest thing to the genuine prewar 'Cheltenham Flyer' that I was ever likely to experience. I suppose it was intended to bring the Oxford intelligentsia up to the city for evening cultural events — plays, the opera, concerts etc — but frankly it was a bit early for that. I don't remember ever seeing swathes of bow-tied gents or women in long gowns awaiting this train.

After my winter jaunts I'd become a bit addicted to this train — if you can be 'a bit' addicted to anything. Whilst still residing in the London Division I was tempted to go out of my way to experience it again, so during my last week of training at Reading station itself, on 18 April 1962 (when I'd been working on a suitable early shift), I made my way to Oxford and waited in anticipation as a resplendent Old Oak double-chimney 'Castle', 5001 *Llandovery Castle*, eased into the platform with its customary rake of six maroon corridor coaches. This 1926-built engine had since had the front half of its frames renewed and at its last works visit in the early summer of 1961 had received a four-row superheat boiler with double chimney. From 1939 to 1958 it had been a Canton resident, but it had come then to Old Oak and since July 1961 had been one of the depot's top-link locomotives. Although nine months had elapsed since its 'Heavy General' repair, and despite having a probable 45,000-50,000 miles already under its belt, it still looked superb as it gleamed in the evening sunshine of this fair April day, appearing sleek and well groomed with its flat-sided Hawksworth tender. I entered the 1946-built Hawksworth SK next to the engine and sat on the window side, facing the engine, on the plump cushions sported by that these coaches. Outline statistics of the ensuing run were given in the previous chapter, and the full log appears in the Appendix (Table 14), but I want to share with you now the emotions I felt on the journey.

Undisturbed in my compartment, I sit pleased with the world as the guard's whistle blows, and the locomotive gives one shrill whistle and a very satisfying

201

series of emphatic exhaust beats. I feel the pull of the locomotive as we accelerate rapidly past the cemetery on the down side. By Kennington Junction we are already at nearly 60mph, and we fly through Radley, five miles out, in 6¾ minutes, already doing 72mph. We touch 80 between Culham and Appleford Halt, with a beautiful even purr from the engine, and my spirits are uplifted, for we're clearly in for a fine run. We've made even time by Didcot — 10½ miles in 10 minutes 40 seconds — and after we have glided swifly around the East Curve and slowed to 48mph over the East Junction the throttle is opened wide. We accelerate up the fast line like a jet taking off from Heathrow; the surge in the front coach is thrilling. Normally I revel in the scenery as the Thames winds under us between Cholsey and Pangbourne, but I've no eyes for the scenery today — my eyes fixed on the second hand of my watch as we pile on the speed, exceeding 90mph at Tilehurst.

The record states that the 27 miles to Reading have been covered in 24 minutes 53 seconds, but the excitement as we tear through the middle road, whistle screaming, exhaust roaring, at a full 91mph, must be truly awe-inspiring to the massed throng of people on Reading station awaiting the next up express. We dash through Sonning Cutting while I'm still savouring the Reading experience, and I scarcely notice the slight easing as we take the reverse curves through Twyford station, whereupon the roar from 5001's chimney erupts once more, and we gradually accelerate from 84 up to 92 as we cross the Thames on Maidenhead Bridge. We continue at this breakneck speed on the level; there's no easing for Slough as we rock over the crossings from the Windsor line and hurl ourselves through the station at 91mph, the 18 miles from Reading having taken just 12 minutes 19 seconds. Surely we're going to pay for this haste — we must catch signals from something soon. But still we charge on, 88 at West Drayton, back up to 90 again by Ealing Broadway, and only then does the driver close the regulator, yet we sweep past Old Oak still doing 70. A slight check to 20mph passing Subway Junction, then it's clear into the station, and we pull up at the stop-blocks a full seven minutes early, having covered the 63½ miles from Oxford in 53 minutes 9 seconds. Why the haste? I don't ask. A good engine, a clear road, an enthusiastic driver and a co-operative and competent fireman. And some very satisfied customers, including this one.

*   *   *

It's 16 May, my 24th birthday, and I'm still fired up after the magnificent run I had yesterday to Wolverhampton and back on the track-testing train, which exceeded 100mph three times on the return journey behind 7030 *Cranbrook Castle* (see next chapter). When I get to Old Oak today I see 7030 is booked for a diagram which includes the 5.30pm 'Oxford Flyer', and after a day spent in Acton Yard on a 350hp diesel shunter (part of my 'compulsory' footplate experience) I get away early to Oxford and show my footplate pass to the driver of 7030 standing in Oxford station on the same six-coach set (188 tons tare, 200 gross) that I experienced last month behind 5001 and again nine days ago when I had Oxford's 7911 on the Saturday equivalent.

Of course I'm still full of the trip yesterday, and I recount to the driver the speeds I timed on the test train. I'm not sure if he believes me, but at least it might encourage him to see what 7030 can do today. The fireman cedes his tip-up seat to me — 'I'll be working pretty hard [or words to that effect], so you might as well have it!' I lean out, relay the 'right away' to the driver, and we're off. Full regulator, no slip, and we're away even faster than 5001 was last month. We're a quarter of a minute up on 5001 at Radley, but then the driver eases back to first port, and I have to be satisfied with 75mph at Appleford Halt before the Didcot Junction slowings. Half regulator and 20% cut-off produces a steady acceleration to 75 by Goring, where we take water at speed, and the driver nudges the regulator on to the second port at Tilehurst, and we approach Reading at 83mph, with me leaning nonchalantly from my perch and feeling the breeze as we sweep through the station, putting on a fine show for the commuters.

The pressure is rock steady at 225lb, and the driver is adjusting the cut-off between 17 and 20%, which induces an acceleration to 84mph by Twyford, 88 at Ruscombe and a full 90 by Maidenhead. I'm looking forward to even more, but the driver then eases the regulator back. 'Enough', he murmurs and later expresses concern at what 100mph+ might have felt like on the footplate, as the engine is rolling too much for his liking. I haven't really noticed this, the movement being slight and even, nothing like some engines I've been on, and the fireman has been having no trouble firing steadily at this speed, although I note that his job seems fairly light and that he spends a lot of time hosing to keep the dust down, sweeping the footplate and generally keeping things neat and tidy, despite our 90mph progress. We're up to 90 again by Burnham, take Slough at 88, shut off steam momentarily at West Drayton, then open out again, back up to 85 by Southall, but we catch sight of double-yellows at Ealing and brake to 70 and then harder, as the Old Oak signals clear only when we're down to 15mph. We run into Paddington still three and a half minutes early, in 56 minutes 19 seconds (53½ minutes net), and I'm pleased, but in my view it would have been so easy to have sustained 95mph on the level from Maidenhead to Southall without significantly more effort. But it was unnecessary, and the driver was a little uneasy. I'm not sure how hard he would have driven 7030 without my encouragement.

Chapter 15

Old Oak Common management training

In the spring of 1962 I was allocated to Old Oak Common for my depot and footplate training — the highlight of most Traffic Apprentices' three-year stint. One objective was to ensure that management trainees had an understanding of operations from a driver's perspective, and the normal arrangement was the provision of a Divisional footplate pass for three weeks of the depot training. As I had been at Old Oak during my college years, and as Ray Sims, the Shedmaster, knew of my interest in locomotive matters, he handed me a driver's Regional route-learning footplate pass (covering Paddington–Penzance, Paddington–Fishguard, Paddington–Chester and all stations between) on my first day, to be returned only on my last. My official pass had got 'lost' somewhere between the Superintendent's Office in Paddington and Old Oak Common in the railway's internal postal system!

I had been surprised to be sent to Old Oak for this part of my training, for two reasons. Normally the HQ Personnel staff in charge of trainee allocations avoided locations where one had previously worked, and also Old Oak had been known to ask Head Office not to send trainees there, as there was a certain degree of hostility towards future bosses at that somewhat militant location. Traffic Apprentices had to be sensitive to the feelings of many ordinary railwaymen and women who sometimes resented the 'fast track' promotion that would follow our training, and Traffic Apprentices were not always the most tactful of individuals. In this case, apparently, because I had worked at Old Oak previously and had got on well with most staff (apart from the guy whose overtime I had usurped in 1958!), I was warmly accepted as 'one of them' and received full co-operation.

In fact I was later censured by the senior management — whose job it was to evaluate the reports I had to write after each period of training — for being too uncritical of my time at Old Oak. I was, as a 'bright young thing', expected to produce reports full of criticism of the way things were done and to come up with lots of new ideas and suggestions which the local management would be expected to implement (or justify rejecting) — a practice which did nothing to endear Traffic Apprentices to many of the local managers. By this time the Traffic Apprentices' mentor at Paddington, Assistant General Manager George Bowles (an avuncular figure, reputed to be a scoutmaster, who actually encouraged trainees to be interested in railways), had been replaced by Lance Ibbotson (assistant to Stanley Raymond), the aim being to to 'de-Great Westernise' the Region and introduce a more appropriate management culture.

Although my training at Old Oak involved experience of rostering, trade-union negotiations, maintenance planning, route learning and training practices etc I made sure to take advantage of the privileges afforded by my footplate pass. On the first Saturday lunchtime (in those days one still worked until noon on most Saturdays) I made my way to Paddington and showed my pass to the crew of 7031 *Cromwell's Castle*, newly transferred from Laira to Worcester and working the 1.15pm Paddington–Hereford. We had a very comfortable and punctual trip to Oxford, where I alighted, the gleaming locomotive and Worcester crew well on top of the job. After I'd had a quick sandwich a Worcester double-chimney 'Castle', 7013 (the real 4082) *Bristol Castle*, rolled into Oxford on time, and I joined the crew. 7013 was one of five 'Castles' with a Davies & Metcalfe experimental mechanical lubricator reservoir sited halfway up the side of the smokebox (the others being Nos 4087, 4088, 5084 and 7014), and because these engines had a good reputation I was keen to see 7013 in action. We had a very straightforward run, economical on coal and water, with sustained running in the mid-70s and an early arrival. 7013 was not quite as smooth-running as 7031, but it was twenty-six years older!

During those first few weeks while my training was constrained to the depot environment I increasingly utilised my pass for evening trips to Paddington, Swindon or Oxford and rode on a number of 'Castle' turns in the main — engines from Old Oak, Worcester and South Wales, like 4088, 4096 (on which I had a firing lesson), 4099, 5008, 5020, 5034, 5056, 5065, 7007 and 7032.

By mid-May 1962 it was my turn for the three rostered weeks of formal footplate training, during which I was required to sample both steam and diesel, freight and passenger, local and main-line work. One of my first days was to be spent on shunting and empty-carriage working (the Old Oak–Paddington 'in-and-outs') with condensing pannier tank 9709. Because of my supposed firing prowess (had my successful showing with No 4096 gone around the Old Oak grapevine?) I was entrusted with looking after the fire while the fireman was despatched to the office to collect the wages of driver and fireman, taking the little brass discs that acted as proof of identity. We were marshalled ahead of a long train of parcels vehicles to form the 2.34pm Paddington–Plymouth parcels from platform 1A, awaiting the road to leave Old Oak carriage sidings. The fireman had been gone a long time, and the driver had engrossed me in a rambling discourse on a number of topics (including, I believe, the correct way to prune raspberries), when we got the road to leave. The fireman was still nowhere to be seen, so the driver said 'You'll do' and went to open the regulator. I decided it was time to put coal on the fire and opened the firebox door — and found, to my horror, that the fire had gone out! To my surprise the driver was not unduly fazed and helped me find some timber and firelighters to relight the fire. Meanwhile, using what steam remained, we travelled at least as far as the bottom of the flyover at North Pole. A mere 80lb of steam plainly was not sufficient to lift fourteen large parcel vehicles up the gradient of the flyover, so we gesticulated to the driver of 5021 *Whittington Castle*, waiting to follow us light-engine, and he gave us an almighty shove up to the top, whereafter I just raised enough steam to keep the brakes off until our arrival at platform 1A. I never heard anything more about it, and the driver did not even tell the fireman (well, not in my hearing anyway) when he returned with their wages upon our eventual arrival back at the depot.

I had worked pretty long hours to make full use of my pass while undergoing depot training, but once my scheduled footplate programme came around I could not squeeze enough hours into the day to do all I wanted. Luckily no-one sought to challenge my 14-15 hour turns of duty, and only once did I appear to suffer, when I nearly fell asleep while trying to fire 6015 on the first up Wolverhampton after an all-night shift on a Paddington–Oxley fast freight. In order to maximise my day (and avoid the anxious entreaties of my uncomprehending landlady) I lodged for three weeks with the jovial stationmaster at Twyford, Bob Poynter, a former Traffic Apprentice in his first substantive post, which covered the Henley branch as well as the main line. Many of the commuter trains were formed of ex-GWR rolling stock with T-shaped door handles that had to be turned, and Bob was much exercised by station overtime while doors were shut and handles operated — he learned from bitter experience that you don't blow whistles to hurry commuters off the Henley branch! Most mornings I would travel up to Paddington in the cab of a 'Castle' or 'Hall' and then stay on the locomotive as it made its way light-engine to to Old Oak shed.

My programme required me to travel on various types of train, and among those stipulated was a steam-hauled stopping service. This seemed a little unnecessary from a training point of view, as by 1962 most local services were DMUs (on which I dutifully travelled from Banbury to Paddington), but I decided to fulfil my remit by turning up for a Saturday Paddington–Oxford train (calling at all stations after Reading), whose DMU was replaced one day a week by an engine and coaches. After an uneventful run from Paddington as far as Reading the driver turned to me and offered me his seat and the controls.

So here I was, in charge of 5986 *Arbury Hall* and eight (fairly empty) non-corridor coaches. We set off on the down relief line in brisk style, and I was bowling merrily along when Tilehurst station came into view. As a novice I had been expecting some tuition, but the driver said nothing, and my somewhat late (albeit increasingly severe) brake application saw us sailing through the station before finally coming to a stand, with only the rearmost coach at the platform! I held my breath, watching to see how many doors opened off the platform, but no-one stirred, and off we went. I repeated the performance at Pangbourne but managed to get three coaches alongside the platform — a distinct improvement. Still the driver seemed totally unperturbed, so I requested guidance for Goring, and he pointed out a white cottage, which he used as a marker for braking. Third time lucky — a perfect stop! By now I was becoming over-confident and was finding the sedate 60mph limit on the relief line somewhat unexciting, so in accelerating away from Cholsey I moved the regulator into second-port position. 5986 responded by almost leaping into the air and producing a lovely roar from the chimney, and this was the only time the driver took any interest in my efforts, a restraining hand on my shoulder being accompanied by the words 'Steady on, lad, steady on!'

Condensing '57xx' pannier 9703 at Old Oak Common, 25 May 1957.

For some reason engines were changed at Didcot, whence I continued to Oxford very sedately with 1015 *County of Gloucester* and a new crew. I mentioned earlier that on Saturdays the 'Oxford Flyer' was not an Old Oak 'Castle' turn but could produce anything that Oxford shed had on hand, spare. On this particular Saturday it turned out one of its own 'Modified Halls', 7911 *Lady Margaret Hall*, and I rode this on my return to Paddington. The engine was on top of the job, running in the low 80s, and we reached Paddington in 59 minutes and 55 seconds, but I learned a major lesson en route. We had a tender full of ovoids (coal dust cemented in ovoid shape, which produced a lot of dust and contained a chemical that had an irritant effect if you got it in the eye). The fireman had been busy with the hose throughout the journey, attempting to control the dust, but as we shot under the station overbridge at Southall at 80mph the swirling coal dust got in my eyes. I had bought myself a pair of motor-cycle goggles to wear as protection but had allowed myself to be laughed into not wearing them by a succession of 'macho' train crews. A visit to the First Aid Room at Paddington was not successful in removing all the dust, and I was sent to the Casualty Department of the adjacent St Mary's Hospital, where I spent a very painful four hours awaiting attention. Thereafter I ignored the teasing and put my own safety first — I wore my goggles.

Another requirement of my programme was that I should experience a footplate run on a night fast freight. Here was a splendid opportunity to travel on one of those marvellous Churchward '47xx', engines the Old Oak men swore by. I chose the 10.55pm Paddington–Bordesley & Oxley, a train that was invariably rostered for a '47xx', and booked on and reported to the crew preparing 4704, which was just ex works and sporting the fully lined Brunswick-green livery. As we backed into Paddington goods depot we joined an array of well-turned-out locomotives ready to

Photographed from the new enginemen's lobby, Churchward '47xx' 2-8-0 4704 enters Old Oak Common shed in July 1958.

depart with a succession of fast night freights. Seeing 4087, my favourite 'Castle', on a West of England Class C fully fitted freight tempted me to change footplates, but I had made my choice and had been made welcome by 4704's crew, so I stuck with the Birmingham train.

We left punctually but spent a long time making up the full load of fifty-five vanfits at Park Royal (a private siding to the tobacco factory). As we left High Wycombe I was again offered the regulator (news of my previous attempts clearly not having reached this particular crew), and I took control for the climb to Saunderton Summit. This was not particularly difficult, involving the insertion of a large lump of coal to keep the regulator opened wide while I manipulated the heavy and somewhat stiff reversing and cut-off lever which obtruded into my space. We went over the summit at 31mph without any fuss and made good time until we reached the Leamington area, where we suffered a succession of signal checks, leaving us to start the climb of Hatton Bank at walking pace. This caused the surefooted 4704 no problem, and the only complaint I have about the locomotive was its frugal cab design — specifically the awkward reversing lever and the severely attenuated cab roof, which gave no protection from the steady rain which soaked me from Leamington onwards. It was after this trip that I made my way back to Snow Hill and boarded 6015 *King Richard III* on the 6.25am Wolverhampton, as I felt too wet and filthy to travel 'on the cushions'. However, when a nasty lurch nearly sent me tumbling through the gap between engine and tender after I had nodded off somewhere around Cropredy I decided to seek refuge in the train at Banbury.

New diesel-hydraulic types were being introduced by the Western Region at around this time, and I had already travelled in the cab of brand-new 'Hymek'

D7025 (on an up South Wales express), which appeared to have little in hand over the previously diagrammed 'Castle'. The 'Warships' were now fairly common but were still causing the fitters some problems, and while I was at Old Oak drawings arrived from Germany — but unfortunately the explanations were in German. Knowing that I was a graduate in the language, the shedmaster asked me if I would translate the sheaf of documents. Unfortunately, as I was no engineer, I didn't know the English for half the engine parts described! Also during my stay the first two 'Westerns' appeared, and I arranged to come in specially on a Saturday to travel down to Plymouth on D1001 at the head of the *Cornish Riviera*. Unfortunately it failed the previous evening on the up run, and when I arrived at the platform end at Paddington I found North British-built 'Warship' No D851. It kept time without trouble, but the North British locomotives in particular were prone to the emission of unpleasant fumes from badly fitted pipes, and by the time we reached Exeter I was suffering from a filthy headache. Seeing 4909 *Blakesley Hall* waiting to back onto the three-coach Kingswear portion of our train was too tempting, so I opted to breathe the ozone along the Dawlish wall. After a pleasant couple of unhurried hours in Kingswear we returned to Exeter with a portion of the 1.50pm Penzance, only to find another fume-filled North British 'Warship', D855. But this was reality; one of the purposes of my training was to experience life as it was for the train crews, and cab design and conditions were important, as I would find later in my career when dealing with trade-union complaints over Health & Safety issues or investigating the causes of SPADs (signals passed at danger).

In the early 1960s the Paddington–Wolverhampton service had been augmented to replace Euston services curtailed during electrification, and most of the Laira 'Kings' had been transferred to Old Oak or Stafford Road for the northern road. One of the extra services was an 8.20am Paddington–Birmingham, scheduled for 2 hours and 10 minutes with one stop and named the 'Inter City'. This was very attractive to me as a day out, and I had two runs with 'Kings' on this train and on a 9.0am Paddington Mondays-only train that was non-stop. Surprisingly both had major problems, although for different reasons. On the first I rode 6016 *King Edward V*. The tender was filled with an appalling load of coal dust, and we struggled for steam throughout. I spent at least half the journey knee-deep in the stuff, mining the odd lump of genuine coal and flinging it forward to the perspiring fireman. We somehow kept time, but it was a struggle, and I doubt we would have made it without the two of us working flat-out to make steam. On the second occasion we had 6000 itself (known on depot as 'KG5') and a load of good Welsh coal, but as we accelerated up to Seer Green the steam pressure dropped ominously quickly. As soon as we shut off for the High Wycombe curves the steam pressure rose again, and we progressed in fits and starts, working hard uphill and drifting downhill while we recovered breath. We roared over Hatton Summit at 53mph and sailed into Snow Hill on time, but again it had been touch and go. We later learned that superheater tubes in the smokebox were leaking. 6000 did not in any case have a very good reputation for steaming, and it was discovered at some point that the double blastpipes were slightly out of alignment. (See Appendix Table 14 for the detailed logs of most

209

of my footplate runs.) I went through to Shrewsbury on a Stafford Road 'Castle' (5047 *Earl of Dartmouth*), returning to London on 6845 *Paviland Grange* and, from Wolverhampton, a beautifully maintained and superb riding 6026 *King John*, which, without any real fuss, turned a nine min-late departure from Leamington (sheep on the line at Lapworth) into an early arrival at Paddington.

Just before my time at Old Oak came to an end I had one last trip up the GW Birmingham route behind my favourite 'King', 6022 *King Edward III*. This was a Stafford Road engine, and we had an crew who were on a punctuality-bonus scheme. Unfortunately, although going well, we failed to pick up any water from the nearly empty troughs just south of Banbury and so tried to take water during the scheduled Princes Risborough stop. The fireman climbed onto the tender to put the bag in the tank, and I was sent to turn on the hydrant. Nothing came. I fiddled with the handle, trying all positions in case I had got it wrong (everyone assumed you knew everything, without instruction, and, as a young trainee, I was sometimes too embarrassed to admit my ignorance) so we abandoned the attempt and set off with great gusto to get time in hand, as we would have to make a special stop for water at High Wycombe. Here I was again sent to operate the water-column hydrant and managed somehow to get the handle off the valve seat, so that it just revolved without connection. The driver saw the mess I was in and immediately assumed I had made the same mistake at Princes Risborough, so I became the target of a few well-aimed epithets. With the water column restored to action we topped up as far as was necessary and then set off for Paddington, the driver taking out his frustration on the locomotive as he saw his bonus disappearing. I have no idea what speed we reached — I just huddled in the fireman's corner and willed myself to disappear! We arrived seven minutes late, and I made myself scarce.

One week during this time I heard rumour of a high-speed test to Wolverhampton and back. The 'Kings' were living on borrowed time, it being anticipated that there would be sufficient 'Western' diesels to cover the winter timetable on the Birmingham line. The Civil Engineer was a little nervous about the state of the track for sustained higher-speed running, and to be sure he wanted a test with the 'Whitewash Car' — the vehicle that would evaluate track condition at speed and let splashes of whitewash fall on track which did not come up to standard. We had two 'Castles' in store in the paint shop, 4098 and 7030; I noticed activity around the latter, and the rumours were confirmed when I was informed that 7030 *Cranbrook Castle* was being prepared for the test run (diesel availability being insufficient to spare a 'Warship'). I asked Ray Sims for permission to travel on the locomotive, but he refused on the grounds that there would be an additional fireman and an inspector in the cab. However, someone overheard my request and suggested I just turn up at Paddington and ask the Civil Engineer in charge if I could travel in the train.

I did as suggested and, permission (surprisingly) having been readily forthcoming, made my way to the front BSK (Brake Second Corridor) in splendid isolation — the engineering party were all in the test vehicle, and the rest of the train was empty. We left Paddington at 10.25, fifteen minutes behind the '*Blue Pullman*', and with five minute stops booked at High Wycombe and Leamington, to ensure the Pullman did not delay us, we were scheduled to reach Wolverhampton in just over two hours. However, in the event even this margin was insufficient, and we caught up with the Pullman in the Black Country, in consequence arriving a few minutes late. Highlights on the down journey were 96mph at Haddenham, acceleration to 70 at Warwick and a sustained 66mph approaching Hatton Summit, before braking for the curve at the top of the bank. However, this was small beer compared with the return journey, which after Leamington became extremely lively. I made it 105mph below Bicester (although I claimed only 103 subsequently, having tested my average speeds against claimed maxima), and after the High Wycombe stop we again touched 103 at Denham and 97 at Greenford. The latter fireworks got both driver and inspector into hot water, as it was claimed that we would never have stopped had Old Oak West Junction signals been against us. I enclose my logs for interest (Appendix Table 15), although these have been published elsewhere, notably in O. S. Nock's classic book on the 'Kings' and 'Castles'. Incidentally, I gathered that, from an engineering-test point of view, the exercise was of very limited value, as the riding south of Banbury on the return journey was so rough that the whitewash splashed onto almost every mile of track (as well as obliterating the rear windows of the test car), breaking the hearts of a number of p-way gangers in the process.

The following day, 16 May 1962, 7030 was on the 'Oxford Flyer' turn (5.30pm non-stop Oxford–Paddington in 60 minutes for the 63 miles), and I decided to use my footplate pass to see what high speed on 7030 was like. We got to Paddington in 56 minutes, with a top speed of 90mph near Maidenhead, but the driver was dubious when I told him of the previous day's exploits. He was not disbelieving that 7030 was capable of such speeds but thought the driver and inspector foolhardy, as the engine rolled quite pronouncedly at 90mph; it was not rough, but it was enough for the 'Oxford Flyer' driver to ease off once that speed was reached. The best bit: sitting in the fireman's tip-up seat on the left-hand side, leaning out of the cab window, as we roared through the middle road at Reading in the mid-80s, whistle howling — what a sight we must have made for the crowds awaiting the next up express!

A week later I sat somewhat nonchalantly in the cab of 5001 *Llandovery Castle* on arrival at Paddington, chatting with my father and a few of his friends who had spent the day at an army reunion in Bristol and whom we had just transported back to London. 5001 had been another star on the 'Oxford Flyer' a month previously, when it had achieved an actual time of 53 minutes (average speed 71.3mph), and the highlight that time had been passing through Reading at spectacular speed (Tableau 8 and Appendix Table 14). The following day I saw No 4082 roaring through Twyford on the 'Flyer', and the Old Oak grapevine later claimed a journey time of 51 minutes (74mph average). The sound effects were akin to that of an automatic machine-gun being fired; there was clearly no slowing for the Twyford curve that day!

On the whole, ex-GWR engines rode extremely well, but I was quite keen to experience a really rough locomotive, to see just how bad it could be for the crew. I had been on a 'Hall' (4917) which rode like a bicycle with a flat tyre, but that was irritating rather than rough. One of Old Oak's older double-chimney 'Castles', 5008 *Raglan Castle*, had been a star but was getting run-down as it neared its shopping date, and as it was rostered for an evening commuter train I decided to go with it to Reading. The first alarm was when I leant against the cab side and found that it moved under my weight. (A few days later 5008 was removed from a South Wales milk train because the crew complained of a dangerous cab — many rivets were found to be missing.) Steam pressure on getting the 'right away' was only 180lb, and the fireman was trying manfully to clean the fire. However, once underway, 5008 proved herself to be very strong, steam pressure recovered, and good time was kept. 5008 was rough but not uncomfortably so. She rolled and pitched in a sort of corkscrew motion, but if you learned to move with it, it was quite predictable and rather fun.

I did eventually find a real shocker — but it was not a GW engine. On one of my very long days I decided to do the 'triangle' — Paddington–Bristol–Shrewsbury via the North & West and back up the Birmingham main line. I picked up the 7.55am Paddington at Reading, with 7021 *Haverfordwest Castle*, which gave me a good steady run to Newport, where I caught a DMU to Bristol. There joined the 7.5am Penzance–Manchester, hauled by an ex-works 6945 *Glasfryn Hall*, the special attraction of this train being that from Pontypool Road it was rostered for a Crewe 'Royal Scot' for the remainder of its journey to Manchester. Sure enough, at Pontypool Road a grubby 46166 *London Rifle Brigade* was waiting, complete with Shrewsbury crew (ex-LMS driver and ex-GW fireman). My first impression was of the comfort and roominess of the cab after the Western engines, but this was soon undermined by its behaviour in motion. Although our running was 'gentle', to put it mildly, the locomotive riding was erratic and unpredictable and over 50mph was decidedly rough. The schedule was very easy, the train on time, and the load only moderate (nine coaches), so little exertion was called for, and our highest speeds on the way to Shrewsbury were 66mph at Tram Inn and 65mph on the descent from Church Stretton at Dorrington. At these modest speeds the ride became very uncomfortable, with a jerky side 'waggle' that caused me to hang on and not relax my grip for fear of being thrown across the cab. The firing technique was very different from that applied to GW engines; large lumps of coal were manhandled through the firehole door until the firebox was full, then a rest was taken while it burned through, whereas Western engines almost invariably were fired little and often. 46166 was taken very easily up the banks (in fact the fireman confided in me that he thought his mate took it too easily), but we arrived in Shrewsbury on time without discovering what the 'Scot' could really do, if pushed.

At the other end of the scale in terms of ride was a run up from Swansea on 5056 *Earl of Powis*, a couple of months out of Swindon after overhaul and thus in its prime. I'd joined the Cardiff crew on 7036 *Taunton Castle* on the 7.55am Paddington from Reading, which ran very energetically and was early at every calling-point. I'd pre-arranged with Driver Ward of Old Oak that I'd return with him on the 11.10am Milford Haven from Swansea — a double-home job, as he would have gone down to Swansea the previous night with 5056 on the 6.55pm Paddington–Fishguard. Despite a load of eleven coaches (420 tons gross) the return journey could not have been made to seem easier. The only source of alarm was a drop in steam pressure as we climbed through Landore and Llansamlet to the summit at Skewen, but on arrival at Neath Fireman Thomas found that the smokebox door had not been sufficiently tightened and was drawing air, and after his attention we had no further problems. Arrival at Swindon was a full five minutes early, and running in the upper 60s was sufficient to get us into Paddington equally ahead of time, with the locomotive running very quietly and riding like a Pullman coach.

As I made my way back to Twyford station house for the night, on the footplate of 7906 *Fron Hall* on a Didcot semi-fast, we passed the next up South Wales express (the 12.5pm Neyland) running equally early behind my favourite Laira 'Castle', 4087, and I found myself wishing I had waited a further hour in Swansea, although this would have meant disappointing my Old Oak crew, who seemed genuinely pleased to have someone on board who took an interest in their work. In fact, one of the lessons I learned during my footplate spell was that managers were often not aware of the attitudes and concerns of footplate staff because they so seldom saw them undertaking their normal duties. Drivers told me all too often that they only ever saw management when they were 'on the carpet' for some sort of misdemeanour. I remembered this when I became Chief Operating Manager of the LMR in 1982 and sought wherever possible to ride with train crews when I had to travel round the Region to get to meetings or conduct other business.

Other memorable journeys included a little gem of a trip on a parcels train with Didcot's 6309 — a competent little locomotive, just back from another Swindon overhaul despite its age — and a hugely impressive run with a heavy load (470 tons) from Shrewsbury right through to Bristol with Canton's best 'King', 6018 *King Henry VI*. During my spell in training at Old Oak my ultimate tally for footplate trips was six 'D8xx' 'Warships', one 'D70xx' 'Hymek', one DMU, one 'D30xx' diesel shunter, six 'Kings', twenty-two 'Castles', ten 'Halls', one 'County', one '47xx', one 'Grange', one '63xx', one '97xx' and one 'Royal Scot'. Logs of some of these runs, with details of the locomotive handling, are included in the Appendix (Table 14).

At the end of this particular period of my training my supervisory managers doubtless felt that I had been much too much the 'enthusiast' rather than the management trainee and had spent too much of my time at Old Oak sampling obsolete steam locomotives rather than the new forms of traction, but as things turned out I would have plenty of opportunities of living with the diesels as they flooded the Western Region over the next couple of years. In retrospect I realise just how much of value I picked up — largely as a result of of my intense interest in all that was going on — that stayed with me throughout my working life. Supremely, the lesson was one of being sensitive to people, their interests and concerns and of respecting the knowledge and experience of those who would not count themselves as managers but whose opinions and views were well worth the effort of canvassing through both formal and informal contacts.

I look back at my time in the old London Division of BR's Western Region with great affection and feel a great sense of gratitude towards all those who gave me opportunities and enabled me to develop my potential yet allowed me to have a lot of fun in the process. Many were the times I found myself thinking in disbelief: 'I'm actually getting paid for doing this!'

Postscript

In June 1962 I moved on to the South Wales Division to complete my basic training at Margam (the London Division having no major freight yard), spending months 'sitting next to Nellie', as it was known — learning by watching clerks do their job and reading files — in the Swansea District and Cardiff Divisional Offices and ultimately becoming a stationmaster in a Welsh valley. These, however, form other stories and, together with tales of my time at Gillingham (Dorset), Aberbeeg and Bridgend, in the Cardiff Divisional Office, as Chief Operating Manager at Crewe and ultimately as Head of Safety Policy for British Rail at 222 Marylebone Road, will form the backdrop of a second volume of my reminiscences, to be published in 2016. The foreground will be taken up by accounts of  my frantic attempts to savour the last swansongs of British steam between 1963 and 1968, a burgeoning interest in Continental steam in France and both halves of Germany, a one-off amazing tour of China's JiTong Railway in 2002 and my experiences of the many special steam trains, both in the UK and of those splendid German phenomena, the 'Plandampfs' of the 1990s.

A final chapter will be describe the railway industry's support for the charity I founded in 1995, Railway Children, which helps street children living on the railway and other transport termini in India and East Africa, and the often hidden runaway children living on the streets of our own country. At a meeting of the United Nations Human Rights Council held in Geneva in 2012 it was stated that Railway Children, with an annual income of nearly £3 million, was now the largest charity in the world working exclusively for children living on the street. Since its inception almost 50% of the charity's income has come from individuals and companies associated with the UK railway industry — both the main-line network and heritage railways.

In common with the royalties and profits from my various novels and non-fictional books on street children, all royalties from this book will be donated to the Railway Children charity.

The author at the launch of the Railway Children charity at Waterloo station, 31 May 1995.

The author sits with street children at their 'platform school' on the Rayagada Goods station platform near Visakhapatnam in the Indian State of Andhra Pradesh, c 2004

Above:
The Child Assistance Booth 'CAB' at Lucknow station manned round the clock by Railway Children's partner project, station staff and members of the Indian Railway Protection Force (RPF) as part of that station's piloted 'Child Friendly Station' scheme, January 2011

Opposite top right:
Street boys demand a photo with the author at Delhi Cantonment station, c2002

Opposite right:
The poster displayed round Lucknow station encouraging passengers to spot lone vulnerable children and bring them for registration at the Child Assistance Booth as part of the 'Child Friendly Station' initiative, a partnership between Indian Railways and the Railway Children, January 2011.

Appendix
Train 'log' tables

Table 1: Salisbury–Exeter with a 'King Arthur' (replacing 34009 — failed, injector problem)

Salisbury–Exeter Central, August 1956
7.38am Waterloo–Ilfracombe (SO)
30449 *Sir Torre* (72B)
11 coaches, 355/385 tons

	Time (min.sec)	Speed (mph)	Remarks
Salisbury	00.00		3min late
Wilton	07.30	35	
Dinton	14.51	60	
Tisbury	19.11	54	
Semley	24.47	53	at summit
Gillingham	29.42	77/20*	p-way slack
Templecombe	38.32	50	
Milborne Port	42.05	35	
Sherborne	45.39	80	
Yeovil Jct	49.34	69/76	
Sutton Bingham	52.46	40	
Crewkerne	59.27	70/58	
Chard	67.08	70	
Axminster	71.31	76	
Seaton Jct	74.19	67	
MP150	-	43	
Honiton Tunnel	83.11	26/28	
Honiton	86.34	51	
Sidmouth Jct	91.24	62	
Whimple	94.54	69	
Broad Clyst	97.59	75	
Pinhoe	99.41	56	easy
			30sec sigs stand
Exeter Central	106.00		3min late

30449 *Sir Torre*, the engine that worked the Ilfracombe express west of Salisbury in 1956, passing Surbiton with a West of England train c1955. *(Robin Russell)*

218

Table 2: Waterloo–Woking ('King Arthurs')

	30796 *Sir Dodinas le Savage* (72B) 2.54pm Waterloo–Salisbury (6 coaches — 210 tons) 8.10.59		30777 *Sir Lamiel* (70D) 5.9pm Waterloo–Basingstoke (9 coaches — 345 tons) 9.2.60		30453 *King Arthur* (72B) 2.54pm Waterloo–Salisbury (6 coaches — 210 tons) 23.3.60	
Waterloo	00.00		00.00		00.00	
Vauxhall	03.08	48	03.30	52	03.16	58
Clapham Jct	06.56	40*	07.08	40*	06.35	40*
Earlsfield	09.28	55	09.34	52	08.56	58
Wimbledon	11.17	64	11.33	62	10.45	25* (sigs)
New Malden	15.07	5* (pws)	14.26	10* (pws)	14.05	15* (pws)
Surbiton	19.26	50	19.28	46	18.30	53
Hampton Court Jct	-	67	-	60	-	65
Esher	21.55	20* (slow line)	22.02	71	21.12	15* (slow line)
Hersham	-	51	-	73	-	50
Walton	25.23	58	24.25	72	24.07	58
Weybridge	27.29	63	26.14	71	26.17	63
West Weybridge	-	74	-	78	-	73
West Byfleet	29.41	72	28.25	76	28.33	72
Woking	32.29 (27 net)		32.04 (27½ net)		31.33 (27 net)	

	30777 *Sir Lamiel* (70B) 5.9pm Waterloo–Basingstoke (10 coaches — 370 tons) 2.6.60		30777 *Sir Lamiel* (70B) 5.9pm Waterloo–Basingstoke (10 coaches — 370 tons) 3.6.60		30765 *Sir Gareth* (70D) 7.54pm Waterloo–Basingstoke (8 coaches — 255 tons) 30.6.60	
Waterloo	00.00		00.00		00.00	
Vauxhall	03.26	53	03.29	56	03.42	
Clapham Jct	06.59	42*	06.53	46*	07.11	10* (pws)
Earlsfield	09.13	55	09.05	56	-	43
Wimbledon	11.06	64	10.59	61	13.32	53
New Malden	13.43	67	13.39	65	-	61
Surbiton	16.17	42* (sigs)	15.46	68	18.58	66
Hampton Court Jct	-	57	17.00	73	-	72
Esher	19.00	67	17.54	73	-	73
Hersham	-	68	-	73	-	75
Walton	21.30	70	20.10	75	23.21	76
Weybridge	23.28	67	21.58	72	25.11	72
West Weybridge	-	77	-	70 (eased)	-	81
West Byfleet	25.47	72	24.17		27.20	74
Woking	29.06 (27 net)		27.41		30.53 (27½ net)	

	30765 *Sir Gareth* (70D) 5.9pm Waterloo–Basingstoke (11 coaches — 390 tons) 15.7.60		30796 *Sir Dodinas le Savage* (72B) 6.54pm Waterloo–Salisbury (5 coaches — 190 tons) 7.2.61		30777 *Sir Lamiel* (70D) 9.54pm Waterloo–Basingstoke (4 coaches — 150 tons) 21.2.61	
Waterloo	00.00		00.00		00.00	
Vauxhall	03.10	50	03.01	58	03.11	57
Clapham Jct	06.41	47*	06.11	46*	06.24	45*
Earlsfield	08.43	58	08.20	60	08.38	58
Wimbledon	10.35	62	10.37	15* (sigs)	10.36	63
New Malden	13.18	64	15.10	64	13.06	72
Surbiton	15.31	65	17.30	60* (sigs)	15.20	62* (eased)
Hampton Court Jct	-	70	18.50	71	16.42	64
Esher	17.48	70	20.02	43* (slow line)	17.41	71
Hersham	-	70	-	61	-	76
Walton	20.14	70	23.00	66	20.01	78
Weybridge	22.10	67	24.58	70	21.41	80
West Weybridge	-	73	-	76	-	82
West Byfleet	24.31	70	27.13	73	23.49	73
Woking	27.41		34.22 (sigs; 26 net)		27.07 (26 net)	

30777 *Sir Lamiel* pictured in May 1960 at the head of the 5.9pm Waterloo–Basingstoke commuter train, which it hauled regularly during the latter part of 1959 and most of 1960.

Nine Elms' 30779 *Sir Colgrevance* arriving at Woking with the 9.48am to Waterloo, May 1959.

Table 3: Woking–Waterloo ('King Arthurs')

	30768 *Sir Balin* (70A) 10.20am arr ex Southampton (9 coaches — 260 tons) 5.59		30799 *Sir Ironside* (72B) 3.27pm arr ex Salisbury (7 coaches — 250 tons) 12.12.59		30788 *Sir Urre of the Mount* (71A) 6.4pm arr (FO) ex Southampton (10 coaches — 340 tons) 6.6.60	
Woking	00.00		00.00		00.00	
West Byfleet	04.02	66	03.56	68	04.02	63
Weybridge	06.14	69	06.10	70	06.29	65
Walton	-	73	07.56	78	08.21	77
Hersham	-	75	-	78	-	76
Esher	10.15	74	10.08	76	10.36	78
Hampton Court Jct	-	74	11.04	73	11.32	77
Surbiton	12.16	69	12.26	45* (sigs)	12.34	76
New Malden	14.20	71	15.38	60/5* (pws)	14.39	70
Wimbledon	16.39	67	20.04	35* (sigs)	16.59	67
Earlsfield	18.16	61	22.03		18.35	66
Clapham Jct	(3min stand* — sigs)		24.09	20* sigs	20.22	40*
Queens Road	26.41	42	-	52	-	35* (sigs)
Vauxhall	28.18		28.00		23.58	(2min sigs)
Waterloo	31.09 (26½ net)		31.27 (26 net)		30.56 (26½ net)	

	30457 *Sir Bedivere* (70A) 2.4pm arr ex Basingstoke (6 coaches — 220 tons) 18.6.60		30803 *Sir Harry le Fise Lake* (71A) 10.20am arr ex Southampton (8 coaches — 260 tons) 1.7.60		30457 *Sir Bedivere* (70A) 10.20am arr ex Southampton (9 coaches — 265 tons) 6.7.60	
Woking	00.00		00.00		00.00	
West Byfleet	04.03	65	04.26	62	04.18	66/70
Weybridge	06.28	63	07.03	60	06.40	69
Walton	08.30	71	09.03	74	08.32	75
Hersham	-	70	-	72	-	73
Esher	10.59	72	11.25	77	10.56	72
Hampton Court Jct	11.59	69	12.25	71	11.58	72
Surbiton	13.06	68	14.52	5* (sigs)	13.10	64* (sigs)
New Malden	15.16	67	-	50	15.28	67
Wimbledon	17.38	69	-	63	18.01	65
Earlsfield	19.14	68	-	65	19.44	68
Clapham Jct	21.32	20* (sigs)	26.08	10* (pws)	21.45	25* (pws)
Queens Rd	-	46	-	47	-	49
Vauxhall	26.00	(3min stand — sigs)	30.35	15* (sigs)	25.53	
Waterloo	34.22 (27½ net)		34.28 (28 net)		29.20 (27½ net)	

	30795 *Sir Dinadan* (70D) 9.45am arr ex Basingstoke (10 coaches — 370 tons) 5.4.61		30798 *Sir Hectimere* (72B) 11.16am arr ex Salisbury (7 coaches — 250 tons) 26.3.62	
Woking	00.00		00.00	
West Byfleet	04.16	68	03.49	69/73
Weybridge	06.44	66	06.05	72
Walton	08.42	74	07.50	78
Hersham	-	75	-	79
Esher	11.00	75	09.59	76
Hampton Court Jct	11.58	73	10.54	74
Surbiton	14.25	5* (sigs)	12.16	42* (sigs)
New Malden	18.10	55	16.25	2* (long pws)
Wimbledon	21.01	61	22.18	57
Earlsfield	22.41	67	24.02	64
Clapham Jct	24.30	40*	25.50	43*
Queens Rd	-	51	-	58
Vauxhall	28.21	15* (sigs)	28.51	
Waterloo	32.05 (27½ net)		31.46 (25½ net)	

Table 4: Woking–Waterloo ('Lord Nelsons')

	30855 *Robert Blake* (71A) 9.39am arr ex Basingstoke (9 coaches — 330 tons) 5.10.59		30864 *Sir Martin Frobisher* (71A) 8.22am arr ex Southampton (10 coaches — 360 tons) 2.60		30861 *Lord Anson* (71A) 8.22am arr ex Southampton (10 coaches — 360 tons) 1.11.60	
Woking	00.00		00.00		00.00	
West Byfleet	04.31	58	05.02	55	04.19	58/64
Weybridge	07.07	60/5	07.44	59	06.45	62
Walton	09.16	61	09.58	62	08.37	73
Hersham	-	60	-	63	-	10* (sigs)
Esher	11.53	59	12.29	62	12.17	38
Hampton Court Jct	13.00	58	13.37	62	14.08	43
Surbiton	15.00	10* (sigs)	14.45	60	15.47	47
New Malden	19.52	15* (pws)	17.12	56	18.26	56
Wimbledon	23.51	50	20.04	58	21.07	62
Earlsfield	25.48	56	22.05	57	22.57	60
Clapham Jct	27.42	45*	24.12	40*	25.02	44*
Queens Road	-	50	-	51	-	50
Vauxhall	31.13		27.46	10* (sigs)	28.30	
Waterloo	34.04 (31 net)		32.06 (31 net)		32.24 (29 net)	
			(average run)		(good average run)	

	30862 *Lord Collingwood* (71A) 8.22am arr ex Southampton (10 coaches — 360 tons) 11.60		30857 *Lord Howe* (71A) 8.22am arr ex Southampton (10 coaches — 360 tons) 26.7.61	
Woking	00.00		00.00	
West Byfleet	04.32	56/63	05.44	43/46
Weybridge	06.59	62	09.05	39
Walton	08.59	69	11.50	48
Hersham	-	71	-	51
Esher	11.11	70	15.07	47
Hampton Court Jct	12.10	68	16.30	46
Surbiton	13.46	25* (sigs)	18.02	44
New Malden	16.22	53	20.47	49
Wimbledon	19.06	60	24.06	30* (sigs)
Earlsfield	21.00	60	26.57	39
Clapham Jct	22.57	40*	29.37	36*
Queens Road	-	52	-	41
Vauxhall	26.20		33.50	
Waterloo	29.36 (28½ net)		37.13 (36 net)	
			(loco short of steam)	

Table 5: Waterloo–Woking ('Lord Nelsons')

	30850 *Lord Nelson* (71A) 10.54am Salisbury (4 coaches — 130 tons) 2.60		30850 *Lord Nelson* (71A) 11.15pm Basingstoke (6 coaches — 165 tons) 9.3.60		30851 *Sir Francis Drake* (71A) 10.35pm Weymouth (15 coaches — 410 tons) 11.60		30854 *Howard of Effingham* (71A) 10.35pm Weymouth (15 coaches — 402 tons) 10.5.61	
Waterloo	00.00		00.00		00.00		00.00	
Vauxhall	02.50	47	02.58		03.48		03.36	
Queens Road	-	45	-	54	-	48	-	40
Clapham Jct	07.08	45*	06.17	48*	07.42	42*	07.31	42*
Earlsfield	09.50	39	08.33	48	10.10	47	10.19	44
Wimbledon	12.48	42	10.33	55	12.18	56	12.36	53
New Malden	16.04	40	13.38	15* (pws)	14.49	62	15.50	54
Surbiton	19.10	40	18.47	44* (slow line)	17.02	67	18.50	44 (short of steam)
Hampton Court Jct	-	42	20.30	52	18.16	70	-	41
Esher	22.42	40	21.48	55	19.14	68	22.23	38
Hersham	-	38	-	54	-	67	-	41
Walton	26.58	35	24.40	51	21.52	68	26.26	40
Weybridge	30.55	31	27.38	42	24.01	64	30.04	33
West Weybridge	-	38	-	50	-	69/72	-	43
West Byfleet	34.52	36	30.37	49	26.32	65	34.07	29/18
Woking (Mosque)							-	8
Woking	39.06 (8min late)		34.14 (31½ net)		30.09		41.56/69.40	
	(top speed Vauxhall)		(short of steam)		(worked very hard)		(brakes on, with only mail vans at platform; departed 89min late after raising steam)	

30852 *Sir Walter Raleigh* at Waterloo with the 10.54am semi-fast to Salisbury, May 1959.

Table 6: Waterloo–Southampton Central ('Lord Nelson')

30861 *Lord Anson* (71A)
12.22pm (SO) Waterloo–Bournemouth
(10 coaches — 335 tons)
17.6.61

Waterloo	00.00		2min late
Vauxhall	03.20		
Clapham Jct	07.10	40*	
Earlsfield	09.36	48	
Wimbledon	11.42	51	
New Malden	14.38	54	
Surbiton	16.52	59	
Hampton Court Jct	18.08	65	
Esher	19.09	64	
Walton	21.58	24* (slow line)	
Weybridge	25.37	41	
West Weybridge	-	55	
West Byfleet	28.26	58	
Woking	31.50		3min late
	00.00	(slow line)	on time
Brookwood	06.57	44	
MP31	-	46	
Farnborough	12.52	62	
Fleet	15.50	70/73	racing 'Bournemouth Belle' on fast line
Winchfield	18.41	65	
Hook	20.52	62/60	
Basingstoke	26.22	57/5* (sigs)	
Worting Jct	32.36	29	very slow acceleration
Wootton 'box	-	38	
Micheldever	42.40	54/63	
Weston 'box	-	66	
Winchester	49.50	74	
Shawford	52.17	78	
Eastleigh	55.20	70	
Swaythling	57.22	69/1* (sigs)	
St Denys	61.33		
Northam Curve	-	15*	
Tunnel Jct	64.08		
Southampton	66.50		1min early

30861 *Lord Anson* at Southampton Central on 14 June 1962 with a Bournemouth–York express, which it will work as far as Oxford. *(Manchester Locomotive Society collection)*

Table 7: Woking–Waterloo (morning commuter runs)

	35004 *Cunard White Star* (72B) 6.45am Salisbury (11 coaches — 390 tons) 12.57		35007 *Aberdeen Commonwealth* (72B) 6.45am Salisbury (10 coaches — 365 tons) 19.11.59		34016 *Bodmin* (71A) 6.04am Southampton Terminus (10 coaches — 365 tons) 1.8.61		30918 *Hurstpierpoint* (70D) 8.25am Basingstoke (9 coaches — 320 tons) 26.10.59	
Woking	00.00		00.00		00.00		00.00	
West Byfleet	03.59	70	04.02	68	04.28	68	04.34	61
Weybridge	06.02	78	06.20	69	06.43	72	07.02	60
Walton	07.33	83	08.09	82	08.23	82	09.01	72
Hersham	-	87	-	84	-	83	-	73
Esher	09.13	88	10.13	84	10.25	84	11.20	74
Hampton Court Jct	-	86	-	84	11.17	81	12.18	72
Surbiton	11.00	78	12.02	82/5* (sigs)	12.17	73	13.21	73
New Malden	12.56	75	16.18	5* (pws)	14.28	58* (sigs)	17.00	5* (pws)
Wimbledon	14.46	73	22.21	53	17.11	54* (sigs)	21.47	56
Earlsfield	-	66	24.11	64	19.08	56	23.34	61
Clapham Jct	18.44	40*	26.10	40*	20.46	15* (sigs)	25.35	40*
Queens Road	-	10* (sigs)	-	52	-	5* (sigs)	-	54
Vauxhall	23.41		30.00	0* (sigs)	26.33		28.50	
Waterloo	26.56 (25 net)		36.52 (26½ net)		29.48 (26¾ net)		31.56 (28 net)	

Table 8: Waterloo–Woking (evening commuter runs)

	35010 *Blue Star* (72A) 5pm to Exeter (10 coaches — 365 tons) 27.5.60		35023 *Holland-Afrika Line* (72A) 5pm to Exeter (11 coaches — 400 tons) 4.3.60		34082 *615 Squadron* (70A) 5.39pm to Salisbury (11 coaches — 400 tons) 10.7.61	
Waterloo	00.00		00.00		00.00	
Vauxhall	03.20		03.12		03.44	
Queens Road	-	57	-	56	-	48
Clapham Jct	06.25	45*	06.38	40*	07.20	43*
Earlsfield	08.33	58	08.48	57	09.35	53
Wimbledon	10.19	63	10.42	61	11.29	59
New Malden	14.03	5* (pws)	13.51	10* (pws)	14.02	65
Surbiton	19.01	51	18.58	46	16.06	69
Hampton Court Jct	-	64	-	64	17.18	75
Esher	21.33	69	21.26	72	18.04	79
Hersham	-	72	-	74	-	80
Walton	23.56	72	23.48	74	20.10	79
Weybridge	25.45	70	25.35	74	21.44	79
West Weybridge	-	81	-	84	-	86
West Byfleet	27.52	75	27.41	82	23 37	84
Woking	30.58 (26½ net)		30.42 (26¾ net)		26.17	

	73114 *Etarre* (70A) 5.39pm to Salisbury (11 coaches — 400 tons) 3.61		30918 *Hurstpierpoint* (70D) 5.9pm to Basingstoke (10 coaches — 375 tons) 15.3.60		30908 *Westminster* (70D) 5.9pm to Basingstoke (10 coaches — 365 tons) 3.5.60	
Waterloo	00.00		00.00		00.00	
Vauxhall	03.28		03.05		03.11	
Queens Road	-	50	-	2* (sigs)	-	50
Clapham Jct	07.11	40*	08.04	40*	06.38	44*
Earlsfield	09.34	48	10.22	52	08.58	52
Wimbledon	11.36	57	12.21	63	10.59	59
New Malden	14.28	65	15.18	15* (pws)	13.56	20* (pws)
Surbiton	16.38	68	19.46	47	18.08	48
Hampton Court Jct	17.52	70	-	62	-	59
Esher	18.47	71	22.21	70	20.50	62
Hersham	-	74	-	70	-	64
Walton	21.05	72	24.56	69	23.28	64
Weybridge	22.54	65	26.50	64	25.30	62
West Weybridge	-	77	-	70	-	74
West Byfleet	25.02	74	29.11	70	27.51	70
Woking	28.03		32.30 (27½ net)		31.02 (28 net)	

35004 *Cunard White Star* draws into Woking with the 1pm Waterloo–Exeter (the return working of the 6.45am Salisbury commuter train), July 1959.

Table 9: 5.9pm Waterloo–Woking (March 1959 'trials', Driver Carlisle of Basingstoke)

	30794 *Sir Ector de Maris* (70D) 10 coaches (375 tons)		75078 (70D) (Standard Class 4 4-6-0) 10 coaches (375 tons)		30923 *Bradfield* (70D) 10 coaches (375 tons)	
Waterloo	00.00		00.00		00.00	
Vauxhall	02.51		03.12		03.24	
Queens Road	-	61	-	58	-	55
Clapham Jct	05.56	46*	06.20	45*	06.46	45*
Earlsfield	08.04	57	08.31	55	08.59	54
Wimbledon	09.52	66	10.24	64	10.52	65
New Malden	12.20	71	12.59	69	13.23	70
Surbiton	14.30	75	15.19	73	15.42	72
Hampton Court Jct	-	75	-	75	-	74
Esher	16.28	75	17.20	75	17.42	76
Hersham	-	76	-	77	-	76
Walton	18.48	76	19.35	78	19.58	77
Weybridge	20.31	73	21.12	75	21.36	74
West Weybridge	-	75	-	78	-	83
West Byfleet	22.46	73	23.22	75	23.33	81
Woking	25.45		26.18		26.22	

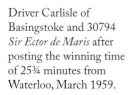

Driver Carlisle of Basingstoke and 30794 *Sir Ector de Maris* after posting the winning time of 25¾ minutes from Waterloo, March 1959.

Table 10: Waterloo–Woking (Basingstoke/Salisbury semi-fast services)

	30919 Harrow (70A)		30489 (70A) ('H15' 4-6-0)		30521 (70A) ('H15' 4-6-0)		31634 (70A) ('U' 2-6-0)	
	12.54pm Waterloo-Salisbury (7 coaches — 240 tons) 29.6.59		1.54pm Waterloo-Basingstoke (5 coaches — 180 tons) 10.59		11.15pm Waterloo-Basingstoke (6 coaches — 200 tons) 10.5.60		12.42pm (SO) Waterloo-Basingstoke (6 coaches — 205 tons) 13.8.60	
Waterloo	00.00		00.00		00.00		00.00	
Vauxhall	03.16		03.09		03.10		02.53	
Queens Road	-	66	-	53	-	58	-	58
Clapham Jct	06.02	40*	06.28	40*	06.18	46*	06.12	40*
Earlsfield	08.01	61	08.52	53	08.26	56	08.55	22* (pws)
Wimbledon	10.09	25* (sigs)	10.58	59	10.15	66	12.55	10* (sigs)
New Malden	-	15* (pws)	14.32	15* (pws)	13.11	15* (pws)	16.12	60
Surbiton	16.22	73	19.04	49	17.48	25* (slow line)	18.37	66
Hampton Court Jct	-	77	-	61	-	55	-	5* (sigs)
Esher	18.21	80	21.44	63	20.52	62	22.01	42
Hersham	-	78	-	63	-	68	-	56
Walton	20.20	76	24.28	62	23.23	70	25.32	60
Weybridge	22.04	70	26.44	59	25.23	66	27.46	61
West Weybridge	-	77	-	66	-	67	-	71
West Byfleet	24.16	74	29.21	61	27.49	68	30.41	25* (sigs)
Woking	27.52 (25 net)		33.16 (29 net)		31.05 (27 net)		34.51 (27 net)	

Another run on the 9.48am Woking, this time with the sole Maunsell rebuild of a Urie 'H15', 30491, May 1960.

Urie 'H15' 30489 arrives at Woking with the 9.48 to Waterloo, a stopping train from Bournemouth, in June 1960.

Table 11: Woking–Waterloo (Basingstoke semi-fast services)

	73087 *Maid of Astolat* (70A) 12.26pm arr ex Basingstoke (3 coaches — 110 tons) 4.59		34039 *Boscastle* (71B) (rebuilt) 12.26pm arr ex Basingstoke (3 coaches — 110 tons) 9.2.60		34041 *Wilton* (71B) (unrebuilt) 4.9pm arr ex Bournemouth (8 coaches — 280 tons) 6.10.59	
Woking	00.00		00.00		00.00	
West Byfleet	03.30	71	03.38	74	04.28	65
Weybridge	05.31	78/75	05.36	83/80	06.48	69/70
Walton	07.12	78	07.06	85	08.33	78
Hersham	-	81	-	87	-	81
Esher	09.18	77	09.06	82	10.38	83
Hampton Court Jct	10.09	75	09.57	82	-	82
Surbiton	11.13	74	10.58	69	12.32	82
New Malden	13.07	75/67	13.53	15* (pws)	15.34	15* (pws)
Wimbledon	15.28	61	19.23	5* (sigs)	19.58	49
Earlsfield	-	65	21.25	65	21.50	60
Clapham Jct	18.45	40*	23.19	30*	23.47	40*
Queens Road	-	64	-	62	-	54
Vauxhall	23.56	5* (pws)	26.53	15* (sigs)	27.17	5* (sigs)
Waterloo	27.13 (25 net)		30.26 (25 net)		31.23 (26½ net)	

	31753 (70A) ('L1' 4-4-0) 10.20am arr ex Southampton (7 coaches — 240 tons) 3.6.60		31628 (70C) ('U' 2-6-0) 2.34pm arr ex Andover (SO) (6 coaches — 200 tons) 6.8.60	
Woking	00.00		00.00	(slow line)
West Byfleet	04.16	61	04.02	67
Weybridge	06.56	63/60	06.26	64
Walton	09.07	66	08.24	71
Hersham	-	68	-	73
Esher	11.42	70	10.48	20* (sigs)
Hampton Court Jct	12.45	69	-	(main line)
Surbiton	13.57	65	14.11	46
New Malden	16.15	64	16.58	58
Wimbledon	18.48	65	19.51	60
Earlsfield	20.30	68	22.35	15* (pws)
Clapham Jct	22.31	30*	25.10	47*
Queens Road	-	0* (sigs)	-	54
Vauxhall	29.27	5* (sigs)	28.28	0* (sigs)
Waterloo	33.20 (28½ net)		32.58 (27½ net)	

'L1' 4-4-0 31786, displaced by the Kent Coast electrification, heads the
1.24pm Saturday Waterloo–Salisbury into Woking, July 1959.

Table 12: 8am Plymouth–Liverpool (via North & West route) 1960/1

5095 *Barbury Castle* (84G)
11 coaches (386/410 tons)
17.11.60
Driver G. Owen, Fireman H. Bound (Shrewsbury)

4037 *The South Wales Borderers* (83A)
11 coaches (386/410 tons)
15.2.61
Driver D. Lewis, Fireman R. Aggett (Newton Abbot)
Inspector H. George (Newport)

Location	Time	Speed	Note	Time	Speed	Late	Regulator/notes
Bristol Temple Meads	00.00		3½min late				
Dr Day's Bridge Jct	02.35	34					
Lawrence Hill	03.20	40					
Stapleton Road	04.21	45	3min late				
Ashley Hill	05.50	33					
Horfield	08.21	24					
Filton	10.56	42	3min late				
Patchway	12.48	53/73					
Pilning	16.20	81					
Severn Tunnel East	17.36	70 (eased)					
Severn Tunnel West	21.52	72/43					
Severn Tunnel Jct	23.32	43					
Magor	27.11	60/20* (pws)					
Bishton	-	58/5* (pws)					
Maindee Jct East	37.15	5*	2min early				
Maindee Jct North	38.50	15* (pws)					
Caerleon	42.38	48					
Ponthir	44.25	49					
Llantarnam	46.30	44					
Llantarnam Jct	-		35min				
Pontypool Road	54.56		7min early				
	00.0		2min early	00.00		10min late	210psi ½ regulator
Little Mill	-	62		-	50/63		½ regulator
Nantyderry	06.01/07.25 (overbraked pws)			06.33	30* (pws)		
Penpergwm	11.30	66/20* (bridge)		09.45	59/52*		2nd port opened
Abergavenny	17.59	36		16.05	10* (pws)	12min late	full regulator, 35% cut-off
Abergavenny Jct	-	34		18.13	34/28		220psi
Llanvihangel	26.08	38		25.00	30/36/40	11min late	30% cut-off, 225psi
Pandy	-	71/35* (pws)		27.45	67/48* (pws)		½ regulator 210psi
Pontrilas	33.41	77/60*		33.01	68/60*	11min late	shut off
St Devereux	-	70		36.48	64		½ reg 15%, 210psi
Tram Inn	-	8* (pws)		39.18	58/60		shut off
Red Hill Jct	45.06	35*		44.11	15*/62 (pws)	13min late	¾ regulator, 25% cut-off
Rotherwas Jct	47.28	56/61		46.45	70		205psi
Hereford	50.11		on time	49.05		11min late	195psi
	00.00		½min late	00.00		9min late	220psi
Barrs Court Jct	02.24	42	½min early	03.05	5* (sigs)		full reg
Shelwick Jct	03.58	51	1min early	04.50	48/56	8½min late	½ regulator, 15% cut-off
Moreton-on-Lugg	06.50	62		07.46	60		210psi
Dinmore	10.21	58/57		11.21	56/53		½ regulator, 20% cut-off
Ford Bridge	13.24	63		14.33	67		15% cut-off
Leominster	15.37	64		16.45	62/64	9min late	220psi
Berrington & Eye	18.50	66		19.48	65/60		pricker used on fire
Woofferton	22.00	73/60		22.47	71	8min late	¼ regulator, 200psi
Ludlow	26.36	59	3min early	27.16	60	6½min late	½ regulator, 215psi
Bromfield	29.05	58		29.30	61		no water from troughs
Onibury	-	49		32.03	62/51		½ regulator, 17% cut-off, 218psi
Craven Arms	35.10	56	4min early	35.26	60	5min late	205psi
Winstanstow Halt	-	54		-	53		pricker used
Marsh Farm Jct	-	54		-	47 (distant sigs on)		
Marsh Brook	40.56	52		42.26/44.01 (crossing failure)			218psi, full regulator, 25% cut-off
Little Stretton	-	44		-	30/35		½ regulator, 20% cut-off, 200psi
Church Stretton	44.32	50	6½min early	49.58	51	8min late	reg just cracked, 195psi
All Stretton Halt	-	64		-	65		shut off, 190psi
Leebotwood	48.18	72		53.40	73		
Dorrington	50.42	81		56.13	64/61		reg slightly opened
Condover	52.33	71		58.18	59		shut off, 180psi
Sutton Bridge Jct	56.28	15*		62.26	(sigs slight)		
Coleham	-			-	5* (sigs/pws)		
Shrewsbury	58.51		13½min early	66.58 (58½ net)		3min late (on time by public book)	

Net gain by locomotive of 44 minutes overall

Water consumption 1,400gal Hereford–Shrewsbury (= 28gal per mile); coal (dust and ovoids) c30-35lb per mile (very light)

Above: 5095 *Barbury Castle* at Pontypool Road with the 8am Plymouth–Liverpool, 17 November 1960.

Opposite page: Churchward 2-8-0 4708 at Reading on the Gloucester – Paddington relief train, on which the author, travelling in the first ex LMS coach just visible, recorded 80 mph between Reading and Maidenhead, 4.8.61. *(A.Wild)*

Table 13: Swindon–Paddington, 1961

2.55pm Cheltenham–Paddington relief
4.8.61
4708 (81A)
(Churchward large 2-8-0, restricted to 60mph)
Driver Instone (Swindon)
8 coaches (258/275 tons)

Swindon	00.00		1min late
Marston Sidings	-	50/55	
Shrivenham	09.29	57	
Uffington	14.58	60/62	
Challow	17.41	66	
Wantage Road	20.54	68/72	
Steventon	24.23	74	
Didcot	27.21	69 (eased)	
Cholsey	31.48	66	
Goring	35.21	67/64	
Pangbourne	38.28	66	
Tilehurst	41.10	68	
Reading	44.46		1½min early
	00.00		2min late
Sonning Cutting	-	53	
Twyford	06.46	69/73	
Waltham Sidings	-	77	
Maidenhead	12.25	80	
Taplow	14.00	69 (eased)	
Slough	17.47	64	
West Drayton	22.56	64	
Southall	27.06	64	
Acton	31.58	64	
OOld Oak Common East	33.59/34.12 (sigs stand)		
Westbourne Park	39.01	15* (sigs)	
Paddington	43.35 (38 net)		3½min late

231

Above: 7013 *Bristol Castle* (the former 4082) at Oxford with a Worcester–Paddington express on 6 May 1962, a week after the author footplated it from Oxford to Paddington on a similar train. (*John Hodge collection*)

Table 14: Footplate runs during OOC management training (April-June 1962)

1.15pm Paddington–Oxford(–Worcester–Hereford)
28.4.62
7031 *Cromwell's Castle* **(85A)**
Worcester crew
9 coaches (306/320 tons)

Paddington	00.00		on time	
Westbourne Park	02.46			full regulator
Acton	06.50	58		heavy firing to build fire up (not much preparation)
Ealing Broadway	08.28	62		
Southall	12.20	48* (sigs)		
Hayes	14.25	60		
West Drayton	16.43	65		¾ regulator, 15% cut-off
Slough	21.44	68/70		
Maidenhead	27.14	68/66		
Reading	37.56	65		½ regulator, 15% cut-off
Reading–Didcot	-	64-68		author firing
Oxford	68.00 (approx)		3min early	

Loco (transferred to 85A from 83D) in excellent condition, riding extremely well; fitted with single chimney and three-row superheater. Coal of poor quality (slack and slaty), but pressure steady at 225psi after Southall.

12.5pm Hereford–Paddington (2.30pm from Oxford)
28.4.62
7013 *Bristol Castle* **85A**
Worcester crew
9 coaches (308/325 tons)

Oxford	00.00		on time	
Radley	07.10	65		½ regulator (1st port)
Culham	09.25	70		
Appleford Halt	10.28	20* (long pws)		
Didcot East Jct	-	35*		
Cholsey	-	66		1st port regulator, 17% cut-off
Goring	-	71		
Pangbourne	-	75		
Tilehurst	-	76		
Reading	33.00		on time	
	00.00		4min late	station overtime unloading mail
Twyford	06.45	66/71		1st port regulator, 20% cut-off
Maidenhead	13.04	75		2nd port cracked, 17% cut-off
Taplow	14.44	73		
Slough	18.20	72/74		
Langley	20.23	74		1st port regulator, 17% cut-off
West Drayton	23.00	72		
Hayes	25.06	72		
Southall	26.48	74		
Ealing Broadway	29.44	75		
Acton	31.04	75		
Ladbroke Grove		0		15sec dead stand (sigs)
Westbourne Park	35.15			¾ regulator
Paddington	38.20 (37 net)		on time	

Loco recently ex Swindon, smooth riding. Steamed well (215-225psi all the way) on poor-quality coal; firing very light. By now fitted with double chimney, four-row superheater and Davies & Metcalfe valveless mechanical lubricator, it had been built in 1924 as No 4082 *Windsor Castle*, which identity it surrendered in 1952 (on account of being unavailable for working King George VI's funeral train) and never regained.

Opposite below: *Bristol Castle* speeds through Sonning Cutting with the up '*Cathedrals Express*' from Hereford and Worcester to Paddington, July 1962. *(R. H. Leslie)*

Table 14 (cont'd)

4.35pm Paddington–Reading(–Swindon)
30.4.62
4917 *Crosswood Hall* (82D)
6 coaches (184/205 tons)

Paddington	00.00		on time	
Westbourne Park	02.45			
Acton	06.55	58		
Ealing Broadway	08.22	63		
Southall	11.40	69		½ regulator, 20% cut-off
Hayes	13.29	70		
West Drayton	15.28	74		
Slough	19.55	15* (sigs; to slow line)		
Ruscombe Sidings	-	65		
Maidenhead	30.30		3½min early	slow into platform

Loco in good condition, steaming well and riding tolerably well.

12.5pm Milford Haven–Paddington (from Reading)
30.4.62
5034 *Corfe Castle* (81A)
12 coaches (412/440 tons)

Reading	00.00		on time	
Twyford	07.35	61		full regulator, 18% cut-off, 225psi
Maidenhead	14.15	70		full regulator, 15% cut-off, 190psi
Slough	19.28	72		pricker used; 170psi
West Drayton	-	64		¾ regulator, 15% cut-off, 180psi
Southall	-	68		full regulator, 18% cut-off, 200psi
Ealing Broadway	-	72		210psi
Acton	-	30* (sigs)		225psi
Paddington	42.01 (39 net)		on time	

Slight knock on right-hand side when notched up to 15%, but ride extremely smooth. Coal very poor; dirty fire accounted for lapse in steaming after Slough, but recovered quickly.

5.38pm Paddington–Reading(–Didcot)
2.5.62
5008 *Raglan Castle* (81A)
10 coaches (312/350 tons)
Driver Marshall, Fireman Stares (Old Oak Common)

Paddington	00.00		on time	170psi
Westbourne Park	03.01			full regulator, 190psi
Acton	07.10	57		full regulator, 20% cut-off, 180psi
Ealing Broadway	08.41	62		
Southall	12.11	68		full regulator, 18% cut-of, 160psi; pricker used
Hayes	13.56	70		180psi
West Drayton	16.05	71		½ regulator, 17% cut-off
Slough	21.00	72		200psi
Maidenhead	26.38	67 (eased)		190psi
Ruscombe Sidings	-	38* (to slow line)		210psi
Twyford	35.00		4min early	225psi
	00.00		on time	full regulator
Sonning Cutting	-	65		200psi
Reading	08.23	15* (sigs)	1min early	225psi

Very interesting trip. Timing from train, all would have seemed very easy. In fact the engine was rough-riding (lurching, everything very loose and rattling). The engine was low on its springs and had run 56,000 miles since last heavy intermediate repair. Coal was very poor, and fire at Paddington was clinkered and in bad shape. Firing was light, and the driver worked loco hard at first to let the fire burn through. Engine very strong, being fitted with double chimney and four-row superheater.

Table 14 (cont'd)

5.38pm Paddington–Twyford(-Didcot)
4.5.62
4088 *Dartmouth Castle* (82C)
10 coaches (312/350 tons)
Driver Radway (Old Oak Common)

Paddington	00.00		on time	225psi
Westbourne Park	03.23			¼ regulator
Acton	08.08	51		½ regulator, 225psi
Ealing Broadway	10.02	55		
Southall	14.20	57		16% cut-off, 225psi
Hayes	16.32	58		regulator eased back, 225psi
West Drayton	19.02	61		
Iver	-	5* (sigs)		cautioned — cow on line
Langley	-	2* (sigs)		engine blowing off steam
Slough	28.02	58		½ regulator, 18% cut-off, 225psi
Maidenhead	33.44	66		
Ruscombe Sidings	-	38* (to slow line)		
<u>Twyford</u>	<u>41.57</u> (39 net)		3min late	

No 4088 had a double chimney, four-row superheater and Davies & Metcalfe valveless mechanical lubricator; rode well. Firing very light, difficult to stop loco blowing off all the way. Driven very easily, fireman badgering driver to 'open her up'.

8.55am Fishguard–Paddington Parcels (from Reading)
May 1962
4099 *Kilgerran Castle* (87E)
Loaded parcel vans (444/500 tons)
Driver Instone (Swindon)

(Timed to nearest half-minute)

Reading	00.00		slow-line platform
Ruscombe	-	50	
Maidenhead	18.00	30* (sigs)	¼ regulator, 15% cut-off
Slough	25.00	3* (sigs)	
West Drayton	37.00	15*	to main line; ¾ regulator, 20% cut-off, 225psi
Hayes	40.30	45	
Southall	43.00	52	
Hanwell	-	60	
West Ealing	45.30	64	
Ealing Broadway	46.30	68	220psi
<u>Acton</u>	<u>48.00</u>		easy; signals onwards to Paddington

Loco in good condition and rode well. It was withdrawn four months later, in September 1962.

4088 *Dartmouth Castle*, at Oxford in 1960 with a Worcester–Paddington express.

Lady Margaret Hall pounds past Fosse Road with a Saturday Wolverhampton–Weymouth holiday express in June 1962, a month after the author footplated it on the 5.30pm Oxford–Paddington. *(R. H. Leslie)*

7911 *Lady Margaret Hall* at its home station of Oxford, at the head of a York–Bournemouth express, 1960. *(R. K. Blencowe collection)*

Table 14 (cont'd)

5.30pm (SO) Oxford–Paddington
5.5.62
7911 *Lady Margaret Hall* (81F)
6 coaches (188/195 tons)

Oxford	00.00		on time	
Radley	07.05	70		½ regulator, 20% cut-off, 210psi
Culham	09.10	72		½ regulator, 18% cut off, 200psi
Appleford Halt	10.06	73/55* (pws)		shut off, 190/220psi
Didcot North Jct	11.44	54*		
Didcot East Jct	13.00	35*		
Moreton Cutting	15.00	62		¾ regulator, 225psi
Cholsey	17.58	70		¾ regulator, 20% cut-off, 220psi
Goring	21.11	75/77		½ regulator, 18% cut-off, 210psi
Pangbourne	23.51	79		17% cut-off, 215psi
Tilehurst	26.09	81		225psi
Reading	28.10	83/80		
Twyford	32.08	80		full regulator, 195psi; pricker used
Maidenhead	37.28	82		¾ regulator, 190/200psi
Taplow	-	84		½ regulator, 18% cut-off, 185psi
Slough	42.03	80		¾ regulator, 205psi
Langley	43.51	78		¾ regulator, 195psi
West Drayton	46.28	75		full regulator, 200psi
Hayes	48.25	74		195psi
Southall	50.00	78		
Ealing Broadway	52.46	82		½ regulator, 190psi
Acton	53.58	80		firing eased
Westbourne Park	56.58	30*		
Paddington	59.55 (59 net)		on time	

Oxford 'spare' loco SO; had stood for some time and had formed clinker. Rode well except rough through Reading and Slough.

Table 14 (cont'd)

8.20am Paddington–Birmingham Snow Hill(–Wolverhampton) 'Inter City'
9.5.62
6016 *King Edward V* (81A)
10 coaches (348/375 tons)
Driver Newton, Fireman Billing (Old Oak Common)

Paddington	00.00		on time	250psi
Old Oak Common West	07.15			
Greenford	-	62		½ regulator, 18% cut-off, 205psi
Denham	-	58		180psi
Seer Green	-	44		155psi
Beaconsfield	-	63		
High Wycombe	36.30			
	00.00			185psi
Saunderton	-	45/43		full regulator, 25% cut-off, 200/160psi
Princes Risborough	-	60*		shut off, coasting
Ashendon Jct	22.00	78		¾ regulator, 18% cut-off
Brill	-	15* (sigs)		190psi
Blackthorn	-	68/70		full regulator, 20% cut-off
Bicester North	-	68		full regulator, 25% cut-off
Ardley	-	56		155psi
Ardley Tunnel	-	10* (pws)		
Aynho Jct	-	52		
Banbury	48.00	62/65		¼ regulator, 18% cut-off, 180psi
Fenny Compton	-	60* 65 (pws)		shut off
Leamington Spa	68.30	48*		injector off, blower on, 160psi
Warwick	-	58		full regulator, 20% cut off, 180psi
Hatton	-	48/42		full regulator, 25% cut-off, 210psi
Lapworth	-	59		full regulator, 18% cut-off, 220psi
Knowle	-	65		½ regulator, 180psi
Solihull	-	68		full regulator, 15% cut-off, 160/190psi
Tyseley	-	72		shut off, 210psi
Birmingham Snow Hill	97.00 (88 net)		½min late	220psi

Coal very poor, mostly dust; author spent much of journey looking for lumps of coal in the tender and throwing them forward for the fireman. Engine rode well and performed best on Hatton Bank, when the fierce draught on the fire livened things up. Author too busy to take accurate timings; speeds taken from loco speedometer and considered accurate.

No 6016 *King Edward* V descends Hatton Bank with the 07.40 Birkenhead - Paddington express on 25 August 1962, a month before withdrawal. *(Manchester Locomotive Society collection)*

Table 14 (cont'd)

9am (MO) Paddington–Birmingham Snow Hill(–Wolverhampton)
14.5.62
6000 *King George V* **(81A)**
9 coaches (312/325 tons)
Old Oak Common crew

Paddington	00.00		on time	250psi
Westbourne Park	03.30			235psi
Old Oak Common West	07.00			220psi
Greenford	12.45	65		½ regulator, 20% cut-off, 200psi
Northolt Jct East	-	61		¼ regulator
West Ruislip	-	66		regulator just cracked, 180psi
Denham	19.35	65		190psi
Gerrards Cross	22.20	54		½ regulator, 180psi
Beaconsfield	27.25	50		¼ regulator/shut off, 165psi
High Wycombe	33.35	35*		250psi
Saunderton	-	43/45		½ regulator, 20% cut-off, 185psi
Princes Risborough	45.18	57*		shut off, 215psi
Ashendon Jct	53.45	78/73		¾ regulator, 17% cut-off, 195psi
Brill	-	62		
Blackthorn	-	76		½ regulator, 185psi
Bicester North	61.50	60		½ regulator, 22% cut-off, 180psi
Ardley	66.15	52		
Ardley Tunnel	-	45* (pws)		shut off, 200psi
Aynho Jct	73.30	50*/63		shut off/½ regulator, 20% cut-off, 250/205psi
Banbury	79.20	15* (sigs)		250psi
Cropredy	-	65/60* (pws)		½ regulator
Fenny Compton	89.46	83		½ regulator
Leamington Spa	99.00	40*		250/235psi
Warwick	-	61/54		220psi
Hatton	106.25	53		full regulator, 20% cut-off, 205psi
Lapworth	-	45* (sigs)		
Widney Manor	-	58/15* (pws)		shut off, 250psi
Solihull	121.10	65		230psi
Bordesley	-	10* (sigs)		full regulator through Snow Hill Tunnel, 250psi
Birmingham Snow Hill	130.56 (118 net)		1min late	240psi

Loco had covered 38,000 miles since last works visit and had a reputation for poor steaming; rallied quickly every time steam shut off. Suspected smokebox problem, blast pipe alignment and/or superheater units blowing. Driver's skilled driving would have got train to Birmingham on time but for signal check at Bordesley.

11.40am Birkenhead–Paddington (Shrewsbury–Wolverhampton)
14.5.62
6845 *Paviland Grange* **(84B)**
6 coaches (211/225 tons)

Shrewsbury	00.00		3min late	
MP169	05.17	45		½ regulator, 30% cut-off, 225psi
Upton Magna	06.44	54		
Walcot	09.39	60/48		
Admaston	12.18	53/45		
Wellington	14.49		1min late	
	00.00		½min late	½ regulator, 35% cut-off, 225psi
Ketley Jct	03.08	33		
Oakengates	06.11	37		
Hollinswood	08.01	32		200psi
Shifnal	12.32	50/30*/44/21* (pws x2)		
Cosford	17.08	57		½ regulator, 30% cut-off, 225psi
Albrighton	18.51	44		
Codsall	22.36	54		25% cut-off
Birches Halt	23.25	60		
Oxley South	26.33	27* (sigs)		
Dunstall Park	27.23	35		
Wolverhampton Low Level	29.32 (25 net)		4min late	

Table 14 (cont'd)

4.35pm Wolverhampton–Paddington ('Inter City')
14.5.62
6026 *King John* (81A)
10 coaches (354/375 tons)
Driver Hinton (Tyseley) — from Birmingham to Paddington

Wolverhampton Low Level	00.00		1min early	
Priestfield	04.09	35/31*		250psi
Wednesbury	08.49	52/43*		
Swan Village	11.10	35		
West Bromwich	12.54	43		
Handsworth	15.34	55		
Soho & Winson Green	16.36	60/20* (sigs)		
Birmingham Snow Hill	20.19		½min early	
	00.00		½min late	250psi
Bordesley	02.41	46		
Tyseley	05.13	50		
Olton Park	07.23	55		
Solihull	09.19	57		
Widney Manor	10.46	62		
Knowle	12.41	56/15* (pws)		
Lapworth	19.31/19.53	2*/0 (cows on line)		
Hatton	26.24	48/60		
Warwick	30.20	72		
Leamington Spa	32.51		9min late	
	00.00		9min late	250psi
Fosse Road	06.12	46		
Southam Road	09.12	51		full regulator, 15% cut-off
Fenny Compton	14.23	62/56		
Claydon Crossing	17.10	64		
Cropredy	19.25	71		
Banbury	22.28	71	6½min late	
Kings Sutton	25.31	69/71		
Aynho Jct	26.58	69		
Ardley	32.07	63/54	5½min late	full regulator, 15% cut-off
Bicester	35.12	81		
Blackthorn	37.22	79/84		
Brill	39.38	75		
Dorton Halt	41.28	67/74		
Ashendon Jct	42.37	55*	3min late	
Haddenham	46.27	65		
Ilmer Halt	48.53	69/56		full regulator, 20% cut-off
Princes Risborough	51.38	63	2min late	
Saunderton	55.10	49		shut off
West Wycombe	58.05	65/38*		
High Wycombe	61.55		½min early	
	00.00		on time	250psi
Beaconsfield	07.10	56		full regulator, 15% cut-off
Seer Green	09.44	63		
Gerrards Cross	11.07	72		
Denham Golf Course	12.30	77		
Denham	13.11	80		
West Ruislip	15.21	71		coasting
Northolt Jct	17.07	69	2min early	
Greenford	19.09	64/70		
Park Royal	22.05	56		
Old Oak Common West	24.09	31*		
Westbourne Park	27.53			
Subway Jct	28.37/28.52 (15sec stand — sigs)			
Paddington	32.35		1½min early	

Loco in excellent condition, riding very smoothly and steaming well throughout. Driver favoured full regulator and 15% cut-off, letting loco find its own speed — a well-judged run, steadily recovering the time lost at Lapworth. Very economical firing.

Table 14 (cont'd)

12.25pm Manchester–Plymouth (between Shrewsbury and Bristol Temple Meads)
9.5.62
6018 *King Henry VI* (88A)
12 coaches (414/450 tons) Shrewsbury–Hereford
12 coaches + van (429/470 tons) Hereford–Bristol
Pontypool Road crew and inspector

Shrewsbury	00.00		7min late	245psi
Sutton Bridge Jct	02.28			½ regulator, 30% cut-off, 220/235psi
Condover	09.15	37		¾ regulator, 25% cut-off, heavy firing, 230psi
Dorrington	12.35	42		30% cut-off, 215/240psi
Leebotwood	17.56	34		32% cut-off, 225psi
Church Stretton	24.51	33/53		¼ regulator, 15% cut-off, 205/185psi
Marshbrook	28.43	65		170psi
Craven Arms	33.11	68		
Onibury	36.16	61		220/240psi
Bromfield	38.50	62		235psi
Ludlow	41.20	58*		shut off, ¼ regulator, 18% cut-off
Woofferton	46.23	59/64		¼ regulator, 15% cut-off
Berrington & Eye	50.00	64		blowing off, 250psi
Leominster	53.13	65		
Ford Bridge	56.03	54 mimimum		½ regulator, 20% cut-off, 250psi
Dinmore	59.05	68		250psi
Moreton-on-Lugg	62.55	35* (sigs)		½ regulator, 20% cut-off
Shelwick Jct	65.50	56		
Hereford	69.55 (67 net)		½min early	200psi
	00.00		4min late	240psi
Rotherwas Jct	03.04			½ regulator, 250psi
Red Hill Jct	06.02	46		235psi
Tram Inn	11.15	53		¼ regulator, 22% cut-off, 245psi
St Devereux	14.09	58/64		½ regulator, 235psi
Pontrilas	17.50	66/57*		shut off, 215psi
Pandy	24.37	20*/32 (pws)		full regulator, 30% cut-off, 240psi
Llanvihangel	29.20	38/37		full regulator, 25% cut-off, 250psi
Abergavenny Jct	32.47	60		shut off
Abergavenny Monmouth Rd	33.55	50*		
Penpergwm	37.08	50* (pws)		shut off, 250psi
Nantyderry	40.55	50		½ regulator, 250psi
Little Mill	-	58		
Pontypool Road	47.00 (42 net)		1min late	
	00.00		2min late	250psi
Lower Pontnewydd	05.25	56		½ regulator, ¼ regulator, shut off
Llantarnam Jct	06.58	60/45* (pws)		½ regulator
Ponthir	09.00	56		shut off
Caerleon	10.48	50*		¼ regulator, 235psi
Usk Bridge	-	30*/3* (sigs)		
Maindee North Jct	14.45	5* (sigs)		
East Usk	16.58/17.30	0 (sigs)		½ regulator, 20% cut-off
Bishton	-	72		shut off
Severn Tunnel Jct	28.25		½min early	
	00.00		on time	235psi
Severn Tunnel West	02.45	52/74		
Severn Tunnel East	07.27	50		½ regulator, 35% cut-off, 190psi
Pilning	09.35	43		½ regulator, 33% cut-off, 180psi
Cattybrook	-	20* (sigs)		slipped in tunnel; 210psi
Patchway	17.43	27		¾ regulator, 35% cut-off, 180psi
Filton Jct	21.25	10*/2* (sigs)		shut off
Horfield	-	58		
Stapleton Road	-	2* (sigs)		
Dr Day's Bridge Jct	31.03/31.55	0 (sigs)		pilotman picked up
Bristol Temple Meads	34.15		2½min early	

Coal fairly good lumps, if a bit 'slaty'. Heavy firing to get fire into shape early; loco then steamed freely, rode perfectly and was very strong. Crew and inspector convinced it was the best 'King'.

Table 14 (cont'd)

7.5am Penzance–Manchester (Pontypool Road to Shrewsbury)
17.5.62
46166 *London Rifle Brigade* (5A)
9 coaches (310/325 tons)
Ex-LMS driver, ex-GWR fireman (Shrewsbury)

Pontypool Road	00.00		on time	
Little Mill	03.03	51		½ regulator, 20% cut-off, 220psi
Nantyderry	05.55	54		shut off, 205psi
Penpergwm	09.04	46*/40		¾ regulator, 25% cut-off, 200psi
Abergavenny Monmouth Rd	13.38			190psi
	00.00			¾ reg 25% cut off, 218psi
Abergavenny Jct	04.22	20/23		¾ regulator, 30% cut-off, 195psi
Llanvihangel	11.32	29		180psi
Pandy	14.34	58/20* (pws)		shut off, 190psi
Pontrilas	21.25	64/58*		¼ regulator, 20% cut-off, 190psi
St Devereux	24.59	63		regulator, 20% cut-off
Tram Inn	27.12	66		195psi
Red Hill Jct	30.55	38*		210psi
Rotherwas Jct	33.32	52		
Hereford	36.44			190psi
	00.00			210psi
Barrs Court Jct	03.12	23		½ regulator, 30% cut-off, 220psi
Shelwick Jct	05.18	38		25% cut-off
Moreton-on-Lugg	08.25	52		200psi
Dinmore	12.22	42		¾ regulator, 25% cut-off, 195psi
Ford Bridge	15.50	57		½ regulator, 25% cut-off, 205psi
Leominster	18.11	61/58		200psi
Wooferton	25.28	45/61		¼ regulator, 20% cut-off, 190psi
Ludlow	31.41	37		½ regulator, 20% cut-off, 215psi
Bromfield	34.15	52/58		½ regulator, 25% cut-off, 220psi
Onibury	37.20	34		½ regulator, 35% cut-off, 200psi
Craven Arms	41.42	48		½ regulator, 25% cut-off
Marsh Farm Jct	46.25	38		210psi
Marshbrook	48.30	36/31		½ regulator, 28% cut-off, 210psi
Church Stretton	53.32	25		215psi
Dorrington	61.17	65/52*		shut off
Sutton Bridge Jct	70.23	1* (sigs)		
Shrewsbury	75.30 (73½ net)		on time	

Loco run-down and rough-riding, prone to uncomfortable 'side-waggle'. Steaming not free but adequate for slack schedule. Coal consisted of large hard lumps; firing involved filling the box and waiting for the fire to burn through. Right-hand injector not functioning properly; loco weak in acceleration and uphill but free-running on level and downhill.

46166 *London Rifle Brigade* at Cardiff General with the 8.55am Cardiff–Manchester express, during a period in March 1962 when engineering work at Shrewsbury made engine-changing there something to be avoided. *(John Hodge)*

Table 14 (cont'd)

7.55am Paddington–Swansea High Street (from Reading)
10.5.62
7036 *Taunton Castle* **(81A)**
7 coaches (238/255 tons)
Cardiff Canton crew

Reading	00.00		on time	
Tilehurst	04.30	64		full regulator, 20% cut-off, 225psi
Pangbourne	-	72		18% cut-off
Goring	-	74		15% cut-off
Cholsey	-	75		
Moreton Cutting	-	77		
Didcot	18.32	0 (sigs)		
Steventon	-	61		full regulator, 20% cut-off
Wantage Road	-	72		18% cut-off
Challow	-	75		15% cut-off, 225psi
Uffington	-	74		
Shrivenham	-	76		
Swindon	<u>43.30</u>	10* (sigs)	3min early	
	00.00		on time	225psi
Wootton Bassett	-	64/51*		
Brinkworth	-	72		full regulator, 17% cut-off
Little Somerford	-	79		
Hullavington	-	72/68		full regulator, 22% cut-off
Badminton	21.00	66		
Chipping Sodbury	-	73/68*		shut off
Winterbourne	-	76		easy
Stoke Gifford	30.30	40*		
Pilning	-	73		
Severn Tunnel East	-	70/74		coasting
Severn Tunnel West	-	30/10* (sigs)		¾ regulator, 18% cut-off
Bishton	-	65		
Newport	<u>60.00</u> (approx)		on time	

Loco fitted with four-row superheater and double chimney, 60,000 miles since last overhaul; strong and steamed perfectly throughout, but coal was ovoids and dust. Author continued on footplate to Swansea but involved in pulling coal forward and helping fireman, so train not timed. Arrived early in Swansea.

Old Oak's 7036 *Taunton Castle* passes Ealing Broadway at speed with the up '*Red Dragon*' (normally a Canton 'King' turn) early in 1962, two months before the author rode it on the 7.55am Paddington–Swansea. *(G. A. Richardson)*

Table 14 (cont'd)

11.10am Milford Haven–Paddington (from Swansea) ('Capitals United')
10.5.62
5056 *Earl of Powis* **(81A)**
11 coaches (384/420 tons)
Driver Ward, Fireman Thomas (Old Oak Common)

Swansea High Street	00.00		on time	225psi
Landore	05.05	15/10*		205psi
Llansamlet	08.47	44/42		¾ regulator, 30% cut-off, 175psi
Skewen	12.13	58		shut off, 185psi
Neath	15.40			smokebox door tightened (two turns); 210/225psi
	00.00			200psi
Briton Ferry	03.35	42/50		½ regulator, 18% cut-of, 225psi
Port Talbot	09.04			225psi
	00.00			½ regulator, 45% cut-off, 210psi
Margam Steelworks	-	10* (sheep on track)		
Margam	04.07	53		½ regulator, 35% cut-off, 225psi
Margam Moors 'box	-	36*/45 (sigs)		½ regulator, 30% cut-off
Pyle	10.39	46		full regulator, 35% cut-off, 215psi
Stormy Sidings	-	44/60*		¼ regulator, 20% cut-off, 210psi
Bridgend	18.35			
	00.00			½ regulator, 30% cut-off, 220psi
Pencoed	06.08	58/48*		
Llanharan	10.00	40*/42 (colliery slack)		225psi
Llantrisant	13.29	35*/58 (sigs)		¼ regulator, 210psi
Pontsarn Crossing	-	60		¼ regulator, 20% cut-off, 225psi
Peterston	18.15	60		
St. Fagans	21.15	64		shut off, 210psi
Ely	22.44	61/5* (sigs)		
Cardiff General	27.40		3min early	225psi
	00.00		on time	

(Train not timed between Cardiff and Newport)

Newport	00.00		3min late	225psi
Llanwern	-	62		
Bishton	-	68		
Severn Tunnel Jct	-	20* (sigs)		
Severn Tunnel West	-	54/77		
Severn Tunnel East	-	42		¾ regulator, 18% cut-off, 225psi
Pilning	-	41/49		22% cut-off
Cattybrook	-	45		
Patchway	-	38		
Coalpit Heath	-	55		¾ regulator, 18% cut-off, 225psi
Chipping Sodbury	-	58		
Badminton	-	60		
Hullavington	-	73/60* (pws)		shut off
Wootton Bassett	-	62		
Swindon	67.00	5* (sigs)	5min early	225psi

Journey not timed from Swindon, as running was so easy — 15% cut-off and first port of the regulator maintained steady running between 62 and 68mph, and train arrived at Paddington 5 minutes early; could easily have arrived much earlier, but the firing — with good Welsh coal — was extremely light, and the engine steamed perfectly (other than the start from Swansea, it being discovered at Neath that the smokebox door had not been properly secured). Recently ex works, loco was fitted with double chimney and four-row superheater and rode very smoothly.

Table 14 (cont'd)

	5.30pm Oxford–Paddington 16.5.62 7030 *Cranbrook Castle* (81A) 6 coaches (188/200 tons)			5.30pm Oxford–Paddington 18.4.62 5001 *Llandovery Castle* (81A) Six coaches (188/200 tons)	
Oxford	00.00		on time	00.00	on time
Kennington Jct	03.59	56		-	55
Radley	06.34	70/69		06.48	62/72
Culham	08.31	72		08.37	78
Appleford Halt	09.23	75		09.26	82
Didcot North Jct	10.37	60*		10.40	58*
Didcot East Jct	11.33	44*		11.35	48*
Moreton Cutting	13.09	58		13.09	66
Cholsey	16.00	70	½ regulator, 20% cut-off	15.48	79
Goring	19.04	75		18.38	85
Pangbourne	21.38	78		21.01	88
Tilehurst	23.49	82	2nd port regulator cracked open	23.04	90
Reading	25.46	83		24.53	91
Twyford	29.23	81/84	17-20% cut-off (varying)	28.27	84*
MP27	-	88		-	86
Maidenhead	34.03	90	steady, 225psi	33.13	90
Taplow	35.16	88	firing very light	34.27	92
Burnham	36.18	90		-	90
Slough	38.00	88/87		37.12	91
Langley	39.29	85		38.42	89
Iver	40.32	88		-	88
West Drayton	41.35	85/81	shut off momentarily	40.50	88
Hayes	43.15	82		42.28	87
Southall	44.34	85		43.48	88
Ealing Broadway	47.13	69 (sigs — double yellow)		46.12	90
Acton	48.28	72		47.13	82
Old Oak Common West	49.58	16* (sigs)		-	70
Westbourne Park	53.12	47/25* (sigs)		50.05	20* (sigs)
Paddington	56.19 (54 net)		3½min early	53.09	7min early

Run with 5001 for comparison purposes; made one month before author's footplate training and timed from first coach behind the engine. Rumours among drivers at Old Oak claimed a 51-minute run the following day with 4082.

Nameplate and numberplate of 7030, now owned by Steven Hayes. *(Steven Hayes)*

245

Table 15: Test runs, 15 May 1962

10.25am Paddington–Wolverhampton
7030 *Cranbrook Castle* (81A), fitted with double chimney and four-row superheater
5 coaches (176/180 tons)
Driver Pimm, Inspector Hancock + two firemen

Paddington	00.00		on time
Westbourne Park	02.55	52	1min early
Old Oak Common West	05.53	42*	¾min early
Greenford	10.33	75	½min early
Northolt Jct East	12.32	71	½min early
West Ruislip	14.14	74	
Denham	16.30	77	
Denham Golf Course	17.17	70	
Gerrards Cross	18.51	69	
Seer Green	21.15	72	
Beaconsfield	22.38	77/82	
High Wycombe	27.39		1min late
	00.00		on time
West Wycombe	03.43	50	
Saunderton	06.48	61/67	
Princes Risborough	09.50	62*/80	¼min early
Ilmer Halt	12.06	90	
Haddenham	13.55	96/92	
Ashendon Jct	-	94	
Dorton Halt	-	90	
Brill	18.58	94/91	
Blackthorn	21.02	92	
Bicester North	23.09	83	½min late
Ardley	26.05	77/88	½min late
Aynho Jct	30.18	66*	¼min late
Kings Sutton	31.50	70	
Banbury	34.45	80	¾min late
Cropredy	37.48	78	
Claydon Crossing	39.50	77	
Fenny Compton	42.00	66* (pws)	
Southam Road	46.04	85	
Fosse Road	47.52	87	
Leamington Spa	51.45 (49.45 net)		2¼min late
	00.00		on time
Warwick	03.04	60/70	
Hatton	06.56	66	on time
Hatton North Jct	-	55*	
Lapworth Troughs	-	72	
Lapworth	11.01	77	
Knowle & Dorridge	13.14	74 (eased)	
Widney Manor	15.03	16* (long pws)	
Solihull	18.56	54	
Olton	20.56	75	
Acocks Green	21.45	77	
Tyseley	22.33	79/64*	4½min late
Small Heath	23.28	63	
Bordesley	24.27	59	
Birmingham Snow Hill	25.59	22* (through line)	4min late
Hockley	27.57	46	
Soho & Winson Green	28.54	56	
Handsworth	30.06	62	1½min late
West Bromwich	32.28	60/41	
Swan Village	34.06	61 (sigs	
Wednesbury	37.23	2* (sigs)	
Bilston Central	41.13	2*/54 (sigs)	
Priestfield	43.07	20*/30*/48 (sigs x2)	
Wolverhampton Low Level	46.55		5min late

Five-minute stops at High Wycombe and Leamington for pathing (10.10 Paddington 'Blue Pullman' diesel train ahead).
Signal checks from Swan Village to Wolverhampton from 'Blue Pullman' ahead.

Table 15 (cont'd)

2.20pm Wolverhampton–Paddington
(Loco, formation and crew as on down run)

Wolverhampton Low Level	00.00		on time
Priestfield	03.25	48/34*	
Bilston Central	05.08	52	
Wednesbury	07.52	58/43*	
Swan Village	10.03	51	
West Bromwich	11.25	63	
Handsworth	13.45	69	1¼min early
Soho & Winson Green	14.34	42*	
Hockley	15.43		
Birmingham Snow Hill	17.08	38* (through line)	3min early
Bordesley	18.58	64	
Small Heath	19.58	67	
Tyseley	20.54	72	3min early
Acocks Green	21.47	77	
Olton	22.34	78	
Solihull	24.02	77/82	
Widney Manor	25.15	74 (eased)	
Knowle & Dorridge	27.23	17* (long pws)	2min early
Lapworth	31.54	76	
Lapworth Troughs	-	83	
Hatton	35.21	86/65*	1min late
Warwick	38.38	84/81* (pws)	
<u>Leamington Spa</u>	<u>41.10</u> (36.30 net)		1¼min late
	00.00		on time
Fosse Road	04.57	65	
Southam Road	07.15	71	
Greaves Sidings	-	80	
Fenny Compton	11.21	80/79	
Claydon Crossing	13.28	82	
Cropredy	15.17	88	
Banbury	17.58	80*	1min late
Kings Sutton	20.45	84	
Aynho Jct	22.14	65*/72	1¼min late
Ardley	26.32	76	1½min late
Bicester North	29.07	102	1½min late
Blackthorn	30.55	105/102	
Brill	32.53	94	
Dorton Halt	34.29	87 (eased)	
Ashendon Jct	35.42	61*/74	1¾min late
Haddenham	39.04	80	
Ilmer Halt	41.12	81	
Princes Risborough	43.31	80/62*	2min late
Saunderton	46.25	68	
West Wycombe	48.48	81/48*/62	
<u>High Wycombe</u>	<u>51.59</u>		1½min late
	00.00		on time
Beaconsfield	05.15	76	
Seer Green	06.28	85	
Gerrards Cross	08.21	94	
Denham Golf Club	09.29	99	
Denham	10.01	103	½min early
Denham Troughs	-	101	
West Ruislip	11.47	91	
Northolt Jct East	13.11	94	¼min early
Greenford	14.40	97	¼min early
Old Oak Common West	18.25	40*/58 (relief line)	on time
Westbourne Park	21.55	15* (pws)	1½min late
<u>Paddington</u>	<u>25.15</u>		¾min early

Table 16: Excerpts from best runs, 1961/2

4.30pm Birkenhead–Paddington
15.3.62
6021 *King Richard II* **(81A)**
11 coaches (376/405 tons) to Banbury, 9 coaches (316/335 tons) from Banbury

Birmingham Snow Hill	00.00	
Bordesley	02.35	51
Small Heath	03.51	55
Tyseley	05.07	55
Acocks Green	06.14	59
Olton	07.18	61/5* (sigs)
Solihull	10.48/11.25	0 (sigs)
Widney Manor	15.25	56
Knowle & Dorridge	17.36	65/71
Lapworth	19.53	78
Hatton	23.41	66*
Warwick	27.25	77/67*
Leamington Spa	30.46	
	00.00	
Fosse Road	06.25	51
Southam Road	09.36	52
Fenny Compton	14.54	60/65/64
Claydon Crossing	-	70
Cropredy	19.48	80/82
Banbury	23.41	
	00.00	
Kings Sutton	05.33	63
Aynho Jct	07.16	67/58
Ardley	12.48	57
Bicester North	16.01	78/84
Blackthorn	18.10	92
Brill & Ludgershall	20.23	80
Dorton Halt	22.16	75 (eased)
Ashendon Jct	23.40	61*
Haddenham	27.29	71/66
Princes Risborough	32.48	63
Saunderton	36.25	56
West Wycombe	39.43	65/38*
High Wycombe	44.10	21* (sigs)
Beaconsfield	50.05	62
Seer Green	51.41	74
Gerrards Cross	54.00	85
Denham Golf Course	55.18	90
Denham	55.54	96
West Ruislip	57.52	88
Northolt Jct	59.20	91
Greenford	60.57	92/94
Hangar Lane	62.42	90
Old Oak Common West	64.59	33*
Westbourne Park	68.08	50/5* (sigs)
Paddington	72.55 (69 net)	3½min early

Table 16 (cont'd)

10.10am (SO) Edinburgh–King's Cross
2.9.61
60094 *Colorado* **(64B)**
13 coaches (462/500 tons)

Edinburgh Waverley	00.00	
Portobello Jct	05.49	43
Joppa	06.42	40
Inveresk	11.12	40* (pws)
Prestonpans	15.07	51
Longniddry	19.22	59
Drem	23.52	66/72
East Fortune	26.25	71
East Linton	28.43	70
Dunbar	33.34	76/63*
Cockburnspath	-	67/52/33
Grantshouse	49.17	64*
Reston	54.42	64*
Ayton	58.36	61*
Burnmouth	60.19	62*
<u>Berwick</u>	<u>66.49</u>	
	00.00	
Tweedmouth	02.47	46/73
Beal	09.43	80/82
Belford	15.39	67
Chathill	21.06	66
Christon Bank	-	60*
Longhoughton	29.49	64
<u>Alnmouth</u>	<u>33.18</u>	
	00.00	
Warkworth	06.33	52/59
<u>Acklington</u>	<u>11.01</u>	
	00.00	
Widdrington	08.02	61
Pegswood	12.19	71
Morpeth	14.32	40*
Cramlington	23.01	55
Killingworth	-	62
Heaton	31.51	(sigs)
Manors	34.12	5* (sigs)
<u>Newcastle Central</u>	<u>37.31</u> (35 net)	

No 60094 replaced at Newcastle by ex-works 60147. Author alighted at York to catch 1.10pm Edinburgh (relief to 'Heart of Midlothian') with 60138 from York and 60063 from Grantham, the latter touching 93mph after Essendine and, despite severe signals at Peterborough and a pw slack to 10mph at Knebworth, arriving 7 minutes early at King's Cross.

Table 16 (cont'd)

4.15pm Liverpool–Euston (from Rugby)
6.8.62
46208 *Princess Helena Victoria* **(8A)**
12 coaches (422/460 tons)

Rugby	00.00		5min late
Hillmorton 'box	05.22	45	
Kilsby Tunnel	-	50/56	
Welton	11.36	63/68	
Weedon	16.39	80	
Heyford Box	-	70	
Banbury Lane Crossing	-	67	
Blisworth	22.54	66	
Roade	25.54	64	
Castlethorpe	30.22	83	
Wolverton	32.20	76/72	
Denbigh Hall 'box	-	72	
Bletchley	37.32	72	
Leighton Buzzard	43.13	74	
Cheddington	46.54	72/66	
Tring	51.15	63	
Berkhamsted	54.40	75	
Hemel Hempstead	57.29	80	
Apsley	59.39	83	
Kings Langley	62.01	15*/60 (pws)	
Watford Jct	<u>67.12</u> (63½ net)		
	00.00		
Bushey & Oxhey	03.33	46	
Carpenders Park	05.27	55	
Hatch End	07.01	64	
Harrow & Wealdstone	08.51	72	
South Kenton	10.32	79	
Wembley Central	11.37	80	
Willesden Jct	14.04	65/16* (sigs)	
Kensal Green	16.52/17.32	0 (sigs)	
Queens Park	19.51	46	
Camden No 1	24.35	20* (sigs)	
Euston	<u>27.17</u> (22 net)		5min early

The train left Crewe on time, touched 85mph after Norton Bridge but was delayed by signals several times between Stafford and Nuneaton and approaching Rugby.

August 1962 was the month of the author's 'Princess Royal' swansong. Four days later he journeyed to Scotland for No 46201 on the 10.00 Euston–Perth from Carlisle, which ran punctually throughout, and a week later he had No 46206 on the 14.00 Liverpool–Euston from Rugby, which regained 10 minutes of lost time on an easy schedule with just 10 coaches.

46206 *Princess Marie Louise* takes over the Fridays-only 8.55pm Glasgow–Euston sleeper at Carlisle, 1 September 1961.

A Privileged Journey – Index

Train Logs:

4037, Pontypool Road – Shrewsbury, 229
4088, Paddington – Twyford, 235
4099, Reading – Acton Parcels, 235
4708, Swindon – Paddington, 231
4917, Paddington – Maidenhead, 234
5001, Oxford – Paddington, 245
5008, Paddington – Reading, 234
5034, Reading – Paddington, 234
5056, Swansea – Swindon, 244
5095, Bristol – Shrewsbury, 229
6000, Paddington – Birmingham, 239
6016, Paddington – Birmingham, 238
6018, Shrewsbury – Bristol, 241
6021, Birmingham – Paddington, 248
6026, Wolverhampton – Paddington, 240
6845, Shrewsbury – Wolverhampton, 239
7013, Oxford – Paddington, 233
7030, Oxford – Paddington, 245, Paddington – Wolverhampton – Paddington, 246–7
7031, Paddington – Oxford, 233
7036, Reading – Newport, 243
7911, Oxford – Paddington, 237
30449, Salisbury – Exeter, 218
30453, Waterloo – Woking, 219
30457, Woking – Waterloo, 221
30489, Waterloo – Woking, 227
30521, Waterloo – Woking, 227
30765, Waterloo – Woking, 219
30768, Woking – Waterloo, 221
30777, Waterloo – Woking, 219
30788, Woking – Waterloo, 221
30794, Waterloo – Woking, 226
30795, Woking – Waterloo, 221
30796, Waterloo – Woking, 219
30798, Woking – Waterloo, 221
30799, Woking – Waterloo, 221
30803, Woking – Waterloo, 221
30850, Waterloo – Woking, 222
30851, Waterloo – Woking, 222
30854, Waterloo – Woking, 222
30855, Woking – Waterloo, 222
30857, Woking – Waterloo, 222
30861, Woking – Waterloo, 222, Waterloo – Southampton, 224
30862, Woking – Waterloo, 222

Photo Index (Locomotives)

Previous books by author

Novels
Religous historical fiction
The Child Madonna, Melrose Books, 2009
The Missing Madonna, PublishNation, 2012
The Madonna and her Sons, PublishNation, 2015

Railway fiction
Lives on the Line, Max Books, 2013

Railway Non-fiction
The Toss of a Coin, PublishNation, 2014

Non-fiction (Street Children)
The Other Railway Children, PublishNation, 2012
Nobody ever listened to me, PublishNation, 2012